Brandon
Zaffuto
570-

A WOLF IN THE CITY

A WOLF IN THE CITY

Tyranny and the Tyrant in Plato's *Republic*

Cinzia Arruzza

OXFORD
UNIVERSITY PRESS

OXFORD
UNIVERSITY PRESS

Oxford University Press is a department of the University of Oxford. It furthers the University's objective of excellence in research, scholarship, and education by publishing worldwide. Oxford is a registered trade mark of Oxford University Press in the UK and certain other countries.

Published in the United States of America by Oxford University Press
198 Madison Avenue, New York, NY 10016, United States of America.

Library of Congress Cataloging-in-Publication Data
Names: Arruzza, Cinzia, author.
Title: A wolf in the city : tyranny and the tyrant in Plato's Republic / Cinzia Arruzza.
Description: New York : Oxford University Press, 2019. |
Includes bibliographical references and index.
Identifiers: LCCN 2018008357 (print) | LCCN 2018028420 (ebook) |
ISBN 9780190678883 (online content) | ISBN 9780190678869 (updf) |
ISBN 9780190678876 (epub) | ISBN 9780190678852 (cloth : alk. paper)
Subjects: LCSH: Despotism. | Plato. Republic. | Greece—Politics and government—To 146 B.C.
Classification: LCC JC75.D4 (ebook) | LCC JC75.D4 A77 2018 (print) |
DDC 321.9—dc23
LC record available at https://lccn.loc.gov/2018008357

1 3 5 7 9 8 6 4 2

Printed by Sheridan Books, Inc., United States of America

To Nicola
κούφα σοι χθὼν ἐπάνωθε πέσοι

CONTENTS

ACKNOWLEDGMENTS

Most appropriately for a book dissecting the soul of a "melancholic drunkard," the idea of writing on tyranny was conceived over drinks. While I was rambling in a bar in Cobble Hill, Brooklyn, in the rather unsuccessful attempt to explain my confused project for a book on philosophy and politics in Plato's *Republic*, my colleague and friend Simon Critchley interjected with some surprise that he thought I had been writing a book on tyranny. He was obviously right; this is what I really wanted to write about. For helping me understand my mind I will always be grateful to him.

Giovanni Giorgini and Nickolas Pappas have been the most careful and engaged readers of this work, which I wrote with my ongoing dialogue with them in mind. I will never be able to thank them enough for their support and friendship.

I am also deeply grateful to my editor at OUP, Lucy Randall, who believed in this project and supported me with her patience, kindness, and expertise, and to assistant editor Hannah Doyle, who helped make this book reality.

My department colleagues at the New School for Social Research—Zed Adams, Dick Bernstein, Jay Bernstein, Omri Boehm,

Chiara Bottici, Alice Crary, James Dodd, Nancy Fraser, and Dmitri Nikulin—have supported me in many ways over the course of the years and have read various drafts of this work. I am grateful for their trust and also their insights and criticisms, which helped me write a better book.

I am also grateful to Emanuela Bianchi, Mauro Bonazzi, Dee L. Clayman, Ryan Drake, Simona Forti, David M. Halperin, Christoph Horn, Filip Karfík, Melissa Lane, Jessica Moss, Dominic J. O'Meara, Christoph Riedweg, Anna Schriefl, Michael M. Shaw, Luciana Soares Santoprete, Euree Song, Franco Trabattoni, Dimitris Vardoulakis, Mario Vegetti (+), and Simon Weber for discussing or inviting me to present parts of this book in Bonn, Fribourg, Milan, New York, Zurich, and Salt Lake City; to Damian Caluori, Mitchell Miller, and John Marry for giving me careful and insightful comments on my work on the tyrant's spirit; and to Daniela P. Taormina for her continuous support. The Alexander von Humboldt Stiftung funded my research stay at the University of Bonn in the fall of 2014, providing me—as usual—with wonderful working conditions.

Joshua Nicholas Pineda and Samuel Yelton have been formidable editors and research assistants and helped a great deal in making my English readable.

Lisabeth During, Johanna Oksala, and Ross Poole have become my New York family, and thanks to them I felt at home while writing this book; for this and for reading and commenting on parts of this work, I cannot thank them enough. My partner, Felice Mometti, stubbornly refused to read my work in progress, but patiently put up with all my work-related neuroses and—strangely enough—is still around. I intended to dedicate this book to him, but life decided otherwise.

On September 29, 2017, my father passed away. Plato would have considered him the perfect example of a democratic busybody. He was a balcony gardener of basil, chili peppers, rosemary, cucumbers, and vegetable sponges, a good fisherman, an even better farmer, and a terrible hunter who mostly brought home mushrooms and wild herbs from his escapades. He was a maker of improvised traps for octopi and carved walking sticks. With almost no formal schooling, he taught himself the natural sciences and mineralogy, healed himself with herbs and plants, wrote some poems, and painted a couple of awful landscapes. He had the uncanny ability to both exasperate those around him and persuade them in the end to follow his lead in his mad initiatives, and he always had a new abstruse scientific theory to explain to you at length. Plato would likely have not appreciated his jumping from one activity to another and his stubborn refusal to do just one thing, but freedom and curiosity are the greatest gifts I received from him. This book is dedicated to his memory.

Pages of previously published articles reappear in this volume. I'm grateful to the following journals and publishers for permission to reprint excerpts of this published material: " 'Cleaning the City': Plato and Popper on Political Change," *Polis: The Journal of the Society for Greek Political Thought* 29, no. 2 (2012), pp. 259–285; "Philosophical Dogs and Tyrannical Wolves in Plato's *Republic*," in *Philosophy and Political Power in Antiquity*, edited by C. Arruzza and D. Nikulin (Leiden: Brill, 2016), pp. 41–66; "The Lion and the Wolf: The Tyrant's Spirit in Plato's *Republic*," *Ancient Philosophy* 38, no. 1 (2018), pp. 47–67.

A WOLF IN THE CITY

Introduction

In the first essay of his *Commentary on Plato's Republic*—the only extant commentary from Greek antiquity on this dialogue—the Neoplatonic philosopher Proclus addresses a number of exegetical issues with the goal of establishing the correct method of interpreting the *Republic*. According to Proclus, the appropriate exegetical method requires the reader to take into account the reciprocal relations among an array of factors. The thesis, form, doctrines, and dramaturgic and narrative components of the dialogue all converge and contribute to the articulation of the dialogue's σκοπός (subject matter).[1] The first difficulty for a reader of the dialogue, however, is precisely the identification of its subject matter, and—as Proclus notes—interpreters have expressed numerous opposing views on this point. Proclus refers in particular to the existence of two main interpretive tendencies, one according to which the dialogue's main subject matter is the justice of the soul, to which the discussion on the just constitution is merely accessory, and the other supporting the opposite view (Procl. *In Rem. Pub.* 7.5–11.4). Proclus' solution to this conundrum consists in harmonizing these opposing viewpoints by arguing that the main subject matter of the *Republic* is *both* the virtue of justice and the forms of government. This, however, does

1. On this point see Abbate 2004, pp. lxiv–lxx.

not mean that the dialogue lacks the unity that a singular subject matter is meant to provide, for the discussion of the justice of the soul and that of the just form of government cannot be separated from each other or ordered into a hierarchy between primary and accessory subject matter. They are, in fact, two aspects of the same justice, as there are no distinctions between justice in an individual, in a household, or in a city, and a complete discussion of what justice is requires addressing all these aspects together. Therefore, we have only *one* subject matter, and not two (*In Rem. Pub.* 11.7–13).

Proclus' remarks are no doubt enlightening from a historical viewpoint. They point to the existence of an ancient tradition of discussions about the correct interpretation of the dialogue in which opposite positions on its subject matter—closely resembling the two opposite sides of the analogous contemporary debate—were defended.[2] In this respect, the history of interpretations of the *Republic* would seem to do justice to the insight of Olympiodorus, who in the sixth century CE compared Plato to a swan that hunters have no hope to catch: Plato can be interpreted in physical, ethical, theological, and many other ways, as "his soul contains all harmonies" (Olymp. *In Alc.*, 2.155–165).

But Proclus' remarks are also enlightening because they are fundamentally correct. As polysemy is a distinct and purposeful feature of Plato's dialogues, the best way to grasp the unity of their σκοπός is not to reduce their complexity to a simplicity that often risks reflecting the interpreter's preferences more than Plato's own intentions but, rather, to try to get a glimpse of the inner connections

---

2. In her brief remarks on Proclus' *Commentary*, which she takes as exemplifying the Middle and Neoplatonic tendency to interpret the *Republic* as a dialogue on moral psychology and not as a political dialogue, Julia Annas neglects to mention the First Essay's discussion of the dialogue's subject matter, which obviously jeopardizes her reading: Annas 2000, p. 317. See also Annas 1981 and 1997 for earlier attempts at reading the *Republic* as fundamentally a moral, and not a political, dialogue.

among the multiple threads that make up the dialogues. This particularly applies to the *Republic*, admittedly one of the most complex of Plato's dialogues, addressing subjects as diverse as education, poetry, the composition of the soul and its virtues, forms of government, the Forms, knowledge and dialectics, and the afterlife.

The dialogue's moral psychology, which has become the preferred object of investigation of recent scholarship, cannot easily be disentangled from its political argument and concerns. Moreover, there is little to be gained in isolating the moral arguments and addressing them as autonomous from the political, epistemological, and metaphysical discussions articulated throughout the dialogue, as well as from its narrative form, its characters, and their interactions. On the contrary, this method of interpretation more so than others faces the risk of obscurity and even gross (and perfectly avoidable) misunderstandings. Even more than other dialogues, the *Republic* presents us with what we may call an "embodied" philosophical conversation: one in which the personalities of the characters participating in the exchange are well delineated, their concerns are explicitly related to a specific, political, social, and cultural context— that of the Athens of the last third of the fifth century—and the detours of Socrates' arguments and the selection of the topics to be addressed are heavily influenced by his interaction with the concerns and diverging positions expressed by his interlocutors. Moreover, with the exception of the eschatology of Book X, the dialogue is consistently concerned not only with embodied souls but also specifically with the souls of people living in political communities under a common constitution.

One may have some hope of grasping the arguments articulated in Book IV in support of the tripartition of the soul while making abstraction from the political argument of the dialogue, but it is more difficult to see how one could gain a deep understanding of the virtues and forms of corruption of the soul without addressing the dynamic transaction between soul and city that is the leitmotif of the *Republic*. It is not just that city and soul are "analogous" but, rather, that they stand in a relation of reciprocal causal determination: specific sociopolitical and cultural contexts shape specific kinds of soul and, vice versa, the citizens' virtues and vices form the moral makeup of the city.[3] As most of the discussion of the various kinds of character and corruption in Books VIII and IX is concerned with their genesis, abstracting from the stated political and social conditions of their formation makes Plato's treatment of moral vice less intelligible. At the same time, it would be difficult to understand what is specifically wrong with each corrupt city without addressing its moral character, as well as its effects on individual souls.

Grasping and unpacking the inner connection of moral and political argument is not the only difficulty faced by the interpreter of Plato. As eloquently noted by Myles Burnyeat, the great difficulty of writing about Plato is

> to combine the depth and strength of the Platonic vision with the Socratic subtlety of the arguments by which it is conveyed. Plato's dialogues are a miraculous blend of philosophical imagination and logic. The interpreter must somehow respond to both, for if the imaginative vision is cut loose from the arguments it becomes grandiloquent posturing, and the arguments on their own are arid, the mere skeleton of a philosophy.[4]

To the danger of falling into either of these two interpretive missteps one should add a further risk, which is more specific to the *Republic*'s seemingly shocking political arguments: that of "pruning," to use Eric Havelock's words.[5] As there are several parts

3. See Lear 1992; Brill 2013, pp. 88–89.
4. Burnyeat 1979.
5. Havelock 1963, p. 7.

of the dialogue that go against the grain of modern readers' taste, the frequent temptation is to try to defend Plato from himself and from the consequences of what he appears to be saying. This particularly applies to Plato's dismissal of poetry, his critique of democracy, and to the drastic measures he envisages for the foundation and organization of the beautiful city. "Pruning" strategies may be and have been of various kinds, from downplaying the relevance of the political argument and proposals and separating them from the more easily digestible moral psychology—as already mentioned— thus denying the seriousness of Plato's intent in creating a beautiful city in speech; to reading Plato's anti-democratic arguments as benevolent critique and as an attempt at improving democratic institutions.

In writing this book I have tried to carefully avoid falling into grandiloquent posturing, argumentative aridity, and pruning. The interpretive approach I adopted combines historical contextual analysis, philosophical examination of the arguments, and attention to the narrative and dramatic aspects of the dialogue. The goal of this book is to provide an in-depth analysis of both the political argument concerning tyranny (and democracy) and the moral psychology of the tyrannical man, maintaining the tight connection between moral and political critique of tyranny that characterizes the whole dialogue. As this analysis focuses on the *Republic* and does not have the ambition of conveying an overview of Plato's political and moral theory across dialogues, this book does not concern itself with problems regarding developmentalist or unitary approaches to Plato's *corpus*. While in this book I do not take a position on this matter, I do draw some insights from a cluster of dialogues that seem to me to share a set of concerns and to put forward partially analogous insights, in particular the *Gorgias, Symposium,* and *Phaedrus,* which—like the *Republic*—address the relations between eros, political oratory and leadership, and tyranny.

The extensive treatment of tyranny in Books VIII and IX of Plato's *Republic*—occupying approximately the same number of Stephanus pages as the treatments of timocracy, oligarchy, and democracy taken together—is carefully anticipated throughout the dialogue. Thrasymachus' praise of the tyrant as the happiest man in Book I and Glaucon's story of Gyges in Book II put forward a problem only solved in Book IX's demonstration of the tyrant's unhappiness and Book X's consideration of his fate in the afterlife. Further references to the ever-present danger of developing tyrannical impulses show that counteracting the fascination that the idealized figure of the tyrant exerts on talented people is an underlying preoccupation in the dialogue's treatment of education. Thus, the *Republic* both begins and ends by addressing the problem of tyranny. In spite of its obvious relevance, and while several volumes have been written on Plato's analysis of democracy, there is no wealth of monographs devoted to an in-depth examination of his diagnosis of tyranny in the *Republic*.[6] The themes of tyranny and of the tyrant represent one of the main threads of the dialogue and are a crucial vantage point from which to understand its overall political and moral argument. By providing an in-depth analysis of the topic, this volume aims to contribute to a better understanding of the dialogue as a whole.

The book intervenes in the contemporary debate about the relation of Plato's political theory to democracy. In recent years a number of publications have provided nuanced readings of Plato's approach to Athenian democracy, challenging the standard view that the *Republic* articulates both a straightforward critique of the democratic practices and principles of fifth- and fourth-century Athens and an anti-democratic political project. One of the aims of this volume is to show that if we analyze Plato's treatment of tyranny against the

---

6. A partial exception is Heintzeler 1927. This small monograph, however, also deals with tyranny in other dialogues.

background of traditional depictions of tyranny in fifth-century literature and the function they played in democratic self-understanding, these interpretations appear unpersuasive. The historical contextualization of Plato's treatment of tyranny focuses, therefore, on two distinct aspects. The first is the fifth-century anti-tyrannical literary tradition, comprising histories, theater, orations, and poetry. The second is the crisis of Athenian democracy in the last third of the fifth century and concurrent transformation of the relation between political leaders and demos taking place in those years. This contextual reading is a crucial part of the philosophical interpretation of the argumentative dimension of the text, as it helps elucidate many of Plato's conceptual moves and helps avoid misreading the key points of his argument. In particular, the analysis of Plato's treatment of tyranny in the light of the literary tropes he mobilizes and the function they played in democratic political discourse leads me to conclude that Plato's critique of tyranny is not a critique of actual tyrannical regimes but, rather, should be understood as a key part of his critique of democracy. The tyrant in the dialogue is in fact a theoretical figure corresponding to a specific form of democratic leadership developed in Athens in the last third of the fifth century.

The book also provides a comprehensive analysis of the tyrant's psyche, addressing all three parts of his soul: the appetitive part in conjunction with eros, the spirited part, and the rational part. Scholarly literature on the tyrannical man's psyche has, for obvious and understandable reasons, focused mostly on the appetites and eros. These are the driving motivational source of the tyrant's psychopathology, and there is little to no explicit mention in the text of his reason or his spirit. However, my contention is that it is possible to decipher the specific roles played by the other two parts of the soul in the tyrant's pathology and, moreover, that such an interpretive approach is necessary to fully appraise the complex psychic dynamic taking place in the description of the tyrannical man in Book IX. Moreover, this analysis contributes to the rich ongoing debate on Plato's moral psychology by addressing much-disputed problems such as the natures of eros and of the spirited part of the soul, the unity or disunity of the soul, and the relation between the nonrational parts of the soul and reason. My reading of the parts of the soul could be defined as a "realist" reading as opposed to a "deflationist" one—that is, I address the parts of the soul as real and distinct and do not downplay or nuance Plato's talking of "parts." However, the debate between realists and deflationists is not the central concern of this book, and insofar as in Books VIII and IX Plato uses language and images that emphasize the distinction and conflict among the parts, my analysis of the tyrant's soul may contain useful and, I hope, persuasive insights for deflationist readers, too.

The book is structured in two parts, each comprising three chapters. The first part addresses the political argument over tyranny and its relation to Plato's critique of democracy. The second part articulates an analysis of the three parts of the tyrannical man's soul. While I opted for dividing the volumes into these two parts for ease of exposition and reading, each should be read as taking the other into account. In fact, the rationale for Plato's political critique of democracy and his discussion of tyranny cannot be fully appraised without taking into account the discussion of the nature of the soul and of what constitutes virtue and vice. Vice versa, the moral discussion of the tyrant's soul cannot be fully grasped in making abstraction from the social, cultural, and political conditions that produce tyrannical souls.

Chapter 1 offers an analysis of both the literary tropes surrounding tyranny and the tyrant in fifth-century Greek literature—with some reference to texts from the fourth century and later—and the function they played in democratic self-understanding. It addresses the still ongoing debate about the existence of a democratic theory of democracy in fifth- and fourth-century Athens, arguing that a proper democratic *theory* did not exist. Within the context of this debate, the chapter argues that the depictions of tyranny in anti-tyrannical literature served the purpose of offering the democratic citizen an inverted mirror with which he could contemplate the key features of democratic practice by way of opposition. In other words, hatred for a highly stylized discursive representation of tyranny played a key role in democratic self-understanding. The chapter further analyzes the various contents of this discursive representation: the privatization of the common good and of the freedom enjoyed by the citizens under a democratic regime, the abolition of freedom of speech and of equality before the law, lack of moderation, excessive and arbitrary violence, subversion of the laws, sexual excess, impiety, and exceptionality.

Chapter 2 addresses the controversial question of the identity of the historical figure depicted by Plato's tyrant and rules out the claim that Plato's main source of inspiration was one of the famous (or infamous) tyrants of Greek history. *Contra* such suppositions, the chapter emphasizes the conventional elements of Plato's description and shows its appropriation of preexisting characterizations of tyrannies and tyrants in Greek literature. The thesis of this chapter is that Plato's adoption of these conventional literary tropes reflects an argumentative strategy best understood by referring to their function in democratic self-understanding. Plato adopts these very tropes in order to subvert democratic discourse by arguing that tyranny is democracy's natural derivation rather than its polar opposite. The chapter further analyzes the historical dimension of this claim, suggesting that the main inspiration for Plato's depiction of the tyrant was not an actual tyrant, such as Dionysius the Younger but, rather, a specific type of opportunistic democratic leader. Seen in this way, Plato's diagnosis of tyranny can be better understood as an intervention in a debate concerning the transformed relation between political leaders and demos in Athenian democracy and the crisis of democracy in the last decades of the fifth century, foreshadowed by the dramatic setting of the dialogue.

Chapter 3 addresses the argumentative dimension of Plato's claim that democracy generates tyranny. It analyzes the botanic terminology employed by Plato in order to describe this derivation and contrasts it with the explanations of the degeneration of the other political regimes. In contrast with readings of Plato's analysis of democracy that suggest a benevolent view of the democratic regime as characterized by gentle pluralism, the chapter unpacks the argumentative logic of Plato's claim that the demos is the tyrant's father. This claim should be understood as referring to two main aspects: first, the corrupting effects of democracy's institutional mechanisms and of the collective action of the demos when acting as a sovereign body; second, the similarity between the appetitive natures of the demos and of its political leaders. The figure of the tyrant privatizes and incarnates a fundamental feature of the demos *qua* collective political body: its freedom understood as both freedom from any superior authority and license of appetitive enjoyment.

Chapter 4 is divided in two parts. The first explains Plato's rationale for characterizing the tyrant as an appetitive and erotic kind of man from a historical viewpoint. In this respect, it addresses conceptualizations of the problem of greed and the adoption of eros as a political category in Greek literature. The second part of the chapter addresses Plato's analysis of the tyrannical man's appetites and eros, situating it within the debate on the soul's tripartition and the nature of the appetitive part of the soul in order to explain the latter's attachment to lawless objects of desire in the tyrant. It answers the controversial question of the nature of the tyrant's eros by arguing that this eros should be considered as sexual, but not be equated to an appetite. It further addresses the connection between this sexual eros and the tyrannical man's relation to political power by examining the politicization of eros in Greek debates between the fifth and fourth centuries.

Chapter 5 offers, first, a discussion of the nature of spirit, dealing with the current range of interpretive options, arguing for a definition of spirit as a drive to self-assertion, and offering some solutions for the various problems that derive from such an interpretation. The second part of the chapter is based on an exegesis of the beginning of Book IX and of the only reference to spirit included therein. The thesis of the chapter is that a hardened and corrupt spirit plays a significant role in the tyrant's psyche, because the latter's condition is determined in part by the spirited part's lawlessness *as inflamed by the appetitive part*. The two parts of the chapter are bridged by a section concerning the animal metaphors related to spirit in the dialogue. This section interprets each animal as corresponding to a different state of spirit, and argues that the wolf—the animal associated with the tyrant in the *Republic*—is a metaphor for the tyrant's corrupt spirit.

Chapter 6 addresses the role of the tyrannical man's rational part. Based on the discussion in Book VI of the *Republic* concerning the danger to the city presented by corrupted philosophical natures, as well as other passages (such as the reference to the role of intelligence in vicious people at 519a1–b5), this chapter explores the hypothesis that the tyrant may be endowed with strong intellectual capabilities. Seen in this light, the tyrant may be an example of reason's complete moral perversion in a highly intelligent person. The chapter further explores the nature of the madness attributed to the tyrant and its connection to bad beliefs regarding the good. Finally, it argues for the identification of the tyrant with a philosophical nature gone astray or, put in other terms, with a denatured philosopher.

In the book's conclusion I draw out the consequences from my reading of tyranny in the *Republic*. As far as the political argument is concerned, my analysis repositions Plato squarely among anti-democratic political theorists, while at the same time refraining from caricaturing Plato's political thought as proto-totalitarian.

The anti-democratic character of Plato's political argument, more-over, does not mean that contemporary democratic readers do not have anything to learn from Plato's critique of democracy. Relevant consequences are also drawn from the viewpoint of the overall argument of the dialogue. If the goal of its treatment of tyranny is to examine the moral corruption of intellectually endowed youth within a democratic context and the perversion of philosophical talents into tyrannical characters, then this analysis bears on the tense relation between the goal of living a philosophical life and the political reality of the corrupt cities in which this philosophical life is seemingly destined to take place. This in turn throws further light on the rationale for articulating an ideal of philosophical rule in the form of Kallipolis and for motivating philosophers to take advantage of those rare opportunities to acquire political power that fate sometimes offers.

Line references for Plato's dialogues are to Burnet, *Platonis Opera* (Burnet 1900–07). All translations from ancient Greek are mine.

PART I

TYRANNY AND DEMOCRACY

After Athens' victory over the Persians, tyranny became the inverted mirror in which Athenian democracy could contemplate itself. This entailed attributing a set of conventional features to tyrants that emphasized their exceptional nature, their transgression of the written and unwritten laws regulating human communities, and their acquisitive and violent behavior (which both appropriated and destroyed the city's common property and the citizens' liberty). Tyranny played a crucial role in the self-understanding of Athenian democracy as it embodied everything that was opposed to it: the privatization of the common good and of the freedom enjoyed by the citizens under a democratic regime; the abolition of freedom of speech and of equality in front of the law; lack of measure, excessive and arbitrary violence, subversion of the laws; and impiety. Along with this polar opposition, however, both the power of the Athenian demos and the imperial domination of Athens over other Greek cities were at times characterized as tyrannical, not only by the internal anti-democratic opposition and by the agitators of pro-Spartan propaganda but also by democratic leaders and writers themselves. While this was certainly a minority view, the importance of which should not be exaggerated, it did coexist alongside the official "party line." Similarly, while despised, hated, and rejected as extraneous to the democratic polis and its morality, the figure of the tyrant attracted ambiguous desires and jealousy, reflected in the idea of the supreme happiness enjoyed by the tyrant in virtue of his unrestrained freedom and access to wealth.

The complexity of these characterizations and their relevance in Athenian institutional and political life should be taken as the background for Plato's own intervention in a debate that, between the fifth and fourth centuries, involved poets, tragedians, comedians, historians, orators, and philosophers. Many of these tyrannical features also inform Plato's description of tyranny in Books VIII and IX of the Republic. *His tyrant is a greedy, licentious, violent, intemperate, and lawless erotomaniac. He exploits the demos, kills or exiles all the prominent and virtuous people living in the city, steals the property of the city and of its citizens, constantly wages wars, lives in paranoid isolation, and eventually devours the city as a savage beast would its prey.*

Interpreters have wondered whether Plato's treatment of the tyrant is, to a certain extent, a historical document carrying a judgment of an actual tyranny belonging to his historical context, and they have tried to detect specific historical references disseminated throughout the text. These readings, however, end up overlooking the significance of Plato's mobilization of a whole array of conventional literary tropes related to tyrants. In fact, as I will argue, the adoption of these conventional literary tropes is a response to a precise argumentative strategy, which can be better understood by referring back to their function for democratic self-understanding. Plato mobilizes traditional anti-tyrannical tropes in order to subvert democratic discourse, by arguing that tyranny is not the polar opposite of democracy but, rather, its natural derivation. His treatment of tyranny should be understood not as a subtextual attack against an actual tyrant but, instead, as a bitter diagnosis of and reflection on a form of democratic leadership, as well as an intervention in a debate concerning the transformation of the relation between political leaders and the demos in Athenian democracy in the last third of the fifth century.

Chapter 1

Tyranny in Athens

Aversion, Fascination, and Fear

No one is free except Zeus.

Aesch. (?) *PB.* 50

1.1 THINKING ABOUT DEMOCRACY

Democratic principles and ideas are enunciated in a number of fifth- and fourth-century orations, poetic texts, and histories. Funeral orations offered the occasion for articulating an idealized image of the democratic city without conflicts and tensions, or to use Nicole Loraux's words, "set in the eternity of a stereotyped image,"[1] while explicit praise of political equality and individual and collective freedom can be found, for example, in Aeschylus' tragedies, Herodotus' *Histories*, or Demosthenes' orations. These texts reveal something essential of the way fifth- and fourth-century Athenians interpreted what they were doing when they sat in assemblies, councils, and popular courts, taking part in collective decision-making processes. But whether a proper democratic theory of democracy existed—that is, a theory understood as a comprehensive study, clarification, and justification of democratic principles, practices, and

---

1. Loraux 2006, pp. 251–252.

institutions defending democracy as the best or the most desirable form of government—is a more controversial problem.[2]

Some authors have identified Protagoras as the most likely candidate for the role of the first democratic political theorist, but unless we rely heavily on Plato's presentation of Protagoras' notion of political virtue in the homonymous dialogue, the extremely fragmentary evidence we have of his work provides a rather poor basis for interpretation.[3] Recent interpretations of Aristotle's *Politics* or Plato's political philosophy as not unsympathetic to Athenian democracy do not, in themselves, amount to evidence that these philosophers were articulating a democratic theory. While there is undeniable heuristic

2. On the nonexistence of a written systematic democratic theory, see Jones 1953; Finley 1973, p. 28; Finley 1974; Raaflaub 1990, p. 34; Loraux 2006. The reason for the lack of a written comprehensive democratic theory is yet another contentious problem. Finley, for example, seems to suggest that this is due to a division between theoretical activity and practice. While critics of democracy wrote and articulated their criticisms, democratic politicians reacted by ignoring these criticisms and continuing with their democratic practical management of everyday affairs: Finley 1973, p. 28. Jones 1953 does not provide any explanation for the phenomenon under discussion. Quoting a passage from Gomme 1962, which identifies democracy with the Athenians' life (p. 193), Loraux notes that life may be taken as not having a theory: Loraux 2006, p. 225. Contrary to this reading, however, Loraux suggests that, in order to find the reasons for the absence of a written and fully articulated democratic theory of democracy, rather, we should pay attention to the status of writing in Athenian democracy, to the fact that political theorists were—as a rule—not directly involved in the affairs of the city, and to what may have been a democratic predilection for speech and distrust for writing as an instrument of theoretical reflection: Loraux 2006, pp. 226–228.

3. Finley 1973, for example, suggests that Protagoras' notion of political τέχνη, as articulated in Plato's *Protagoras*, represents an exception to the lack of a democratic theory in fifth- and fourth-century Greece. Farrar 1988 argues that Protagoras, Democritus, and Thucydides articulate a distinctive and neglected form of democratic thought, which while not having the abstract character usually assigned to political theory, elaborates an understanding of politics based on an account of human psychology, human beings' desires and interests, and cosmology: Farrar 1988, p. 2. Her reconstruction of Protagoras and Democritus' democratic theory, however, remains unpersuasive, because of the insurmountable problems posed by the highly fragmentary state of the texts we have. Concerning Thucydides, her interpretation alternatively abstracts from or downplays the passages of the text that more clearly reveal Thucydides' open criticism of Athenian democracy. Finally, her reconstruction is based on a peculiar notion of democracy that has little resemblance with what we know from literary texts and orations about the way Athenians interpreted democracy.

value in interpretations emphasizing the entanglement of these theories with the framework of democratic practices and values that was their immediate context, these considerations are insufficient basis for the claim that these texts develop arguments on behalf of democracy.[4] Josiah Ober argues that democratic theory never achieved independent textual evidence in Athens, and fourth-century political theory was either anti-democratic or critical of democracy. According to Ober, however, a form of democratic theory was actually part of democratic public discourse and it was embedded in democratic rhetoric.[5] But if we take political theory to be the kind of systematic study I have just mentioned, rhetoric can hardly count as democratic theory proper. It certainly enunciates democratic notions and principles, but these, to use Moses Finley's expression, do not "add up to a systematic theory."[6]

The absence of a systematic and comprehensive democratic theory does not amount to the absence of a "clearly perceived democratic idea,"[7] of democratic reflection about the new questions and conflicts posed by the experience of democracy, or of democratic ideology.[8]

4. See, for example, Sara Monoson's fine book: Monoson 2000. The author provides the reader with brilliant and mostly persuasive analyses of the connection between Plato's political philosophy and a number of democratic tropes and values. However, at the end of the volume it remains unclear what we should make of this evidence or in what way it may challenge a more traditional reading of Plato's political philosophy as articulating both a criticism of and an alternative to the Athenian democratic system and ethos. The author herself does not make a claim stronger than emphasizing these entanglements.

5. Ober 1998, pp. 32–51.

6. Finley 1974, p. 9.

7. See Raaflaub 1990, p. 34.

8. Farrar persuasively rebukes Finley's suggestion that there was no ideology in Athens as Athenian consciousness was a clear reflection of the institutions of democracy (Finley 1973, pp. 50–51 and 65–66). Farrar insists that the democratic political community was as reflective and ideological as any other community with unresolved conflicts. As she writes, the ancient citizen "did not live contentedly inside his skin, part of a world wholly unified and integrated, protected by his innocence": Farrar 1988, p. 5. See also Raaflaub's critique of Finley's claim in Raaflaub 1990, p. 34. For the relevance of the existence of a specific popular ideology for the stability and well functioning of the Athenian political process, see Ober 1993, pp. 82–83.

I adopt the notion of ideology here to refer neither to systematic belief nor to false consciousness but, rather, to a flexible set of discursive practices that provided Athenians with a democratic ideal in which they could identify, by offering an interpretation of their conditions of existence and their own relation to them.[9] In this meaning, in contrast to systematic beliefs and to political theories proper, ideology need not be assessed in terms of its inner coherence, and is not necessarily organized into a unified system. Moreover, it encompasses a number of discursive forms of expressions, including poetry, theater, histories, orations, decrees, and rituals, and it is characterized by the recurrence of specific kinds of tropes. The core of this popular, democratic ideology was the belief in the intrinsic value of popular rule and of the sovereignty of the demos; in the political equality of all citizens, which granted them the dignity and freedom denied to slaves, protected them from socioeconomic exploitation, and limited the claims of elites;[10] in the political effectiveness of collective opinion and collective deliberation; in the educational function played by the assembled demos through its deliberations; and in a virtuous harmonization of public and individual interest.

Fifth- and fourth-century anti-tyrannical literary tropes contributed in an important way to the development of this democratic idea and of this self-understanding of democratic practices and way of life. In these literary depictions, tyranny embodied everything that was opposed to democracy. As we will see, by criticizing

---

9. For a summary of the various and at times incompatible meanings of the notion of ideology, see Eagleton 2007, pp. 1–31.

10. By elite I understand to be those members of the Athenian society who enjoyed a higher degree of education, significantly greater access to material wealth, or higher status and social recognition than ordinary citizens. In the case of Athens, however, the existence of a wealth, ability, and status elite did not equate to the existence of a ruling elite, forming a cohesive group over time and developing continuous control over the bureaucratic infrastructure and decision-making processes, as such a group never developed in the democratic regime. See the discussion of this point in Ober 1989, pp. 11–17.

and fearing tyranny, the Athenians could by the same token define themselves, by way of contrast, as democratic citizens characterized by a set of moral features and sharing in common the principles of equality and freedom.

1.2 TYRANTS EVERYWHERE

In the *Wasps*, Aristophanes parodies democratic Athens' obsession with tyranny in a mordant speech from the mouth of an exasperated Bdelycleon:

> Oh, everything is a "tyranny" or a "conspiracy" for you, no matter whether the accusation is of a big or of a small deed! For the last fifty years I haven't even heard the word 'tyranny', and now it's way cheaper than salt fish, and its name is tossed from mouth to mouth in the market! (Aristoph. *Wasps* 488–492)

Wasps was produced at the Lenaia festival in 422. Bdelycleon's remark suggests that the Athenians' paranoia with tyranny suddenly reemerged in the last decades of the fifth century (that is, almost a century after the end of Hippias' tyranny in 510).[11] But the ambiguous

---

11. Whether the Athenians' fear of tyranny was unrealistic is a controversial matter. Andrewes, for example, identifies the "age of the tyrants" with the years between the beginning of Cypselus' rule in Corinth (650 BCE) and the end of Hippias' tyranny in Athens (510 BCE). Andrewes interprets this "age of the tyrants" in terms of a quasi-teleological account of historical development, as a transitional period between aristocratic rule and the mature constitutional regimes of the fifth century: "The tyrants mark a turning-point in the political development of Greece, the moment when an old order was breaking down and a new order was not yet established": Andrewes 1963, pp. 8 and 14. On this account, later tyrannies would be incidental to the course of Greek history. The idea of an almost simultaneous end of the tyrannical period draws on Thucydides: in 1.17–18, Thucydides first implausibly states that all over Greece tyrannies led to a long paralysis owing to the fact that tyrants are always concerned about their and their family's self-interest and security, rather

hatred that tyranny inspired had already become part of Athens' institutional and political life in the immediate aftermath of Hippias' fall, as evidenced in particular by the civic cult devoted to the two so-called tyrant-slayers, Harmodius and Aristogeiton. Indeed, already in the late sixth century or early fifth century, a group statue by Antenor depicting the two lovers in the act of killing Hipparchus was placed close to the orchestra in the agora, where, until the beginning of the fifth century, most public activities took place. Hipparchus was one of Peisistratus' sons, who erotically pursued the young Harmodius and, after being rejected, publicly insulted Harmodius' sister by chasing her away from the Κανηφόροι (the maidens who carried ceremonial baskets at the Panathenaea festival), implying that she was unfit for the role because she was not a virgin. In revenge, Harmodius killed him in 514 with the help of his older lover, Aristogeiton.

However, tyranny did not end with Hipparchus' death: it lasted four more years, during which, according to Thucydides, Hipparchus' brother, Hippias—who was the actual tyrant—shifted from a moderate rule to a violent, harsh, and ruthless tyranny.[12]

than being interested in accomplishing something notable. Then, he makes the largely ungrounded claim that "eventually the Spartans deposed not only the Athenian tyrants but also those in the rest of Greece, which for the most part had fallen under tyrannies earlier than Athens—at least they deposed the majority of them: with the exception of those in Sicily these were the last of the tyrants." In this way, Thucydides uncritically accepts the Spartan propaganda presenting Sparta as the liberator of Greece from tyranny (Lewis 2009, pp. 46–47). On different grounds, Raaflaub (2003, p. 63) and Henderson (2003, p. 155) have recently argued that the Athenians' fear of tyranny, albeit real, was unrealistic, as the threat of establishing a tyranny in Athens ended with the end of the Persian War. For an alternative view challenging the idea of the "end of tyranny" in the Greek mainland and defending the credibility of the Athenians' suspicions about tyrannical attempts, see Osborne 2003; and Lewis 2009, ch. 2.

12. Thucydides' first report of the assassination of Hipparchus (Thuc. 1.20.2), is given as an example of the unreliability of hearsay regarding old events: Thucydides, indeed, complains that the Athenians mistakenly believe Harmodius and Aristogeiton to be two tyrant-slayers, while the truth is that Hippias, and not Hipparchus, was the tyrant. Thucydides, however, contradicts himself in 6.53–54, where he claims that the Athenians knew, by oral tradition, that the end of the tyranny was the result of the Spartan intervention, and that

Hippias was overthrown and forced to flee Athens in 510 by the Spartans, whom the oracle of Delphi (opportunely bribed by the Alcmeonids) had persuaded to intervene in Athens' internal affairs. Nonetheless, irrespective of historical credibility, Harmodius and Aristogeiton became the objects of a civic cult and were honored in the city's collective memory as courageous citizens bonded together by eros who had liberated the city through tyrannicide.[13] For roughly a century their statue remained the only one depicting citizens to have the honor of being placed in the agora. It was seized during the second Persian War by Xerxes' troops, an act that may suggest Xerxes' recognition of the enormous value that the Athenians placed in the cult of the two tyrant-slayers.[14] In 477/476, shortly after the end of the Persian War, the Athenians commissioned a replacement of this statue from Critius and Nesiotes. Moreover, an annual sacrifice in honor of the two heroes took place every year at their tomb in the Kerameikos, although it is uncertain when this rite was established. A number of privileges and honors were accorded to Harmodius' and Aristogeiton's direct descendants as well. Already in mid-fifth century they had the right to have meals at public expense in the Prytaneion, and later on, further honors were added: exemption from taxes and special seats at public events.[15]

in consequence of this knowledge they were in a state of constant suspicion. Thucydides proceeds then to give a detailed account of how the events really unfolded, insisting on the private motivations of Harmodius' and Aristogeiton's act, but also giving a relatively positive image of Peisitratus' and Hippias' tyranny, blaming the assassination of Hipparchus as the cause for the violent degeneration of Hippias' rule (Thuc. 6.59). The same concern about correcting the mistaken and commonly shared beliefs about the end of tyranny is displayed by Herodotus, who insists on the decisive role played by the Alcmeonids in the liberation of Athens and on the fact that the assassination of Hipparchus had only negative consequences and did not end tyranny: Hdt. 6.123.1–2.

13. For the erotic aspect of Harmodius' and Aristogeiton's cult, see Monoson 2000, ch. 1.
14. Raaflaub 2003, p. 63.
15. Raaflaub 2003, p. 66.

The civic cult of the two tyrant-slayers was echoed in the oaths that members of the various political institutions of the city were required to take. By the late sixth century or mid-fifth century,[16] an anti-tyrannical clause was included in the Bouleutic Oath. Moreover, a clause against tyrants was contained in the oath pronounced by the heliasts, the jurors of the supreme court (Heliaea), and at the beginning of each meeting of the Assembly, a curse was pronounced against all those who aspired to become tyrants or to help restore tyranny.[17] Thus, anti-tyrannical sentiment played an important role in shaping democratic political self-understanding well before the eruption of the fear of tyranny signaled by Aristophanes' *Wasps*.

The Persian invasions under Xerxes in 480/479 contributed in a decisive manner to shaping the Athenian negative attitude toward tyranny, as the Greek success against a much wealthier and more numerous enemy was reinterpreted as the victory of freedom against the autocracy of the tyrannical Persian king. As noted by Giorgini, it is only after this event that a new conceptual constellation emerged. This new Panhellenic ideology characterized the Greek world in terms of the combination of ἐλευθερία (freedom), ἰσονομία (equality of political rights), and ἰσηγορία (equal right of speech) in contrast to the Persian δουλεία (slavery).[18] The interpretation of the Persian War as liberation from slavery is suggested by Herodotus' account, which often equates resistance to the Persians and revolt against the tyrant. This juxtaposition was reinforced by the fact that Hippias found refuge in Persia, and even helped Darius' army arrive at Marathon in 490. Darius' expedition was meant to punish Athens' offer of aid to the Ionian Greek cities revolting against Persian rule and, in many

---

16. The date is unfortunately uncertain.
17. Henderson 2003, p. 156; and Raaflaub 2003, pp. 69–70. For a parody of curse at the beginning of the Assembly meetings, see Aristoph. *Thes.* 338–339.
18. Giorgini 1993, pp. 142–145.

cases, against the tyrants appointed and controlled by the Persian satrap. In Herodotus' account, Miltiades evokes Harmodius and Aristogeiton in order to persuade the polemarch Callimachus to cast his vote in favor of engaging the Persians in battle at Marathon, emphasizing how not fighting the Persians would mean delivering Athens to Hippias (Hdt. 6.109.3).

Given this conceptualization of the Persian invasions as the attempted enslavement of the free Greek cities to tyranny, it is not surprising that pro-Spartan propaganda during the Peloponnesian War both implicitly and explicitly compared the Athenian empire to Persia and conflict with Athens to the war for Greek liberation from Persian enslavement.[19]

From the Persian War onward, tyranny and the figure of the tyrant underwent a process of progressive transformation into a political insult and an accusation with potentially serious consequences. By the end of the fifth century, the hatred of tyranny had become so ingrained in Athenian political discourse that, according to Thucydides, the Athenians went so far as to recall Alcibiades from the Sicilian expedition, suspecting him of tyrannical conspiracy and impiety and, after Alicibiades' flight into exile, condemned him to death in his absence (Thuc. 6.60–61).

1.3 THE DEPICTION OF TYRANNY IN ATHENIAN DEMOCRATIC IDEOLOGY

In 410, twelve years after Aristophanes' *Wasps* and in the immediate aftermath of the oligarchic coup guided by Theramenes in 411, the Assembly passed a decree redacted by Demophantus. This decree

---

19. See, for example: Thuc. 1.69.5, 3.62.5, 3.63.3; and Scanlon 1987.

included an oath that all Athenian citizens were required to take over a sacrifice:

> If it is in my power, I will slain by word and by deed, by casting my vote and by my hand whomever will abolish democracy in Athens, whomever will hold a public office after the suppression of democracy, and whomever will aim at becoming a tyrant or will join in setting up a tyrant. And if another will slain him, I will consider him to be without sin in front of the gods and the deities, as having slain an enemy of the Athenians. And, after selling all the goods of the slain, I will give one half to the slayer, and I will rob him of nothing. And if anyone will die while slaying him or trying to slay him, I will benefit him and his children in the same way as Harmodius and Aristogeiton and their descendants. And I annul and dissolve all the oaths against the people of Athens that have been sworn in Athens or in the army or elsewhere. (Andoc. 1.97–98)

Demophantus' decree, branding anyone who would aspire to overthrow Athenian democracy as a public enemy, identified the city with its democratic regime and condemned any opposition to democracy as tyrannical. A similar conflation will characterize Eucrates' much later anti-tyrannical law, which was passed in 337/336 as a reaction to the defeat in the battle against the Macedonians at Chaeronea. Both decrees identified the dissolution of democracy with tyranny and did not discriminate between oligarchy and tyranny.[20] The oligarchic regime, established in 404 and backed by Sparta after the end of the Peloponnesian War and the defeat of Athens, was characterized as a tyranny already in the immediate aftermath of its collapse in 403.[21] In

---

20. McGlew 1993, pp. 185–186; Ober 2003, pp. 222–223.
21. According to Aristotle, the sophist Polycrates praised Thrasybulus for overthrowing the thirty tyrants (*Rh.* 1401a35f). The definition of the thirty oligarchs as tyrants recurs in a few

his speech *Against Eratosthenes*, Lysias calls the participants in the oligarchic coup "tyrants of the city" (τύραννοι τῆς πόλεως; Lys. 12.35) and, moreover, attributes to them features typically used to characterize tyranny: insatiable greed, plotting against the citizens, enmity to the city, violence, cruelty, and monstrous deeds.[22] In Book II of the *Hellenica*, whose date of composition while uncertain cannot be later than the 350s, Xenophon explicitly attributes a tyrannical attitude to Critias, by putting the following words in his mouth: "But if you think that, since we are thirty and not only one, there is less need to take care of this power as if it were a tyranny, you are a fool" (Xen. *Hell*. 2.3.15).[23] A few pages later, Xenophon further emphasizes the degeneration of the Thirty into a shameless tyranny (οἱ δὲ τριάκοντα, ὡς ἐξὸν ἤδη αὐτοῖς τυραννεῖν ἀδεῶς) following the death of the moderate Theramenes (Xen. *Hell*. 2.4.1).

This conflation of attempts to overthrow the democratic regime and tyranny can be explained by looking at the ideological role that discourses about tyranny progressively came to play in the self-understanding of Athenian democracy in the fifth century. In political discourses, tragedies and histories, tyranny and the figure of the tyrant were increasingly constructed as the negation of the founding values of democracy.[24] Athenians progressively came to define their identity as citizens of the democratic polis by way of its contrast with the inverted mirror provided by tyranny. This contrast was organized around a series of polar oppositions: order versus disorder and civil strife, law versus lawlessness, freedom versus slavery, ἰσονομία,

---

fourth-century texts: in addition to Xenophon's *Hellenica*, see *Mem.* 1.2.12 and 56; Aristot. *Ath. Pol.* 41.2; and Diodorus Siculus reporting on the historian Ephorus using this terminology: Diod. Sic. 14.2.1, 14.3.7, 14.5.6, 14.32.1.

22. Lys. 12.19, 12.21, 12.44, 12.51, 12.78.
23. See Bearzot 2009.
24. See along these lines Lanza 1977, pp. 62–63; Giorgini 1993, pp. 30–31; McGlew 1993, p. 183; Henderson 2003, p. 155; and Raaflaub 2003, p. 59.

ἰσηγορία, and ἰσοκρατία versus the tyrant's absolute and arbitrary power, the common versus the private. Many of these oppositions are apparent in two passages of Herodotus' *Histories*: the speech made by the Persian general Otanes in the aftermath of the victory against the Magians, and the Corinthian Socles' speech opposing the Spartan proposal to reinstall a tyranny in Athens. In front of the generals gathered to discuss the form of regime that Persia should adopt, Otanes voices the cause of democracy by pointing out all the dangers and negative aspects of rule by a single man. In his speech, the monarch (βασιλεύς), even if originally one of the most noble of men, is corrupted by the absolute power he holds and rapidly turns into a tyrant. Once so corrupted, his power becomes arbitrary and, moreover, a perversion of the laws of the land (νόμαιά τε κινέει πάτρια). Through Otanes' words, Herodotus stresses the corrupting effects that absolute and unaccountable power inevitably has: the main focus of Otanes' speech is not (as it is elsewhere in Herodotus) the exceptional and violent character of the tyrant, which makes his rule unbearable for his subjects; rather, it is the inner logic of the absolute power of a single man, which corrupts even the best people. This rather typological presentation of the nature and consequences of monarchy makes it an oppositional foil against which to evaluate and praise democracy.[25] Otanes, indeed, opposes both the equality in front of the law characterizing democracy (ἰσονομίην) and the accountability of the rule of many to the tyrant's disrespect for the laws (Hdt. 3.80).

Socles' speech is of the most interest on many levels. The occasion for the speech is an assembly of Spartans and envoys from their allied cities called by the Spartans after they learned that the Alcmeonids had bribed the Pythian priestess in order to persuade Sparta to liberate Athens from tyranny. Dismayed by the discovery of the truth

25. See Raaflaub 1990, p. 43.

about the Alcmeonids' plot, the lack of gratitude shown by the Athenians and the predictions of certain oracles that Athens would be the cause of great sufferings for Sparta, the Spartans presented Hippias to the assembly of the envoys and suggested that they should reinstall tyranny in Athens. Rather than being motivated by revenge, the rationale for this proposal was the concern that, if free, Athens would flourish and become a likely enemy of Sparta. Tyranny, on the contrary, would make the city weak (Hdt. 5.90–91). Herodotus himself equates tyrannical rule and weakness at 5.78. Here he remarks that the growth of Athens' power is the effect of ἰσηγορίη: under tyrannical rule Athens wasn't militarily superior to the other cities because its citizens conducted themselves the way people who work for a master do. Breaking the embarrassed and hostile silence with which the Spartan proposal is received by the allies, Socles begins his long speech on the history of the Cypselids' tyranny in Corinth with such words:

> The sky will fall beneath the earth and the earth will rise above the sky, men will be living in the sea and fishes will be living where men used to live, now that you Spartans are preparing to abolish equality of rights (ἰσοκρατίας) and restore tyranny in the cities. There is nothing more unjust (ἀδικώτερον) or bloodier (μιαιφονώτερον) among men than tyranny. (Hdt. 5.92α.1)

This passage introduces an opposition between tyrannical violence and rule of law. Bloodthirst and violence are, indeed, two of the typological characteristics of tyranny.[26] Violence marks both the tyrant's (frequently illegitimate) ascent to power and his subsequent policies, given that the illegitimacy of his rule renders it perpetually precarious

---

26. The conceptual couple violence/tyranny can already be found in Solon, fr. 32.2 and 34.7 West.

and compels him to violently suppress even his potential enemies and adversaries. The tyrant's violence may be depicted in two ways, one focusing on external constraints and the other on his personal exceptionality: on the one hand, the tyrant exerts excessive violence because he is compelled by the circumstances of his rise to power and by the necessity to maintain his power and protect himself and his family; on the other hand, his violence is an expression and consequence of his character—that is, of his disposition to bloodthirsty ruthlessness.

These topics—violence, suppression of freedom, excess, and arbitrariness—appear in the tragic depiction of tyrants and tyrannies as well and, once again, implicitly or explicitly oppose these features to the freedom, rule of law, moderation, and equality characterizing democracy. In *Prometheus Bound*, for example, the violence and cruelty of Zeus' tyranny is connected to the negation of everybody else's freedom.[27] As Kratos ruthlessly says to Hephaestus, in order to urge him to stop indulging in piety and to bind Prometheus to the rock: "No one is free except Zeus" (Aesch. (?) *PB.* 50). Indeed, tyranny is often depicted as the active abolition and privatization of ἐλευθερία, understood as the freedom benefiting all Athenian citizens under the democratic regime. The tyrant abolishes freedom for his subjects, while at the same time privately enjoying absolute freedom, in the sense of not being subject to anybody else and of being able to do whatever he pleases, whenever he pleases.

This opposition characterizes theatrical representations of the Theban saga. Thebes had been an enemy of Athens since the end of the sixth century, when it attacked Attica immediately after the establishment of democracy in Athens. After the battle of the Thermopylae,

---

27. On the violence of Zeus' tyranny, see Aesch. (?) *PB.* 12–14, 34–35, 163–164, 221–223, 323–324.

where a Theban contingent fought alongside the Spartans, Theban aristocracy allied with Xerxes and fought alongside the Persian army during the Battle of Plataea, in 479. During the Peloponnesian War, Thebes allied with Sparta and defeated Athens at Delium in 424. The longlasting enmity between the two cities resonates in Athenian tragic theater. As argued by Froma Zeitlin, on the tragic scene Thebes became a topos, in the double sense of being a designated place and a commonplace—that is, a recurrent theme or literary trope. In particular, Thebes played the role of the antithesis to Athens, of the negative model, of the "other city," where the relations between *genos* and city are mismanaged and the lines and distinctions among them blurred, and where political power is always tyrannical. The theatrical Thebes offered the opportunity to explore fundamental conflicts—such as those internal to the *genos* or that between *genos* and city—and to investigate the nature and limits of political rule over others, as well as over oneself.[28] Theban rulers such as Oedipus, Creon, and Eteocles, but also Pentheus—who refuses to recognize his own inferiority to the god—exemplify an imperative desire to have absolute power over others at all costs and a tendency to identify the state with themselves.[29] The nature of this theatrical Thebes is exemplified in particular by the figure of Oedipus and his vicissitudes. Sophocles' *Oedipus the Tyrant* combines the topics of incest and parricide—typical tyrannical misdeeds—with those of the aspiration to autonomous rule and of an inclination to excessive anger and disrespect for the gods.[30] Not by chance, the only time Oedipus is referred to as a king, rather than as a tyrant, is after he discovers that he is the legitimate son of

---

28. Zeitlin 1990, p. 131.

29. Zeitlin 1990, p. 149; see also: Soph. *OT.* 628–630 and *Ant.* 733–739.

30. See Edmunds 2006, p. 50: Edmunds notes that Sophocles' Oedipus can be seen as the typical tyrant and presents some similarities with the descriptions of the rise and fall of tyrants in Herodotus' *Histories*.

King Laius, which is also the moment when his rule has to come to an end.[31]

Euripides' *Phoenician Women* was staged in 410 or 409, shortly after the disastrous conclusion of the Sicilian expedition, the exile of Alcibiades, and Theramenes' first oligarchic coup of 411. These were also years of a heated debate about whether Alcibiades should be recalled to Athens and granted immunity, and perhaps we should read an echo of it in the figure of Polynices trying to return to Thebes. In this tragedy, Euripides freely reinterprets the Theban saga and the clash between Eteocles and Polynices in the politically charged terms of the opposition between justice and tyranny—that is, between the interests of the city and Eteocles' thirst for power. When Jocasta asks Polynices, exiled due to Eteocles' greed for absolute power, to tell her what the greatest evil in being deprived of one's country is, her son/grandson answers without hesitation: "One is the greatest: he doesn't have freedom of speech (οὐκ ἔχει παρρησίαν)." Not being able to speak one's mind, agrees Jocasta, is the lot of a slave (Eur. *Phoen.* 391–392).

More than a decade earlier, in *Suppliants*, probably staged between 424 and 421, Euripides had Theseus present a sort of Athenian democratic manifesto, once again in opposition to Theban tyranny. *Suppliants* makes explicit the tight connection between the Labdacids' dynasty and tyranny, and contrasts the Labdacids' tyrannical and monstrous destiny to the Athenian democratic model of equality and the rule of law. Theseus debates with the Theban herald about the virtues of democracy and of people's rule, which he derives *e contrario* from a critique of tyrannical regimes.[32] His

---

31. See Ahrensdorf 2009, p. 9. According to Vernant, the whole Theban saga is marked by the category of "lameness," which indicates both a defect and an extraordinary destiny. This connects the saga to other stories concerning tyrannies and tyrants—for example, the story of Cypselus, who was born from a lame mother: Vernant 1982.

32. See Raaflaub 1990, p. 45.

rebuttal of the Theban herald's arrogance provides an eloquent summary of the negative traits commonly attributed to tyranny and contrasted to democracy. Theseus first responds to the herald's mistake of looking for the tyrant of Athens by arguing that there are no tyrants to look for, as Athens is a free city (ἐλευθέρα πόλις), where people share in ruling with no discriminations or distinctions between wealthy and poor (Eur. *Supp.* 403–408). Then, in response to the herald's dismissal of people's rule as a government of ignorant incompetents, Theseus launches a full-fledged attack on tyranny. For a city, being ruled by a tyrant is the greatest evil, for under a tyrant there are no shared laws (νόμοι κοινοί), but only his arbitrary and personal rule. The tyrant takes possession of the law for himself (τὸν νόμον κεκτημένος αὐτὸς παρ' αὐτῷ), and in doing so abolishes equality (ἴσον). Finally, the tyrant wastes the resources of the city: because they could undermine his power, he eliminates the best people, appropriates their wealth, and abuses young women as his personal sex toys. On the contrary, under democracy, written and shared laws grant equal justice (τὴν δίκην ἴσην) to the rich and to the poor, and the weaker can prevail over the stronger if justice is with them. Moreover, freedom and equality find their highest expression in everybody's equal right to present a resolution in front of the Assembly, in this way contributing to what is useful to the city (Eur. *Supp.* 426–472).

Theseus' words oppose equality, justice, and the rule of law to slavery, arbitrariness, private appropriation of the law, and violence. Freedom is here defined as both freedom from subjection to the despotism of a single ruler and as the equal right of participation in governing the city. The theme of the tyrant's private appropriation of the rights and benefits that belong to all citizens under democratic regimes is one of the main threads of the democratic critique of tyranny. Characterized by a limitless ὕβρις, the tyrant elevates himself above all other citizens; moreover, behaving as a possessive and jealous owner of the city, he turns the κοινόν (the city as a common and shared possession of all the citizens) into an ἴδιον (his own private possession).[33] However, as the private appropriator of the freedom of the citizens, the tyrant also mirrors the shared freedom of the Athenian citizens. Indeed, as McGlew suggests, Athenian democracy did not simply condemn the tyrant's extraordinary freedom but also accepted and exploited it as the conceptual model for the Athenian idea of citizenship, in this manner incorporating the tyrant's freedom into the definition of citizenship. Within a democratic regime every citizen is, in a sense, a tyrant. By this logic, the tyrant overturns democracy through the expropriation and private appropriation of the tyrannical privilege of the demos.[34] Of course, the citizens' freedom is regulated by written and unwritten shared laws, and cannot simply be conflated with the arbitrariness displayed by the tyrant. However, the presence in the literature of the two notions of πόλις τύραννος (tyrant city) and δῆμος τύραννος (tyrant demos) may suggest that, in an ambiguous and contradictory way, the democratic city could identify itself with the tyrant. In fact, while condemnation of tyranny was certainly the majority viewpoint in Athenian democratic ideology, these notions suggest that this pervasive fear and hatred for tyranny was accompanied by an ambiguous fascination with unrestrained and absolute power. As we will see, we can find significant traces of this fascination in Thucydides and Aristophanes, as well as in the idea of the happiness of the tyrant, attributed to Polus, Callicles, and Thrasymachus in Plato's *Gorgias* and *Republic*, and of which we find an echo in Xenophon's *Hiero*.

33. See Giorgini 1993, p. 62.
34. McGlew 1993, pp. 187–190 and 211.

1.4 TYRANNICAL CITY, TYRANNICAL DEMOS

In his widely influential article of 1977, Robert Connor drew attention to three passages in Thucydides, in which three democratic leaders—Pericles, Cleon, and Euphemus—explicitly adopt a comparison between Athens' imperial power and tyranny that used to be polemically employed in anti-Athenian and pro-Spartan propaganda.[35] Connor's explanation for these rather surprising speeches is that a view of tyranny as good *for the tyrant* (albeit bad for the subjects) coexisted alongside the hatred and dislike for tyranny in the fifth-century Athenian collective consciousness. Thus, according to Connor, the view that tyranny was desirable when considered from the perspective of the ruler was present in Greek literature, and we can find traces of it, for example, in Archilochus (fr. 19 West),[36] Aristophanes' *Knights*, and Euripides' *Phoenician Women*. On the basis of this interpretation, Thucydides' passages can be read as exploiting the notion of the desirability of the absolute power over others.

Albeit influential, Connor's interpretation is also controversial.[37] While most scholars agree that positive appraisals of tyranny and of the life of the tyrant were present in fifth-century Athens, there is much disagreement as to whether they played a role in the employment of the τύραννος πόλις metaphor by prominent democratic leaders. Both Tuplin and Raaflaub, for example, admit that a theoretically favorable perspective did exist; however, they both insist that

35. Connor 1977.

36. This is the first occurrence of the word τυραννίς in Greek literature. The poet says that he is not attracted to the wealth of a Gyges nor is he a lover of tyranny; this may mean that Archilochus is responding to a conventional view about the attractiveness of tyranny.

37. Along the lines of Connor's thesis, see McGlew 1993, ch. 6. For criticisms, see Raaflaub 1979 and 2003; Schuller 1978; Tuplin 1985. For a recent defense of his view, referring more to the δῆμος τύραννος metaphor, see Henderson 2003; and Kallet 2003.

this is not pertinent for the interpretation of Thucydides' passage.[38] According to Raaflaub, the positive appraisal of the figure of the tyrant by some sophists in the fifth century was a minority position, which did not have currency in democratic political discourse. Even praises of monarchy and positive assessments of monarchic rule were extremely rare in this period, only becoming more common in the fourth century. These considerations lead Raaflaub and Tuplin to argue that Thucydides' passages should be read as rhetorically employing a negative metaphor in order to install fear, and not desire, in the interlocutors, the aim being to force them to take a realist political stance.[39]

While Raaflaub and Tuplin are certainly right in emphasizing that a fundamental goal of Pericles' and Cleon's speeches was to force Athenians to be realistic about the present circumstances, this observation is compatible with Connor's suggestion, given both that political rhetoric is not generally based on the inner coherence one would expect from a theoretical treatise, and that such rhetoric generally plays with different semantic levels appealing to diverse emotions. The first of Thucydides' passages portrays Pericles talking to the Assembly after the second Peloponnesian invasion and the plague, in order to dissuade the citizens exasperated by the devastation caused by the war from making unilateral concessions to Sparta in a desperate search for peace. As Thucydides recounts Pericles' speech:

> As you all feel proud of the honor that your city receives from ruling an empire, you should also come to its rescue. You cannot decline the burdens and still pursue a share in its glories. Do not think that the stake of the fight is only slavery or freedom: the fight is also about the loss of the empire, and the dangers coming

---

38. Tuplin 1985, p. 362; and Raaflaub 2003, pp. 74–77.
39. Tuplin 1985, p. 362; and Raaflaub 2003, p. 81. See also Seaford 2003, p. 108.

from the hatred you incurred in its exercise. You cannot longer give your empire up, should anyone out of fear of the present circumstances think of sitting at home and playing the honest man. *For the empire you possess is already like a tyranny*: to acquire it is perhaps unjust, but it is certainly dangerous to let it go. (Thuc. 2.63.1–2)

These words are echoed in Thucydides' account of Cleon's ruthless discourse in support of the decision to kill all the adult men of the rebellious city of Mitylene, and to enslave all women and children. Here, Cleon, addressing the Athenian citizens gathered in the Assembly and ready to reach a less savage decision about Mitylene's fate, brutally states:

You do not consider that the empire you have is a tyranny and that you rule over unwilling and conspiring subjects, who do not obey in virtue of the concessions you made to your own disadvantage: your domination over them is based on your force rather than on their goodwill. (Thuc. 3.37.2)

By comparing it to a tyranny, both Pericles and Cleon characterize the Athenian empire as rule over unwilling subjects, based on force rather than legitimacy, and consequently exposed to conspiracy and plotting, hence compelled to defend itself through additional force. Moreover, as Pericles baldly states, a tyrant cannot abdicate: once in power, the tyrant has no choice but to rule, for his enemies will not forgive his weakness.

The third passage portrays the Athenian envoy Euphemus justifying the Athenian empire in front of the assembly of Camarinaeans and trying to convince them to ally with Athens. In response to the Syracusan envoy's accusations that Athens not only substituted Persia in enslaving the Ionian cities, but also aspired to do the same in Sicily, Euphemus, rather than denying the implicit suggestion that the Athenian empire acts like a tyranny, exploits the notion of ξυμφέρον (advantage) presented as the main guideline of a tyrannical behavior:

> For a tyrant or a city holding an empire nothing advantageous is unreasonable, and the only kinship is trustworthiness: in every case friendship and enmity are determined by the circumstances. And in the present circumstances it is to our advantage not to weaken our friends, but to neutralize our enemies by means of our friends' strength. You have no reason to distrust us. (Thuc. 6.85.1)

It is undeniable that, as Raaflaub and Tuplin claim, these three speeches are hard lessons in political realism and (at least in two of the three cases) are meant to induce fear in their audiences. However, the implication that the association between tyranny and imperial power *only* appeals to the audience's fear is unpersuasive. Euphemus plays with the semantic resonances of ξυμφέρον in order to suggest that the Camarinaens would benefit from Athenian imperial tyranny. While the remark on advantage is inspired by political realism, fear is certainly not the only feeling mobilized by the analogy. Of course, one may suggest that a precise threat lurks behind Euphemus' offer of Athens' imperial protection to Camarina, as the ξυμφέρον is the criterion not only for choosing friends but also for determining enemies. But Camarina has a choice to make: either enjoy the advantages offered by Athens' tyrannical empire or run the risk of becoming its enemy. Both persuasion *and* compulsion—carrot and stick—work together in Euphemus' analogy. While in Cleon's speech, the appeal to fear is the dominant thread, Pericles' discourse is a sophisticated combination of appeals to fear, courage, and pride. Before the tyranny metaphor, Pericles first humiliates the advocates of peace for wavering at the first difficulties, losing sight of the well-being and safety of the community as a whole (Thuc. 2.60), then encourages the citizens to reflect the glorious reputation of the city and not to show weakness of spirit (2.61), and continues by reassuring them through reference to Athens' intact naval power, which constitutes the real treasure and strength of the city (2.62). Pericles only suggests the identification between tyranny and empire after this complex appeal to the courage and pride of the Athenians.

The conclusion of the comparison is telling (Thuc. 2.63.3): a policy of disengagement is akin to safe servitude (ἀσφαλῶς δουλεύειν) and is proper to a subject city, rather than to an imperial one (ἀρχούσῃ πόλει). The reference to the servile attitude Pericles attributes to the disengaged and the advocates of peace should not escape our attention. The comparison of the empire to a tyranny is not exclusively meant to induce fear at the possible loss of the empire and force the listeners to open their eyes to the real circumstances of Athens' rule; it also, and by the same token, evokes the polar opposition between slavery and freedom, insisting on the contrast between the freedom of an imperial city and the safe servitude of a subject one.

These ambiguous relations between freedom, power, and tyranny can also be found in Aristophanes' characterization of Demos as a tyrant in *Knights*, where the poet attacks Cleon for his radical pro-war stance. Demos is the capricious and elderly master of three servants, one of which is the subtle flatterer Paphlagonian (representing Cleon) who is accused of prolonging the war out of fear of being prosecuted once the conflict is over. In this context, the chorus addresses Demos as a tyrant whom all men fear and obey, but who is too easily flattered and led astray by orators (Aristoph. *Kn.* 1111–1120). As noted by Henderson, Aristophanes' characterization is not meant to question the Athenian's right to rule over its allied cities. On the contrary, the demos' right to be the absolute ruler at home and abroad is usually justified with references to the role played by Athens in the liberation of Greece from Persia. Aristophanes' critique is, rather, addressed to demagogues and politicians such as Cleon, who stand accused of trying to take advantage and fool the demos-tyrant while expropriating it of its prerogatives.[40]

What sense, then, did the definition of the demos as tyrant have? From a positive viewpoint, this identification expressed both the absence of a ruler governing over the demos and the concentration of all decisional powers in the latter's hands (a concept expressed later on, for example, in Isocrates' *Areopagiticus* 7.26). It is reasonable to think that the logic of this identification was that the citizens collectively shared the absolute power, wealth, and freedom enjoyed by the tyrant.[41] Of course, a negative sense of this comparison coexisted with the positive one: in anti-democratic literature, the tyranny of the demos is understood as the poor segment of the population's domination over the aristocratic elite.[42] However, this polemical indictment of the demos as a tyrant as part of the anti-democratic propaganda should be carefully distinguished from the possible positive identification we find a trace of in Aristophanes.

1.5 THE TYRANT'S EXCEPTIONALITY

The tyrant staged in fifth-century tragedies was a figure who condensed an ensemble of features that opposed him to the dominant model of the wise and free man. In this sense he became a scapegoat, a negative and polemical idol embodying everything the polis rejected

---

40. Henderson 2003, p. 160.
41. Kallet 2003, pp. 138–143. According to Kallet, this was a kind of democratic ideology, although not the one that could be spoken overtly.
42. Ps.-Xen. *Ath. Pol.* 1.1 See also the Old Oligarch's claim that Athens' allies were slaves to its demos: Ps.-Xen. *Ath. Pol.* 1.16. A negative association between the demos and the tyrant can be found also in Aristot. *Pol.* 1274a5–7 and *Pol.* 1313b38.

as external to it.[43] Tragic depictions of tyrants share several common traits with those found in Herodotus' *Histories*, and the description of the tyrant as a moral monster was a widespread commonplace.

Excess is probably the main feature characterizing him: excess greed, excess freedom, excess arrogance, excess fear, and erotic excess. The excessive nature of the tyrant seems to constitutively disrupt the order of the polis, turning its laws upside down, breaking its conventions, perverting blood ties, subverting the order of generations, and questioning the separation of the divine and the human. As a man who conceals a wild beast in the depths of his heart, he is a menace threatening to devour the entire city.

It is possible to isolate a number of recurrent traits used to characterize tyrants in biographies, narratives, and tragedies: bestiality, impiety, hubris, greed, παρανομία (transgression of laws and customs), and excessive eros. These negative traits overlap with a more positive aspect—namely, the tyrant's distinctive intellectual capabilities. Exceptionality is the tyrant's most common attribute, and in some narratives great intellectual capabilities are an integral part of it. Simply put, the tyrant is no dummy.

The tyrant is often associated with wild beasts—often with wolves and to a lesser extent with lions—to emphasize his savagery, which turns all his subjects into possible prey.[44] This association is an ancient one: we can find an early example of it in Alcaeus' anti-tyrannical poetry, where the poet depicts Pittacus of Mytilene as intent on devouring the city. This description echoes the Homeric Achilles' derogatory reference to Agamemnon as a δημοβόρος (a devourer of his

---

43. Lanza 1977, pp, 161–162 and 190–191.
44. For a good collection of occurrences, see Catenacci 2012, pp. 174–178. Catenacci also remarks that λύκος (wolf) is an onomastic component recurring in the names of various tyrants and, perhaps, also in the name of Peisistratus' bodyguards, λυκόποδες: Catenacci 2012, p. 176. I will discuss the significance of the wolf metaphor in more depth in chapter 5.

own people).[45] In Aeschylus' *Agamemnon*, Cassandra calls Aegisthus a "wolf": Aegisthus personifies a set of tyrannical traits, as he is a hubristic figure, sleeps in a bed that does not belong to him, and aspires to rule over Argos without having any religious or dynastic justification for his rule (Aesch. *Ag.* 1258–1260). Moreover, immediately after the assassination of Agamemnon, the chorus mentions tyranny twice: first to denounce Aegisthus' and Clytemnestra's tyrannical plot, and then to emphatically declare that death is preferable to tyranny (1354–1355 and 1364–1365). The trope of the wolf reappears much later, in Diodorus Siculus' account of an episode from Gelon of Syracuse's childhood (Diod. Sic. 10.29).[46]

Contrary to the wolf, in antiquity the lion was often associated with royalty, hence with legitimate rule. Depictions of the tyrant as a lion are, accordingly, less frequent, although telling: in many cases in which it is associated with the tyrant, the lion—like the wolf— symbolizes the repeated contact with blood inscribed in a tyrant's destiny and the future destruction that awaits the city. In Herodotus, both Cypselus of Corinth and Hipparchus of Athens are associated with a lion (Hdt. 5.56.1).[47] According to the story of the Cypselids' tyranny narrated by Socles, oracles sent to Corinth warned the ruling aristocratic family (the Bacchiadae) that a flesh-eating lion had been conceived and would loose the knees of many in the city (Hdt. 5.92β.15–21).[48] Cypselus lived up to this prophecy: upon seizing

---

45. Alcaeus, fr. 70; Hom. *Il.* 1.231; and Lentini 2002, pp. 5–6. See also Aristot. *Pol.* 1305a concerning Theagenes of Megara, who slaughtered the flocks of the aristocrats of the city (hence behaved like a wolf).

46. Gelon was once saved by a wolf, which came to his school and snatched away his tablet. While Gelon was running after the wolf in order to get the tablet back, the school building collapsed because of an earthquake, killing the teacher and all the other students·

47. Hipparchus has a dream in which a tall man calls him "lion."

48. The image of the lion growing in the city into a wild beast that will devour it is employed by the Chorus in reference to Troy's destiny of destruction in Aesch. *Ag.* 717–736. Cassandra uses a similar metaphor later, in reference to the bloody destiny of the Atreids' house, caused by the contamination following Atreus' atrocious and impious vengeance against

power he exiled many Corinthians, expropriating them of their goods while killing many more of them (Hdt. 5.92ε.11–ζ.1). Cypselus' son, Periander, committed even more atrocious crimes than his father. After his father's death, Periander sent a herald to the court of Thrasybulus (the tyrant of Miletus) to seek advice about the best way to ensure the safety of his tyranny. Instead of giving an explicit answer to the herald, Thrasybulus led Periander's herald outside of town into a sown field:

> Coming to a cultivated land, he passed through a cornfield, while repeatedly asking the messenger questions about his arrival from Corinth, and he kept cutting every ear of wheat he would see overtopping the others. After cutting them off he threw them away, until he destroyed the finest and strongest part of the crop in this way. After he went through the field, he sent the messenger away without proffering any word. (Hdt. 5.92ζ.2–3)[49]

Periander immediately understood Thrasybulus' tacit advice; soon thereafter, he murdered all the outstanding people of the city and became, in Socles' words, more bloodthirsty (μιαιφονώτερος) than his father (Hdt. 5.92ζ.1). Among his many crimes, he ordered the castration of three hundred boys belonging to the aristocratic families of Corcyra in vengeance for the murder of his son, and even killed his own wife (Hdt. 3.49 ff).

The violence of the tyrant is not only brutal but also often impious, as it involves abuse of rituals or the murder of one's own kin. The killing of Agamemnon orchestrated by Clytemnestra and

his brother Thyestes, who had slept with Atreus' wife. Atreus killed Thyestes' children and fed them to their father: Aesch. Ag. 1223–1226.

49. In Aristotle's account of this story, it is Periander who gives the advice to Thrasybulus: Aristot. Pol. 1013a.15–20.

Aegisthus in their tyrannical coup[50] combines both forms of impiety. Among the abuse of rituals include the rather hilarious story of the ruse orchestrated by Peisistratus: in his second attempt to gain power, he had a tall girl dressed like Athena with armor and equipped with various paraphernalia, riding on a chariot in procession in the streets of Athens and accompanied by two heralds asking the citizens to welcome Peisistratus in the name of the goddess (Hdt. 1.60). Polyaenus gives a detailed version of Polycrates of Samos' rise to power, which combined extreme cruelty and impiety: On the occasion of a religious festival, which, as was the tradition in Samos, was attended by a procession of men in arms, Polycrates' two brothers, Syloson and Pantognostus, took the lead in the procession. Then, when the other men deposited the weapons next to the altar in order to participate in the rites, the brothers gave the signal to their accomplices and, with their help, killed them all. The massacre at the festival was timed to coincide with Polycrates' seizure of the strategic places in the city (Polyaenus 1.23). Although Herodotus' account of Polycrates' rise to power makes no mention of this episode, the tyrant is described as particularly bloodthirsty in the *Histories* as well (Hdt. 3.39.1). Polycrates exiled and executed those Samians whom he suspected of rebellious intentions, and even went so far as to imprison the children and wives of a group of rebellious Samians and threaten to burn them alive to prevent the citizens from joining the rebellion. In addition to all this, he committed further impious violence by killing one of his brothers and exiling the other in order to remain the sole tyrant of the island (Hdt. 3.44–45 and 3.39).

The story of Polycrates' treatment of his two brothers is exemplary of impiety, and also of the tyrant's greed for both power and wealth. We have already seen that Cypselus expropriated the possessions of his exiled or executed adversaries, and a conventional

---

50. Seaford 2003, pp. 100–101.

view about the tyrant's conflation of the interest of the city with his own private interest is present in Thucydides' criticism of archaic tyranny (Thuc. 1.17). This immense desire for wealth and power is most suggestively displayed on the tragic stage. In the *Phoenician Women*, Eteocles powerfully expresses the unbounded nature of the tyrant's desire for power:

> If what is beautiful or what is wise were exactly the same for everybody, there would be no strife involving dispute among human beings; but, as it is, everything is similar or the same for the mortals only in name, but not in reality. I will speak, mother, without hiding anything: I would go to the rising of the stars and the sun and beneath the earth, if I were able to do so, in order to possess Tyranny, the greatest of the gods. Therefore, mother, I have no intention to yield this advantage to another rather than to keep it for myself; for to lose the greater and to win the less is cowardice. (Eur. *Phoen.* 499–508).

Impiety also characterizes Aegisthus in Euripides' *Electra*. In spite of never being on the stage, his tyrannical presence haunts the entirety of the piece: he is accused of having plotted to murder Electra and Orestes in the manner that tyrants do in order to eliminate potential adversaries, he has given Electra in marriage to a peasant in order to prevent her from giving birth to a noble child, and his ὕβρις does not know any boundaries.[51] Electra depicts him completely drunk, leaping on Agamemnon's grave while asking: "Where is your son Orestes? Is he perhaps here to bravely defend your tomb?" (Eur. *El.* 330–331). Later on, she gives a ruthless funeral "eulogy" over his dead body, where she accuses Aegisthus of impiety (926–927),

---

51. Eur. *El.* 14–28, 31–36, 58.

attachment to wealth (χρήματα, 939–941), and, finally, of committing sexual outrages on the women of the house (ὕβριζες, 947).

Hubristic sex and paraphilia are among the traits that better characterize the tyrant's excessive attachment to power. As suggested by Philip Holt in his analysis of Hippias' incest dream reported in Herodotus' *Histories* 6.107, illicit sex is a constitutive part of the combination of power, abuse, and corruption that marks the tyrant as an exception and detaches him from the rest of humanity. Having absolute power, the tyrant can have sex with anyone he pleases; his monopoly on violence gives him the possibility of sexually abusing his subjects; his general παρανομία translates into sexual intercourses and desires that violate the written and unwritten norms regulating sexual behavior.[52] Thus we read of Periander having sex with the corpse of his wife Melissa whom he had just killed (Hdt. 5.92 η);[53] Peisistratus had intercourse "not according to custom" (οὐ κατὰ νόμον) with his wife in order not to have children with her (Hdt. 1.61); Dionysius the Elder married two wives in one day and his son Dionysius the Younger married his half-sister Sophrosyne (Plut. *Dio*. 3.1–2 and 6.1); the tyrant of Orchomenus, Aristomelidas, tried to sexually abuse a girl who killed herself to escape this fate (Paus. 8.4.6); tyrants are accused of sexually abusing women in Otanes' speech (Hdt. 3.80.5) and in Euripides' *Suppliants* (Eur. *Supp*. 452–454); and the same accusation is addressed to Aegisthus in the *Electra* (Eur. *El*. 947).

This connection between the tyrant's power and his eros is more comprehensible against the background of Paul Ludwig's observation that, in classical Greece, eros was a political category of the utmost public relevance. Indeed, eros was believed to be the underlying

---

52. Holt 1998, pp. 226 and 237.
53. Herodotus attributes illicit sex to eastern monarchs as well: Hdt. 3.31–32 (on Kambyses marrying two of his sisters); 2.131 (on Mykerinos raping his daughter), 9.108–113 (on Xerxes falling in love with his sister in law and then having sex with her daughter).

origin of an array of different passions, from ambition to patriotism, and was conceptualized along a continuum spanning love for the city, citizen lovers and sexual license and tyranny.[54] Hippias makes the connection between eros and political power explicit in his own interpretation of the incest dream he had the night before guiding the Persian army to Marathon, where the Athenians would eventually defeat it: dreaming of sleeping with his mother becomes, in his interpretation, a prediction of his imminent regaining tyrannical power in Athens (Hdt. 6.107.1–2). The interpretation of a dream of sexual intercourse with one's own mother as a prediction of political possession of the motherland is not infrequent in ancient sources, and of course the myth of Oedipus was the archetypical model for the conflation of sexual possession of the mother with political possession of the city.[55] More generally, illicit sex was a specific manifestation of the general παρανομία characterizing the tyrant, which also includes extravagant behavior, frequent drunkenness, excessive luxury, and unusual clothing. We have a clear indication that these traits of extravagance and license were considered signs of tyrannical behavior in the fifth-century Athenian suspicion of citizens from the aristocratic elite who displayed an inclination to excess and disrespect of accepted social norms. The explanation given by Thucydides for the Athenians' suspicions that Alcibiades was cultivating tyrannical ambitions is telling:

> The many started fearing the greatness of his license in his demeanor and lifestyle (φοβηθέντες γὰρ αὐτοῦ οἱ πολλοὶ τὸ μέγεθος τῆς τε κατὰ τὸ ἑαυτοῦ σῶμα παρανομίας ἐς τὴν δίαιταν) as well of

---

54. Ludwig 2002, p. 2.

55. Artemidorus interprets the incest dreams of politicians in this manner: 1.79. Analogous dreams attributed to Julius Caesar can be found in Suet. *Iul.* 7.2; and Dio Cass. 37.52.2, 41.24.2. For a discussion of this point, see Holt 1998, pp. 222–224.

his ambition in every single area in which he got involved: they thought he was aiming at tyranny (ὡς τυραννίδος ἐπιθυμοῦντι), and became his enemies. Even though his conduct of war in the public domain was the most excellent, everybody was appalled by his behavior in private, and, having entrusted the command to another, they caused the city's ruin not long afterwards. (Thuc. 6.15.4)

Alcibiades' figure combines two traits: on the one hand, the transgression of rules, great ambitions, and sexual license; and on the other, the presence of exceptional skills. As Thucydides opines, Alcibiades' revocation from the Sicilian expedition and his subsequent exile were the cause of the disastrous outcome of the expedition and of the consequent downfall of the city. Thus, while license, greed, excessive violence, and impiety all distinguish the tyrant as exceptional, in some cases it is the tyrant's exceptional intellectual capabilities that mark him as distinct.[56] This trait can be noted already in some representations of tyrants mentioned earlier. Polycrates' plot to take over Samos required not only a great deal of ruthlessness but also a capacity for strategic planning. While it is true that Herodotus wonders at the foolishness of Peisistratus' second attempt to seize Athens, which involved the somewhat farcical procession of the girl dressed like Athena,[57] his third successful attempt required significant strategic capacities: Peisistratus managed to collect money, acquire allies, hire mercenaries, and attract supporters from both the

---

56. See McGlew 1993, p. 29; and Gray 1996, p. 381. McGlew notices that tyrants are seldom considered to be stupid and they were rather credited with extraordinary acuity and Gray stresses the importance of the capacity to decipher signs as a common attribute in Herodotus' depiction of tyrants.
57. Herodotus wonders how Greek men, who are well-known for being more clever than foreigners, could conceive of such a stupid plan to deceive the Athenians, the subtlest of all Greeks: Hdt. 1.60.3. It must be said, though, that the plan did work.

countryside and the city—all feats accomplished while in exile—before launching his attack on Athens and seizing power (Hdt. 1.60–63). Intelligence plays a major role in the mythical tyrant Oedipus' accession to power, granted to him by the Thebans in recognition of his superior intellect, which was displayed in the resolution of the Sphinx riddle (Soph. *OT*. 396–398). Quick-wittedness is also required to be able to preserve power by fooling internal and external enemies; as we have seen, Periander immediately understands Thrasybulus' tacit advice and acts accordingly; Herodotus also tells the story of Pittacus of Mytilene, who—by using his wit—managed to persuade Croesus to stop building ships and threatening the Greek islands.[58]

The story of the end of the Cypselids' tyranny is particularly interesting from this viewpoint, because quick intelligence is one of the key points of Herodotus' narrative. At the ages of eighteen and seventeen, respectively, Periander's two sons were invited to Epidaurus by their maternal grandfather, Procles, who was tyrant there. As they were leaving to go back to Corinth, Procles asked them whether they knew who had killed their mother, Melissa. While the elder of the two didn't pay attention to this question and then rapidly forgot it, the younger, Lycophron, immediately understood that Procles was implying that the murderer was their father. As the story goes on, Periander sent away Lycophron as soon as he realized that his younger son had understood Procles' question: Lycophron's quick intelligence, combined with his grudge for his mother's murder, had

---

58. Pittacus himself was one of the seven sages. Other instances of the tyrant's capacity of understanding messages that escape common people's attention and of excogitating plots and devices to deceive the enemies are, for example, the story of Histiaeus of Miletus' stratagem to give the signal of starting the Ionian insurrection escaping Darius' control (Hdt. 5.35.3ff.), and of Polycrates of Samos liberating the island from the Spartan siege by giving the enemies gilded lead coins (Hdt. 3.56.2). For a discussion of the intelligence of the tyrant, see Catenacci 2012, pp. 156–166.

become a danger to him. What is interesting is the conclusion of the story. When Periander grew old, he came to realize that his elder son was too dull (νωθέστερος) to become a tyrant, and he tried to recall Lycophron and persuade him to take over the tyranny of the city. As suggested by Vernant, Lycophron is a copy of his father, in that he has quick intelligence, an accurate memory, and an obstinate character:[59] these capabilities are necessary for a successful tyrant—they are needed to seize power and, as important, to keep it in the midst of the common hatred, fear, and jealousy directed at him.

1.6 THE UNHAPPY TYRANT

The pervasive negative connotation of tyranny in fifth- and fourth-century Athens coexisted with a more ambiguous attraction to the idea of absolute power. I have already discussed how this may have played a role in the metaphors of the tyrant city and the tyrant demos. This attraction to tyranny can be identified in the recurrent belief that the tyrant, being absolutely free and not subject to anybody, enjoys a godlike happiness. From Plato's *Gorgias* and *Republic*, it appears that a number of fifth-century sophists provided immoralist arguments for the justification of tyranny that identified tyranny and supreme happiness.[60] Other sources do not clearly identify the proponents of such a view, which was certainly not limited to the Athenian context. Pindar's and Bacchylides' epinician odes celebrating the victories of Hiero of Syracuse are good examples of idealization of the figure of the tyrant, which contributed to the elaboration of a propagandistic tyrannical self-presentation.[61]

---

59. Vernant 1982, p. 31.
60. As Plato's dialogues are the primary sources that attribute this position to the sophists, I will discuss these immoralist arguments in the next chapters.
61. Pind. *O*.1 and *P*.1 and 2; Bacchyl. *Ep*. 3 and 4.

In fifth-century Athens, we find traces of such a view in some of Euripides' tragedies. Eteocles' praise of tyranny and his idealization of it as the greatest goddess in the *Phoenician Women* is one of the clearest instances of this view. As the tragedy was staged soon after the collapse of the first oligarchic coup, it is not unjustified to see in Eteocles' hubristic attitude an echo of these events and of the passions they aroused. In *Hippolytus*, Theseus' son answers the false accusation of his father, deceived by Phaedra, rebutting the insinuation that he may have aspired to tyranny and that this aspiration led him to try to seduce his stepmother: power, Hippolytus argues, ruins the minds of those who love it (Eur. *Hipp.* 1013–1020). In the *Ion*, when the king of Athens, Xuthus, announces to Ion that he will inherit the kingdom, Ion answers with a proper refutation of the belief that power bears happiness: tyranny may have a pleasant appearance, but is only suffering when seen from within. Among the reasons provided by Ion to reject power are the solitude of the tyrant and the jealousy of his subjects (Eur. *Ion* 595–597). We can find these two observations, together with the contrast between the apparent happiness of the tyrant and his actual condition of misery, spelled out in the later Xenophon's *Hiero*. When Hiero complains that tyrants do not enjoy more pleasures than common citizens, the poet Simonides answers that this cannot be, as everybody desires to rule as a tyrant and is envious of tyrants (Xen. *Hiero* 1.9). Hiero proves his point to Simonides through a series of arguments, some of which we have already found in other sources: the tyrant cannot travel abroad to enjoy festivals in neighboring cities due to his fear of conspiracy (1.11–12)[62] and he takes no pleasure in conversations because his knowledge of his subjects' hatred for him reveals their praise as empty flattery (1.15). Opposing the commonly held views about a tyrant's

---

62. See also Xen. *Hiero* 2.8–11. Hiero argues that tyrants move in the city as if they were constantly at war and surrounded by enemies.

sexual license, Hiero laments that his love cannot be spontaneously reciprocated by his beloved boy (1.33): a tyrant, indeed, can never be sure that he is genuinely loved at all (1.37). Later on, Hiero echoes Ion's words: it is easy for the multitude to make judgments based on appearances and believe that the tyrant is supremely happy, but the tyrant conceals his misery inside his heart (2.3–4). A thread running through the first part of Hiero and Simonides' conversation is the tyrant's solitude: he cannot know whether he is loved or not, he lives in a constant state of suspicion directed at even his closest associates, and friendship is entirely denied to him (3.1–4.2). Xenophon simply exploits commonplace discussions of the admiration enjoyed by the tyrants and its refutations and, thus, a theoretical treatment of the tyrant's soul is entirely absent from his *Hiero*. However, many aspects of Xenophon's descriptions appear in Plato's own treatment of the tyrant's misery, which appears, at times, like a *controcanto* to Xenophon's treatment of this theme.

Chapter 2

Plato's Tyrant and the Crisis of Athenian Democracy

Therefore, this is the reason why the allies have rather become the slaves of the Athenian demos.

Pseudo-Xenophon, *The Constitution of the Athenians*

2.1 IDENTIFYING PLATO'S TYRANT

Plato's tyrant is characterized—as I will examine in greater detail in part II—by lawless appetites, a strong sexual eros, greed, anger, violence, and impiety. His policies include waging continuous wars, creating a personal bodyguard, stealing the resources of the city, eliminating all most prominent citizens, and oppressing the demos. At first sight, it would be obvious to think that the historical models Plato had in mind for this portrait were the famous tyrants of the sixth century BCE or the Syracusan tyrants of the fifth and fourth centuries. However, as persuasively argued by Marcel Meulder, attempts at identifying a single, specific historical tyrant as the referent of Plato's analysis result in hypotheses that do not stand careful historical or textual examination.[1] While some elements of Plato's description may recall the deeds and character of a specific

---

1. Meulder 1989.

tyrant, other elements immediately challenge or contradict this impression. Identifying one single historical tyrant as Plato's target or model compels interpreters to focus selectively on certain aspects of the text while excluding others, and interpretations that take this approach run the risk of appearing arbitrary or question-begging. Some traits of Plato's tyrant echo available information on Periander and Peisistratus. Like Plato's tyrant, both Periander and Peisistratus had personal bodyguards.[2] Periander got rid of the best men in the city in order to eliminate potential internal enemies and competitors, and he was known for his sexual and paraphilic excesses.[3] Peisistratus was exiled, but then managed to come back and seize power, and once in power he imposed heavy taxes.[4] All these features characterize Plato's tyrant as well. However, the dissimilarities and discrepancies are equally important. While in the *Republic* tyranny is portrayed as the degeneration of democracy, Periander, by contrast, inherited his tyranny from his father Cypselus, who established it after a conflict with the aristocratic family ruling Corinth (Hdt. 5.92.β). While Plato's tyrant is a paradigmatic figure for greed, Peisistratus adorned Athens with magnificent buildings rather than wasting the city's resources (Hdt. 1.25). Moreover, Peisistratus was not considered intemperate, nor was he singled out for his erotic or appetitive excesses. More generally, it is unclear why Plato would have targeted two historical figures in the distant past whose specific deeds and biography did not seem to play a prominent role in the political and philosophical debate of the fourth century. It is also significant that Plato never cites Peisistratus and his sons as examples of tyrants, greed, and tyrannical abuse.[5] Given these considerations, identifying the Platonic tyrant with either of these two historical figures seems implausible.

---

2. Hdt. 1.64 and Aristot. *Pol.* 1285a and 1311a; Plat. *Rep.* 566b–c.

3. Hdt. 5.92γ–η, 3.48–53; *Rep.* 567a–c, 571b–d, and 576b.

4. Hdt. 1.64; and *Rep.* 568e–569b.

5. See Vegetti 1998a, p. 34.

Socrates' claim, in Book IX, that the best judge of a tyrant's happiness is one who had an intimate acquaintance with him—as this enabled him to closely observe the tyrant in his everyday life actions—has been taken to suggest that Plato's tyrant is a reference to either Dionysius the Elder or Dionysius the Younger. As he spent some months at their court during his travels to Syracuse, Plato certainly had the opportunity to observe their way of life and character.[6] Moreover, there are some evident similarities: Dionysius the Elder had a personal bodyguard, his tyranny was the outcome of the overthrow of the previous democratic regime, he waged several wars, and he repressed internal enemies. Dionysius the Younger, on the other hand, was known for his erotic excesses and debauchery.[7] Both these two theses have significant conceptual consequences for interpreting Plato's aim in criticizing tyranny, for, in this interpretation, the philosophical and psychological analyses of Books VIII and IX would appear to be the outcome of Plato's travels to Syracuse and of his disappointment with his attempt to reform the Syracusan regime. This disappointment would have caused him to write a full-fledged attack on tyranny, identified as the wickedest form of government. A piece of evidence in support of this thesis would be the fact that discussions about the Syracusan tyranny did play a relevant role for fourth-century moderate circles, as the military, political, and economic successes of Dionysius the Elder represented a good point of reference for those moderate authors who were engaged in a significant positive revaluation of monarchic power.[8]

---

6. *Rep.* 577a–b; Plat. (?) *Ep. VII*, 329b–350b.

7. See Aristot. *Pol.* 1312a.

8. Among the texts belonging to this tendency, see Xenophon's *Cyropaedia* and Isocrates' speeches on Nicocles, Evagoras, and Philip (Isoc. 2, 3, 5, and 9). See also Isoc. *Ep.* 1, an incomplete letter addressed to Dionysius the Elder to persuade him to adhere to a panhellenic program and to ally with the rest of Greece against Persia. Xenophon's *Hiero* can also be interpreted along the lines of a re-evaluation of autocratic power, in that it portrays the possibility for a wise man to counsel and positively condition a tyrant. According to

However, supporting these hypotheses poses numerous difficulties. Various chronological considerations challenge the identification of Dionysus the Younger with Plato's tyrant. While Plato's second and third travels to Syracuse date from around 367 and 361, the current consensus is that Plato wrote the dialogue after his return from his first travel to Syracuse in 387 and the establishment of the Academy (c. 385), but before his second travel to Syracuse. According to various hypotheses, the most likely dates for the composition of the *Republic* are either the decade between 380 and 370, or the one between 385 and 375, or (if we accept the hypothesis that Book I was composed early on) the twenty years between 390 and 370.[9] In support of the claim that Plato's sections on tyranny reflect his negative experience with Dionysus the Younger, Holger Thesleff has argued that they were written during the last stage of the composition of the *Republic*, which, according to Thesleff, took place in the 350s, after Plato's second travel to Syracuse.[10] However, as Meulder stresses, this thesis is problematic, for two sets of reasons. The first is that Books VIII and IX are not characterized by the stylistic features belonging to the late dialogues, which Thesleff himself accepts as a criterion for their demarcation from previous dialogues. The second consists of the relevant discrepancies between Plato's tyrant and Dionysius the Younger. Unlike Plato's tyrant, Dionysius the Younger dismissed his father's bodyguard of mercenaries, intended to lower the taxes and to carry on a less belligerent foreign policy than his father, and was generally willing to soften his father's tyrannical regime.

Bearzot, part of the initial positive appraisal enjoyed by the Syracusan tyranny in Athens was linked to the city's attempt to persuade Dionysius the Elder to loosen his alliance with the Spartans, and build an alliance with Athens: see Bearzot 1981, pp. 118–123.

9. For the discussion on the date of composition of the *Republic* see, for example, Diès 1932, pp. cxxii–cxxxviii; Kahn 1998, p. 59; Vegetti 1998a, pp. 18–23 and 20n13; Wallach 2001, p. 216; Vegetti 2006, p. 9.

10. Thesleff 1982, p. 185.

Moreover, Plato's description of the aspiring tyrant's exile and return to the city cannot allude to Dionysius the Younger's own exile from and return to Syracuse, which took place in 354 and 346.[11]

Furthermore, while it is true that Plato was commonly believed to have continually reworked his dialogues, it is less plausible that he reformulated his views on tyranny only *after* his unfortunate experiences with Dionysius the Younger. The critique of tyranny is a thread that runs through the entirety of the dialogue and decisively contributes to its overall structure and meaning. Even if the latter stages of the *Republic* were, as Thesleff contends, composed in the 350s, the characterization of the tyrant's psychology in Book IX develops the critique of appetitive greed that structures the discussion about injustice from the very beginning of the dialogue and is associated with the figure of the tyrant throughout. The treatment of tyranny in Books VIII and IX is the culminating point of its argument concerning the nature of injustice and its relation to happiness and unhappiness. As this argument is one of the main threads of the *Republic,* the treatment of tyranny in its last books cannot be considered an accessory feature of the dialogue. Given these considerations, the hypothesis that Plato arrived at his conclusions about tyranny following his Syracusan experiences with Dionysius the Younger is highly implausible.

Various scholars have suggested the more plausible identification of Plato's target with Dionysius the Elder. However, there are relevant discrepancies in this case as well.[12] For example, in contrast to the *Republic*'s depiction of the tyrant as a leader of the demos (προστάτης

---

11. Meulder 1989, pp. 49–50.
12. Bearzot, for example, argues that Plato's description of tyranny was inspired by Dionysius the Elder, but she also claims that this description is motivated by Plato's alarmed admiration and fascination for him rather than contempt. The proof of this enduring fascination would be Plato's subsequent travels to Syracuse. This reading, however, ignores the unequivocal indictment of the tyrant in the *Republic*: see Bearzot 1981, pp. 137–142.

τοῦ δήμου), Dionysius the Elder was a general with full powers (στρατηγὸς αὐτοκράτωρ).[13] The phrase προστάτης τοῦ δήμου more closely evokes Athenian radical democratic leaders. While it is true that Dionysius came to acquire autocratic power following a decision by the assembly dictated by fear—which may confirm the Syracusan reference contained in the description of the genesis of tyranny in Book VIII of the *Republic*—this fear was motivated by the external threat represented by the Carthaginians, and not by an embryonic civil war perceived by the demos as an imminent oligarchic threat to popular rule. Moreover, in contrast to the *Republic*'s depiction of tyrannical rule, Dionysius' tyranny lasted several decades and was characterized by political stability and impressive military and economic achievements of which Plato's contemporaries in Athens were perfectly aware.

In addition to the discrepancies mentioned here, there is a further difficulty to be taken into consideration: this difficulty concerns, more generally, the interpretation of Plato's critique of tyranny as a critique of historical Greek tyrannies. In Plato's diagnosis, tyranny is the form of regime proper to a specific kind of appetitive man, whose degree of moral corruption makes it difficult, if not impossible, to envisage a process of moral reform. This psychological pathology is exacerbated by the corrupting impact that the mechanisms of absolute power have on the tyrant's soul. Plato's indictment of tyranny is, therefore, double: it is both the regime most apt for a lawless man driven by his basest appetites and a regime that nourishes the specific psychic disease affecting the tyrannical man, leading him to accomplish the most dreadful deeds. Given the intransigent and self-propagating character of tyranny entailed by Plato's psychosocial diagnosis, taking it as a constitutional analysis of a historically attested form of regime characterized by specific institutional and political

13. Diod. Sic. 13.94.5.

features would raise major interpretive problems concerning both Plato's political dialogues and his own biography. While he refused to take direct part in the political life of a democratic Athens, which was characterized by a relative political stability after the fall of oligarchy in 403, Plato traveled to Syracuse three times. If the information provided by Plato's (?) *Seventh Letter* is reliable,[14] the second journey was motivated by the (albeit weak) hope of reforming the Syracusan regime by educating Dionysius the Younger into philosophy.[15] Moreover, Plato still wanted to test Dionysius' capacity for a philosophical life at the time of his third trip. Even admitting that the letter's account of his motivations cannot be trusted,[16] if his experience with Dionysius the Elder had such a major impact on his philosophical conceptualization of tyrannical power, reconciling with it Plato's decision to return twice to Syracuse is a difficult task. Moreover, while the *Republic* identifies the philosophical reform of a δυνάστης—which may be used here as just a polite word for

14. The authenticity of the *Seventh Letter* is controversial. Michael Frede has provided some rather strong arguments for its spurious character and for the unreliability of some of the information conveyed by it: Burnyeat and Frede 2015. The strength of Frede's analysis may indeed have shifted the burden of proof to those who want to defend the letter's authenticity. For earlier defenses of its authenticity, see Brinckman 1911; Pasquali 1938; Jaeger 1955, p. 111; Isnardi 1955; Von Fritz 1968, p. 110ff.; Isnardi Parente 1970; Brisson 1987. For a review of the debate about the authenticity of the letter, see Isnardi Parente and Ciani 2002, pp. xi–xxxiv; and Huffmann 2005, pp. 42–43. Given the reasonable doubts about the letter's authenticity, in this chapter I use the biographical information the letter offers only insofar as it seems reliable on historical grounds, when confirmed by other sources, or when consistent with indications contained in the dialogues.

15. See along these lines Plutarch account of Plato's second and third travels to Syracuse: Plut. *Dio.* 12.1–20.1. Diogenes Laertius, on the contrary, gives a different motivation for Plato's second travel—namely, that Plato intended to ask Dionysius the Younger for land and people to realize his ideal constitution. The third trip, instead, was aimed at reconciling Dion and Dionysius: Diog. Laert. 3.21 and 3.23.

16. Frede makes strong, although not necessarily conclusive, arguments that this information cannot be trusted, in particular as—according to him—it is highly implausible that Plato saw either Dion or Dionysius the Younger as actual or potential philosophers of the kind that would have been necessary for the realization of even an approximation to the ideal city of the *Republic*: Burnyeat and Frede 2015, pp. 59–65.

"tyrant"[17]—as *a* possibility for realizing the beautiful city, the *Laws* explicitly identifies tyranny as *the best* starting point for the implementation of radical political reforms (*Laws* 710c–711c). As the *Laws* are the last of Plato's dialogues and were written long after the failure of his attempts to morally reform both the Elder and the Younger Dionysius, it would seem that the notion that these troubling experiences led him to indict autocratic power per se does not stand. By this I do not intend to claim that Plato had, in fact, a positive opinion of tyrannies in general but, rather, that he did think that under specific circumstances, tyrannies could be significantly reformed and used as a starting point for the implementation of beneficial policies or the realization of radical political programs. On the other hand, it is hard to see how the kind of tyranny Plato discusses in the *Republic* could be reformed at all.[18]

A further source of puzzlement, moreover, can be found in the—perhaps partially biased—information provided centuries later by Athenaeus concerning the tyrannical entanglements of Plato's

---

17. In Thuc. 3.62, the Theban spokesmen employ the term δυναστεία to indicate an extreme form of lawless oligarchy, which is defined as ἐγγυτάτω δὲ τυράννου, the nearest to tyranny, as opposed to isonomic forms of government. Thessalian δυναστεία is opposed to Athenian isonomy in Thuc. 4.78. In the *Politics*, Aristotle classes it as an extreme form of oligarchy, which is akin to monarchy and where men's power is above the laws: Aristot. *Pol.* 1293a.

18. Giorgini 2009 correctly notes the problem of the coherence between the passages on tyranny in the *Laws* and Plato's indictment of tyranny in the *Republic*, and in order to address this discrepancy he argues that Plato thought that it was possible to reform the soul of the tyrant through a therapy of the soul—that is, the teaching of philosophy. Giorgini is correct in thinking that the tyranny passage in the *Laws* can be better understood by taking into account the possibility of a conversion of the tyrant's soul. The tyrant of the *Republic*, however, seems to me an intractable case, impossible to be reformed. See along these lines Larivée 2012, p. 2n2. The whole architecture of education in the *Republic*, moreover, displays some skepticism about the possibility of educating adult people once they are morally corrupted. As I will argue in this chapter, a different way to make Plato's position on tyranny consistent across the two dialogues is to interpret tyranny in the *Republic* and tyranny in the *Laws* as referring to two very distinct political phenomena.

Academy.[19] Athenaeus (Ath. 11.508) conveys a less sympathetic portrait of Dion's intentions about Syracuse than the one offered by Plutarch in the *Life of Dion* (Plut. *Dio.* 54.1–57.1), as he suggests that Plato's student, Callippus, killed Dion because the latter had tyrannical ambitions in Syracuse, and moreover, that he tried himself to become a tyrant. Athenaeus mentions other students of the Academy who either became tyrants or attempted to establish a tyranny: Chairon, who studied with Plato and then Xenocrates, and was made tyrant of Pellene in c. 335; and Euagon of Lampsacus and Timaeus of Cyzicus, who tried to become tyrants in their respective cities.[20] Athenaeus, therefore, concludes that the Academy was a school of misdeed. Furthermore, from Aelianus we know that another of Plato's students, Clearchus, became a cruel tyrant of Heraclea and ended up being killed in 353 by Chion, another student of the Academy, inspired by Plato's teachings to hate tyranny.[21] Finally, Plato sent two members of the Academy, Erastus and Coriscos, to advise Hermias, tyrant of Atarneus and Assos.[22] The apologetic tone of the *Seventh Letter*—regardless of its authenticity—further shows that the Academy and Plato himself were the objects of suspicion concerning political entanglements with tyrants, confirming in this way the seriousness of the passages from the *Republic* and the *Laws* where Plato justifies collaborations with autocratic rulers for the sake of implementing radical political reforms.

---

19. For a short discussion of the sources concerning the political entanglements of Plato's Academy, see Schuhl 1946.
20. It seems that, once in power, Chairon expelled the rich from the city and distributed their property and women to their slaves: Athenaeus attributes the motivation for these acts to Plato's political teachings. On Chairon, see also *Index Academicorum*, coll. xi–xii; and Frede, in Burnyeat and Frede 2015, p. 13.
21. Aelianus fr. 86 Hercher (Suda, s.v. Klearchos).
22. See Plat. (?) *Ep. VI*.

2.2 THE CRITIQUE OF TYRANNY AS A CRITIQUE OF DEMOCRACY

The difficulties we face are of a double nature. On the one hand, discrepancies with the historical record make it difficult to conclusively and univocally identify Plato's tyrant with an actual tyrant. On the other hand, reconciling Plato's harsh judgment of tyranny in the *Republic* with both his decision to travel to Syracuse for a second and third time and his belief that tyranny may be the most appropriate starting point for the political and moral reform of a city raises another set of interpretive challenges. Faced with these two sets of problems, we must change interpretive approach to see whether different questions offer more promising outcomes. Whether the text contains allusions to one or more specific historical tyrants may bear little theoretical significance. Rather than investigating *who* is the historical tyrant that hides under Plato's flamboyant description, we may try to begin by asking *what* Plato's tyrant is and what we should understand by "tyranny" in the *Republic*.

Books VIII and IX do not articulate a constitutional theory proper, of the kind we can find, for example, in Aristotle's *Politics*. Neither of these books focuses on an empirical and historical analysis of different constitutional forms of regime, nor do they attempt to elucidate and systematize the institutional features of such regimes. These pages include no details about citizenship rules, deliberative institutions and mechanisms, or the distribution of offices. Instead, they address two interrelated questions. On a political level, they investigate the specific kind of sociopolitical disunity affecting the city as an illness, illustrating both the unruly genesis of each regime and the nature of the conflict of interests between the ruling part of the city and the ruled. On a moral psychological level, they articulate a sociopsychological taxonomy and critique of the moral principles governing each form of regime displaying each of their insufficiencies, and showing the reciprocal interaction between moral corruption of the individual soul and political and moral sickness of the city. The specific sociopolitical disunity of each kind of regime contributes to shape specific character types and specific forms of individual moral corruption have effects on the nature and dynamic of the regime as a whole, in a circular process. This is why the moral psychology articulated in these books can hardly be decoupled from the political argument, and vice versa.

If we contrast Plato's tyrant with the tropes typical of anti-tyrannical literature examined in chapter 1, it emerges that Plato freely combines features belonging to fifth- and fourth-century conventional representations of tyranny and tyrants, some of which refer to the perception, representations, and memory of actual tyrants, while others describe mythical and fictional tyrants.[23] This also explains why Plato's description of the tyrannical regime does not match any historical tyranny, albeit presenting features that do appear in historical narratives and other sources concerning an actual tyrant or another. In democratic literature, these conventional tropes combined together to give birth to an ideological figure of tyrannical power that incorporated features diametrically opposed to isonomy, democracy, and popular rule. Attending to the discursive and political *function* of these tropes (rather than focusing on their *content*) puts us in a better position to understand why Plato adopts them and his specific manner of intervening in this tradition. His genetic account of tyranny, which emphasizes its natural derivation

---

23. Vegetti reaches a similar conclusion, on partially different grounds, in Vegetti 1998a, p. 34. Heintzeler does not attempt to identify Plato's tyrant with a historical tyrant but, rather, reads Plato's critique of tyranny in the light of previous representations of tyranny in Greek literature. In Heintzeler's interpretation, the core of Plato's critique of tyranny is an attack against egoism, individualism, and ethical relativism as undergirding power-based politics; see Heintzeler 1927.

from democracy, indicates that Plato's purpose in mobilizing these tropes is to destabilize the dichotomy between democracy and tyranny that organizes democratic discourse. While the democratic representation of tyranny emphasized its radical opposition to an idealized democracy, Plato claims that tyranny is its natural child. This claim would scandalize democratic ears, particularly given that Plato purposively adopts traditional depictions of tyrannies in order to subvert their function in democratic literature. Moreover, this subversion and conceptual reorganization of democratic discourse highlight the contradiction contained within it: that between fascination and fear. As examined in the previous chapter, the tyrant was both an object of fearful disgust and a mirror for the collective power and freedom of the demos, as well as that of imperial Athens. Plato exploits this fascination in Thrasymachus' speech and in Glaucon's version of Gyges' story, in order to show later in Book VIII the hidden truth behind it: the tyrannical aspect of Athenian democracy.

Plato's critique of tyranny should be taken not so much as a critique of actual, historical tyrannical regimes but more as an important part of his critique of Athenian democracy. As such, it exposes the extreme form of moral and political corruption of a sector of the Athenian elite and provides a diagnosis of its causes. The tyrant is an ideal-type corresponding to a specific kind of extreme moral corruption with a political dimension that takes place *within* democracy. For Plato, this corruption is the natural development, rather than the subversion, of Athens' democratic ethos, principles, and institutional mechanisms.

Plato's diagnosis of this form of moral and political corruption articulates two distinct and intertwined levels. The first level consists of a contextual reflection on a historical moral, political, and institutional crisis, which I suggest should be identified with the crisis of Athenian democracy during the last third of the fifth century and the beginning of the fourth.[24] The dramatic setting and some historical references disseminated within the dialogue, as well as the biographical information conveyed by the *Seventh Letter*, strongly suggest that Plato considered this period to be a decisive political and ethical crisis with lasting consequences for fourth-century Athens. Plato's tyrant figures as a kind of political opportunist who cultivates an instrumental relation to the demos and aspires to acquire absolute power in order to satisfy his hedonism. While it would be misleading to try to identify Plato's tyrant with a single Athenian politician, some of his traits do allude to actual political opportunists—in particular, to Alcibiades—who alternately championed democracy, flirted with oligarchy, and aspired to absolute power, all in accordance with changing circumstances.

The second level may be defined as political-philosophical; at this level, the diagnosis of this process of moral and political corruption articulates a complex interpretation of the nature of political power and its abuse, and of the relationship between social and political conditions and the formation of kinds of characters, thus acquiring a larger and less historically specific scope. In this sense, Plato's tyrant is the child of two main aspects of Athenian democracy. The first consists of the institutional mechanisms proper to democracy conferring, in the name of political equality, supreme political authority to the demos and its opinions. This makes political leaders subaltern to the democratic ethos, forcing them to become assimilated to it, rather than playing an educational role vis-à-vis the masses. The second is the content of this democratic ethos, which Plato takes to consist of appetitive and hedonistic self-interest conjoined with the identification of freedom with license. From this viewpoint, in addition to challenging the traditional polar opposition

---

24. According to John Wallach, the thirty years between 415 and the foundation of the Academy (c. 387–385) provided Plato with his major impressions of Athenian politics, as well as with the burning ethical and political problems he addresses in the dialogues; Wallach 2001, p. 50.

between democracy and tyranny, Plato's attack on tyranny clearly displays the core reasons for his critique of the democratic regime.

As Plato's treatment of tyranny combines these two dimensions—one which we may define as contextual, in that it articulates a situated intervention in a historically specific debate stimulated by a set of historical events; and the other, which can be seen as political-philosophical and of a scope that transcends its historical context—my analysis of it is divided into two parts. In the remainder of this chapter, I focus on Plato's contextual intervention by discussing the historical context evoked by the dialogue through its dramatic setting and the explicit and implicit references to salient historical events and figures. The next chapter provides an analysis of the function of the figure of tyranny within the dialogue, of the conception of political power it conveys, and of the relationship between it and the moral principles, values, and institutional mechanisms presiding over democracy.

2.3 THE ATHENIAN CIVIL WARS AND THE *REPUBLIC*'S DRAMATIC SETTING

The beginning of the *Seventh Letter* attempts to justify Plato's abstention from political life: it acknowledges that in his youth Plato had political ambitions, and it explains why he changed his mind. The need for justification is understandable, as a man in fourth-century Athens belonging to an aristocratic family as prestigious and political as Plato's was certainly expected to take part in the political affairs of the city.[25] Issues of authenticity aside, the *Seventh Letter*'s justification

---

25. The fact that the *Letter* begins with a justification of Plato's abstention from active political life may suggest that, even if inauthentic, the letter was written relatively early: justifying one's abstention from politics would not be such a strong concern in much later periods in which members of aristocratic families were not implicitly required to participate in direct political activity.

is consistent with the rationale offered in the dialogues for Socrates' refusal to be a traditional Athenian politician and with the *Republic*'s prescription that the philosopher should abstain from politics in corrupt cities.[26] This justification relies on the events occurring in 404, a few months after Athens' capitulation to Sparta at the end of the Peloponnesian War: the overthrow of democracy and the establishment of a government of thirty men, endowed with absolute powers, and assisted by ten officials (ἄρχοντες) presiding over the Piraeus and ten over the city (*Ep. VII*, 324c–d). Two of Plato's relatives were involved in the government: Critias, his mother's cousin, was among the most prominent politicians of the Thirty, especially after the execution of his rival, Theramenes;[27] Charmides, Plato's maternal uncle and Critias' first cousin, was one of the ἄρχοντες presiding over the Piraeus. These two relatives, along with Plato, were part of the company of friends, admirers, and students of Socrates. This company also included Xenophon, who was perhaps involved in the council of

---

26. See Plat. *Apol.* 31c–d, 32a, and 32e–33b; *Gorg.* 473e–474b; *Rep.* 592a5–b6.

27. Diodorus Siculus writes that Theramenes studied philosophy with Socrates, and that Socrates was the only one who intervened to try to stop his execution: Diod. Sic. 15.5. But this text is unreliable, and is part of a process of political rehabilitation of the figure of Theramenes, increasingly described in late fourth-century literature and by sources dependent on it as the proponent of a moderate constitutional solution, probably consisting in a combination of the limitation of political participation to property owners, a democratic assembly, and an oligarchic council. Holding this position, Theramenes would have represented the alternative both to demagogic radical democracy and to the tyrannical oligarchy of Critias and his friends (see Aristot. *Ath. Pol.* 34.3; Diodorus Siculus goes as far as to present Theramenes as a defender of democracy who ended up voting for its abolition only because threatened by Lysander and the Spartans; Diod. Sic. 14.3.6–7). The association with Socrates served the purpose of reinforcing the image of a wise Theramenes, who faced death with dignity and self-control. One can see the outcome of this process of rehabilitation in Cicero: Cic. *Tusc.* 1.96–97 and 100. For a discussion of Theramenes that emphasizes his decisive role in planning both oligarchic coups, in 411 and the 404, and in leading Athens to accept the worst possible peace conditions with Sparta, see Bearzot 2013, whose thesis is that Theramenes was not a coherent moderate but, rather, a political opportunist motivated by thirst for power. For a discussion of Theramenes' moderate program, see Canfora 2013, part 1, ch. 7.

five hundred nominated by the Thirty.[28] Given Plato's social and familial acquaintance with members of the Thirty and of their council, the letter's report of his attraction to the new government also seems credible. While it is true that the letter makes clear that Plato's fascination for the Thirty had a very short life, this admission of guilt would make no sense if it were a mere forgery, given the overall justificatory ambitions of the text. The letter may even underplay Plato's relation to the Thirty; it is possible that Plato was more than a sympathetic spectator and that he was initially more actively involved in the enterprise, hence the need for self-justification.

According to the letter, the Thirty's regime initially appeared to him to be a welcome alternative to a democratic regime that was "reviled by many" (*Ep. VII*, 324c2–3: ὑπὸ πολλῶν γὰρ τῆς τότε πολιτείας λοιδορουμένη). The letter's allusion to the democratic regime's crisis of credibility clearly refers to hostility from oligarchic and moderate circles, but may also indicate more widespread disillusion caused by the disastrous war supported by the radical democratic faction. However, the *Letter* notes, the crimes and brutality of the new regime soon made the overthrown democracy appear like a golden age, explaining why Plato either broke with the oligarchic government or refused to take direct part in it. As we will see, this negative judgment of the Thirty's government is confirmed by several critical references to conspiracies and aristocratic clubs disseminated in his dialogues.

After a period of turmoil and violence during the months of civil war between the oligarchic forces and the democratic partisans organized by Thrasybulus, the restored democracy showed itself willing to avoid its previous excesses. In a formidable display of restraint, Thrasybulus and the other democratic leaders ended the civil war by reaching an agreement aimed at restoring concord (ὁμόνοια) in the

---

28. On this hypothesis, see Canfora 2013, part 1, ch. 12.

city.[29] This agreement left the remaining supporters of the Thirty with political and civil rights and allowed them to move to the oligarchic enclave of Eleusis if they chose.[30] Moreover, the agreement decreed that all past crimes accomplished by the Thirty and their supporters, excepting murders, were to be *forgotten*: μὴ μνησικακεῖν (literally "not to remember injuries"). In addition to the general amnesty for the remaining supporters of the oligarchic revolution, the decree legally abolished resentment.[31] During these years the democratic faction cooperated with Athenian moderates,[32] such as Anytus, Archinus, and Phormisius, whom the Aristotelian *Athenian Constitution* mentions as collaborators of Theramenes. These moderates participated in the civil war against the Thirty, and thus came to acquire some influence over the political life of the subsequent years (Aristot. *Ath. Pol.* 34.3).[33] In light of this collaboration, and the restored democracy's evident moderation and will to rebuild concord and unity, it is not surprising that—as the *Seventh Letter* claims—Plato thought that the new democratic regime would provide a propitious framework for his involvement in political affairs (*Ep. VII*, 325a–b). But Socrates' subsequent trial and execution in 399 settled the issue once and for all, particularly given that Socrates' accuser, Anytus, was one of the

29. On the ideal of ὁμόνοια pursued by the restored democracy, see Loraux 2001.
30. In order to have a place to flee in case of a fall of the oligarchic government, Critias and the others had created this enclave through extremely violent means: they had killed all adult men of the *deme* and taken over their possessions and houses. The story of the extermination of the Eleusis' population reported by Xenophon is both troubling and instructive. The elimination of all adult men was carried out in a bureaucratic and highly organized manner, as all men were first required to register their name under a pretext, and then they were seized by the cavalry and carried to Athens for execution. After combing Eleusis, Critias spoke in the Odeum at a meeting of hoplites and knights, urging them to vote for the death sentence, in order to force them to be accomplices of the deed; Xen. *Hell.* 2.4.9.
31. On the reconciliation agreement, see Aristot. *Ath. Pol.* 39.1–6; and Shear 2011, pp. 190–207.
32. Athenian moderates were a loosely cohesive cultural and political tendency supporting the political reform of Athenian democracy based on the restriction of citizenship rights to property owners and middle class, with the exclusion of the *thetes*.
33. On the collaboration between moderates and democrats in the restoration of Athenian democracy, see Bearzot 1981, pp. 18–24.

most prominent moderates formerly associated with Theramenes. The involvement of a moderate in the prosecution of Socrates may have persuaded Plato that institutional and political collaboration between democrats and moderates could only lead to the moderates' assimilation of the democratic ethos and political practices. Unlike them, Plato made the more radical choice of withdrawing from active political participation in the affairs of the city (*Ep. VII*, 325d–326a). While we may doubt whether Plato cultivated illusions about the restored democracy, there are good historical reasons to consider this possibility, and to believe that Anytus' involvement in Socrates' trial may have come as a shock.

Several elements of the *Republic* suggest that these tormented years toward the end of the fifth century should be taken as the historical background for Plato's investigation of justice and political rule, and an interpretive key to his treatment of tyranny:[34] the repeated evocation of the dangers of civil war (στάσις) throughout the *Republic*,[35] the dramatic setting of the dialogue, *and* a precise reference to the aristocratic clubs and conspiracies in Book II all suggest this historical reference.

Determining the dramatic date of the dialogue (assuming, of course, that Plato kept a specific date in mind over the years in which he wrote the dialogue) could specify this historical context. The two main hypotheses that have been put forward are that the dramatic date is either 411 or 421.[36] While the evidence for both dates is inconclusive, 421 seems the more likely of the two; Cephalus probably

---

34. Heintzeler takes the crisis of Athenian democracy in 404 to be a decisive event for Plato's reflection on justice (and on the injustice of the tyrant): Heintzeler 1927, pp. 49–50.

35. References to political στάσις and to στασιάζειν can be found in *Rep.* 351b–352a (in the discussion between Socrates and Thrasymachus); 464e–465b, 470b–471a, 488b (in the famous image of Athenian democracy as a ship, where the sailors struggle against each other for the wheel), 520c (as civil war for the conquest of political power), 545d–e, 547a–b, 556e. The term is also applied to the conflict in the soul; see, for example, 440e.

36. For a review of the literature on the dramatic date of the dialogue, see Nails 1998 and Vegetti 1998a, pp. 22–23. See also Pappas 2013, pp. 33–35.

died around 420–415 and the cult of Bendis, which is presented as a novelty at the beginning of the dialogue, was introduced in Attica in 429/8, so it is plausible that the first formal celebration took place in the Piraeus in 421. These two different dramatic dates yield different readings of the context of the conversation about justice. In the first case, the conversation would take place under the oligarchic government of the Four Hundred—that is, in a moment of crisis for the city's institutions. In the second case, it would take place in the summer during the Peace of Nicias with Sparta and in a moment of relative political stability before the disaster of the Sicilian expedition, the deep crisis of Athenian democracy, and the first oligarchic coup. In this latter case we would have a conversation that prefigures and alludes to those troubled events, but that takes place at a moment when it was still possible to avoid them, and that gives a ruthless diagnosis of their deep moral and political causes while opening up a space for thinking about alternatives, if only in the form of a city in words.

At the beginning of the dialogue, Socrates recounts that he went down to the Piraeus with Glaucon in order to participate in the festivities in honor of the goddess Bendis. Bendis was a Thracian goddess who was integrated into Athens' pantheon. While the Athenians tended to resist changing their pantheon, the introduction of Bendis' cult may have been politically motivated. The alliance between Athens and Thrace was strategically important, as Athens imported cereals and the timber for its fleet from Thrace. Considering that the Athenians were competing with the Spartans to ensure the alliance of the Thracian king, Sitalces, the introduction of the official cult of Bendis may have been an attempt to consolidate the relations between Athens and the relatively large Thracian community living in the city.[37] As Socrates would be accused of introducing new divinities some years after the dramatic date of the dialogue, the reference to

37. See Campese and Gastaldi 1998, pp. 119–120.

the cult of Bendis may also be an ironic allusion to the hypocrisy of Socrates' formal indictment. It may also be meant to stress the heterogeneity of democratic life perfectly symbolized by the dialogue's location, the Piraeus.

The Piraeus may be taken as a symbol of Athenian democracy. It was Pericles who assigned Hippodamus of Miletus the task of designing a plan for the Piraeus, and who decided to double the walls connecting it to Athens so as to transform the city into an island.[38] The key to his military strategy in the Peloponnesian War was to ensure the city's self-sufficiency through maritime trade, so as to move a great part of the population from the surrounding environs to the city and abandon the countryside to the Spartan hoplites raids. Unsurprisingly, the peace agreement dictated by the Spartans after Athens' defeat in 404 included the destruction of the Long Walls and the reduction of the Athenian fleet to only twelve ships. The fleet had been the heart of Athens' military power during the war and, moreover, the basis of its radical form of democracy. Its sailors belonged to the *thetes*, the class of property-less people who were the most politicized and radicalized part of the demos, whose role in maritime warfare eventually gave them a decisive political and social relevance. In 411, the democratic fleet played a crucial role in the fall of the first oligarchic government. Moreover, the Piraeus was the base of Thrasybulus' partisans during the bloody civil war against the oligarchs in 403, and the decisive battle between the two factions took place at Munychia, the hill dominating the port: both Critias and Charmides were killed there and the oligarchic forces, while more numerous than the democrats, were forced to flee.

---

38. Pappas suggests that, as Hippodamus is reported by Aristotle to be the first non-philosopher to have inquired into forms of government and city planning (Aristot. *Pol.* 2.7), it is possible that Plato, by choosing the Piraeus, wanted to suggest that we should read the *Republic* against the background of a tradition of city planning and of debate about the future of Greek cities: Pappas 2013, pp. 22–23.

Yet another important reference to the political turmoil of those years is that the conversation takes place in Cephalus' house. Cephalus' family, while not having Athenian citizenship and thus being excluded from direct political participation, had long been connected with the Athenian democratic faction. The wealthy Cephalus was a personal acquaintance of Pericles, who invited him to move to Athens.[39] His son Polemarchus—a key figure in the dialogue as the one who compels Socrates to go to his house in order to have conversations and celebrate the festivity together—was one of the many victims of the Thirty. While, according to his brother Lysias' vehement oration *Against Eratosthenes*, the Thirty executed Polemarchus without a trial in order to take over his properties and wealth, he may actually have been killed because he was a well-known supporter of democracy and, along with his brother, was helping the democratic partisans. It may be significant that, in the dialogue, Polemarchus initially defends a notion of justice as helping friends and harming enemies—that is, a conception of justice of which he himself would become an illustrious victim. Lysias, who is silently present during the conversation, managed to escape to Megara, and continued supporting the democratic counterrevolution by supplying shields and money: for this reason, he was awarded Athenian citizenship by a decree promoted by Thrasybulus, repealed soon after by the Athenian Assembly. After democracy was restored, he authored some of the harshest texts denouncing the brutality and crimes of the Thirty and defending Athens' radical democracy.[40]

Plato chose to set the dialogue in a symbol of Athenian democracy and of democratic resistance (the Piraeus) and at the home of a family of wealthy associates of the Athenian democrats, one of whom would be a victim of the oligarchic terror, and the other

39. See Lys. 12.4.
40. See Lys. 12, 13, 34.

a prominent and vehement accuser of the Thirty. Moreover, he populated the dialogue with figures connected to the tormented years of the civil wars: Clitophon, who in the dialogue speaks in support of Thrasymachus' account of political power, was a member of the council under the 411 oligarchic government and a supporter of Theramenes; while Niceratus of Nicias—who is silent throughout the conversation—was another victim of the Thirty. The prefiguration of these somber years haunts from the very beginning the conversation about justice.

2.4 CRITIAS AND THE OLIGARCHIC CLUBS

A further explicit reference to the tormented last decades of the fifth century can be found in Adeimantus' long speech in Book II. This passage is particularly relevant because, in line with the *Seventh Letter*'s account of Plato's stance toward the Thirty, it places the oligarchic factions that plotted to subvert democracy among those who follow the paradigmatic conception of injustice:

> But in any case, if we are to be happy, we must pursue the path indicated in these accounts. We will organize secret societies and political clubs (συνωμοσίας τε καὶ ἑταιρίας) in order to remain hidden. And there are teachers of persuasion who can impart the art of speaking in assemblies and law courts (σοφίαν δημηγορικήν τε καὶ δικανικὴν διδόντες): therefore, using partly persuasion and partly force, we will not pay a penalty while outdoing others (πλεονεκτοῦντες). (*Rep.* 365c8–d6)

In Plato's works, the words ἑταῖρος and ἑταιρεία indicate three concepts: a generic notion of companionship, a more specific notion of philosophical or doctrinal friendship (which may be either negative or positive), and the historically specific notion of secret co-operation among friends and relatives with the purpose of influencing and even determining political and judiciary life.[41] In Adeimantus' passage, the term has this last meaning, as it appears clear from the other word with which it perhaps builds a hendiadys: συνωμοσίας, or secret societies or conspiratorial groups. From Thucydides we know that ξυνωμοσίαι were involved, under Peisander's lead, in the preparation of the oligarchic coup of 411 (Thuc. 8.54.4).

The *hetaireiai* were originally informal and exclusive groups of Athenians who met to spend time in private symposia and in philosophical, literary, and religious activities: they gathered wealthy aristocrats, were characterized by the practice of homoerotic love, and did not have an eminently political character. In this meaning of the word, the *hetaireia* was opposed to a συνωμοσία, in that the former operated within the constitutional and legal system of the city, while the latter term indicated conspiratorial activities taking place outside of, and in opposition to, the shared constitutional framework. The two terms came to be conflated in the years subsequent to the oligarchic coup of 411.[42] According to Thucydides, the *hetaireiai* became conspiratorial during the Peloponnesian War (Thuc. 3.82.6) and in the last decades of the fifth century, these clubs brought together aristocrats and elite citizens hostile to democracy.[43] In 415, the clubs got involved in two major interconnected scandals: the mutilation of the herms and the imitation of the Eleusinian Mysteries in private houses. The mutilation of the herms took place just before the Sicilian expedition and was probably motivated by the intent to jeopardize an expedition that the philo-oligarchs saw as the extreme expression of the demos' and its leaders' immoderate imperial ambitions. The

41. For an analysis of all the meanings of the two terms in Plato's *corpus*, see Sartori 1958.
42. Sartori 1957, p. 17.
43. Connor 1971, pp. 25–29.

Athenian demos connected the mutilation to the clubs' second act of impiety, the imitation of the Eleusinian Mysteries, in which Alcibiades was involved. According to Thucydides, the demos suspected that both acts indicated the existence of oligarchic conspiracies (Thuc. 6.60–61). The suspected connection between the two events may appear paradoxical, given Alcibiades' involvement in the profanation of the Eleusinian Mysteries. Alcibiades bore the main responsibility for the Assembly's decision to undertake the imperialistic expedition to Sicily and was at that time one of the most prominent democratic leaders. His *hetaireia*, which was implicated in the parody of the Mysteries, was most likely not oligarchic, or at the very least it did not share in the oligarchic and philo-Spartan hostility to the war and to Athens' imperialistic ambitions. Thus, it would have been nonsensical for Alcibiades' *hetaireia* to jeopardize an expedition that the Assembly had approved under his impulse.[44] Thucydides explains this inconsistency by virtue of the citizens' obsessive fear of tyranny and their jealousy and suspicion for Alcibiades' talents, successes, and ambitions (Thuc. 6.61, 6.15.4). Isocrates will, instead, present Alcibiades as a victim of an oligarchic conspiracy (Isoc. 16.5–6).

However, as McGlew argues, there are several reasons why the demos' suspicions connecting the two acts of impiety may not have been entirely irrational. First, the imitation of the mysteries was not necessarily a mockery of them; on the contrary, the intent may have been to actually perform the initiation rite and, by doing so, to privatize and politicize the ties that religious initiation to the mysteries created among the initiated. Seen in this light, it is clear why the demos reacted to what it saw as the creation of secret bonds of loyalty competing with the public bond uniting all citizens. In McGlew's interpretation, the two impious acts were connected insofar as they both challenged the democratic public space: the anonymous

---

44. Sartori 1957, pp. 91–92.

mutilation of the herms was an act of symbolic terrorism that pub-licly expressed a secrecy, while the imitation of the Mysteries was the privatization of a public rite that established bonds of loyalty and si-lence among the initiated. Both acts were addressed against Athenian democracy, rather than against religion.[45]

The aristocratic clubs became significantly involved in the preparation of the two oligarchic revolutions of 411 and 404. In Thucydides' account of the 411 coup, Peisander managed to unite the clubs under the shared purpose of overthrowing democracy or—more literally—of dissolving the demos (καταλύσουσι τὸν δῆμον). In the months immediately preceding the coup, the clubs were most likely involved in a series of criminal acts, most notably a number of political assassinations accomplished in secret with the aims of terrorizing the demos and of eliminating the democratic leaders who might pose a threat to the oligarchs. Moreover, they managed to in-filtrate democratic institutions and manipulate the procedures for choosing magistrates in order to place trustworthy oligarchs in the *boule* and among the elected generals.[46] In all probability, they also played a role in the manipulation of the assemblies that voted to re-strict political rights based on property and establish a government of Four Hundred.

We can find an echo of these events in Aristophanes' *Lysistrata*, performed in 411. The play warns the Athenian public about the dan-gerous activities of the oligarchic clubs at two different moments. In the first passage, Lysistrata suggests that, in order to solve the crisis of the city, it is necessary, among other things, to card like wool those who get together to conspire for public offices—that is, to dissolve the clubs (Aristoph. *Lys.* 577–578). Later (*Lys.* 616–623), the chorus

---

45. McGlew 1999. For an interpretation of the mutilation as an attack against the Athenian democracy see also Osborne 1985.
46. See Bearzot 2013, ch. 2.

claims that it can feel the smell of tyranny because some Spartans are meeting in the house of Cleisthenes and trying to persuade the women to plot together in order to steal the demos' wage—μισθός, the monetary compensation for participation in political activities, which was one of the pillars of Athens' participatory democracy. The reference this time, although more obscure, is still intelligible: the oligarchic faction was notoriously philo-Spartan and the mention of the house of Cleisthenes (whom Aristophanes mocks in the comedy for his effeminacy) contains a reference to homoeroticism, which was a practice typical of the aristocratic members of the clubs. A further reference to the role played by the clubs can be found in Demophantus' decree, passed in 410, after the restoration of democracy. The decree contains a collective oath of loyalty to democracy and a formula that annulled any other oath sworn in Athens for the dissolution of democracy, most likely a reference to the oaths sworn in secret by oligarchic *hetaireiai* (Andoc. 1.97–98).

These clubs played an important role in the preparation of the 404 coup as well, and used methods very similar to those of 411, with the exception of political assassinations;[47] instead, they resorted to political trials (which they probably manipulated) in order to eliminate the democratic leaders and generals opposed to the ratification of the peace agreement Theramenes brought to Athens. In *Against Eratosthenes*, Lysias also reports that the clubs formed a shadow government by nominating five *ephori*, who infiltrated and manipulated democratic institutions in preparation of the coup: Critias is mentioned as one of the five (Lys. 12.43–44). On both occasions, the clubs operated by controlling the democratic institutions and leading

---

47. See Bearzot 2013, ch. 4. The *hetaireiai* are also mentioned in Aristotle's *Athenian Constitution*, which speaks of three positions in the city after peace was made: the democrats, an intermediate moderate position represented by Theramenes, and the nobles organized in the clubs together with the exiles (philo-Spartan oligarchs who had taken part in the 411 coup and had been exiled) who wanted an oligarchy: Aristot. *Ath. Pol.* 34.3.

the Athenian Assembly to vote for its own dissolution and the establishment of an oligarchic government.[48]

In addition to Adeimantus' remark, there are other passages in the Platonic *corpus* in which Plato seems to signal his and Socrates' distance from the aristocratic clubs and their conspiracies. In the *Apology*, Socrates tells the jurors that, for all his life, he avoided participation both in public offices, as a general or a public speaker, and in *conspiracies* and factions: συνωμοσιῶν καὶ στάσεων (Plat. *Apol.* 36b–c). As, besides the official accusation of impiety and corruption of the youth, the main reason for Socrates' indictment was his association both with Alcibiades and with key figures of the two oligarchic coups, it is plausible that this passage is meant to exonerate Socrates from any participation in these plots.[49] A reference to the clubs' symposia, and to their efforts to manipulate public offices, can be found in the *Theaetetus* description of the philosopher's distance from active politics. While the passage does not directly refer to Socrates, it does indicate that the "chorus leader" among philosophers will stay away from the clubs' plots for power and offices (σπουδαὶ δὲ ἑταιριῶν ἐπ᾽ ἀρχὰς) (Plat. *Theaet.* 173d). In a different context, the Athenian Stranger's definition of the worst enemy of the constitution as he who tries to enslave the laws and to make the city into a servant of an ἑταιρεία by arousing a civil strife (Plat. *Laws* 856b) likely expresses the same hostility toward the conspiratorial activity carried on by the clubs.

---

48. Some members of the Thirty had also been members of the Four Hundred: Critias, Theramenes, Melobius, Mnesilochus, Charicles, Aristoteles, Onomacles, and perhaps Eratosthenes: Krentz 1982, p. 55. There may have been more, but as we do not have the list of the Four Hundred, their identity is difficult to verify. Lysias insists, with some exaggeration, on the identity between the oligarchs involved among the Four Hundred and the Thirty and their *boule*: Lys. 13.74.

49. A similar preoccupation with the disassociation of Socrates' memory from the turbulent events of those years and their protagonists is expressed by Xenophon, who in the *Memorabilia* insists on the incompatibility between Critias' and Alcibiades' violence and lack of self-restraint and Socrates' lived example of moderation and use of persuasion instead of force: Xen. *Mem*.1.2.12–16.

The dissemination of these passages indicates that Adeimantus' remark about clubs and conspiracies is not an anomaly but, rather, is part of a pattern extending from what may be the very first of Plato's works to his final dialogue. This pattern is consistent with Plato's political biography in the *Seventh Letter*, in that it is meant to signal his distance from active participation both in democratic institutions and in the oligarchic plots that shook the Athenian political order in the last decade of the fifth century. But Adeimantus' remark is also extremely relevant for our analysis of tyranny in the *Republic*. Indeed, it contains a straightforward evaluation of the unjust nature of these practices. In Book II, Adeimantus' speech follows Glaucon's long tirade in support of injustice and tyranny. This tirade was meant to compel Socrates to find better arguments to defend justice against Thrasymachus' idea that one should only practice justice in the presence of witnesses. Taking up this point, Adeimantus adds that, as the sole concern of justice is reputation, the unjust man who can appear virtuous lives the life of a god (θεσπέσιος; *Rep.* 365b6–7). According to Adeimantus, this idea will especially appeal to smart young people endowed with a good nature (εὐφυεῖς; *Rep.* 365a7), a suggestion that already anticipates Socrates' discussion of the corruption of philosophical natures in Book VI. Adeimantus goes on to characterize conspiracies and political clubs as a tactic to succeed in this enterprise: those who gather together in clubs in order to use both persuasion and force to outdo others in law courts and assemblies are the perfect example of unjust men who cover themselves with virtue in public while secretly acting unjustly. These people share three aspects with Thrasymachus' tyrant: injustice, impunity, and πλεονεξία. As we have seen, in the work of Thucydides and Aristophanes, and in Demophantus' decree, the oligarchic activity of the *hetaireiai* is consistently associated with suspicions of tyrannical ambition, as every attempt to overthrow democracy is considered to be tyrannical. This corroborates the suggestion that, in Adeimantus' remark, the political activities of the aristocratic clubs and of secret conspiracies are an instance of complete injustice and part of the discussion of tyranny as its most perfect political instantiation. The allusion to the role and practice of the *hetaireiai* and conspiracies within the context of the discussion of complete injustice and tyranny suggests that Plato viewed oligarchic conspiracies as a symptom and part of the crisis of the city, and certainly not a solution to it.

As Critias was one of the most prominent oligarchic conspirators and in the fourth century was depicted as a particularly vicious and greedy tyrant, the hypothesis that Critias may be one of those opportunist politicians that Plato had in mind while describing his own tyrant may appear as an attractive one. It is significant, for example, that some of the tyrant's deeds Socrates describes recall the crimes and behaviors frequently attributed to the Thirty: the murder of all potentially hostile prominent citizens, the persecution of the rich, and notably greed.[50] Although speaking from two different political perspectives, both Lysias and Xenophon indict the greed motivating the Thirty's oligarchic opposition to democracy. In *Against Eratosthenes*, Lysias claims greed motivated the Thirty's murder of his brother Polemarchus, which they hypocritically justified on political grounds. This unrestrained greed appears even grotesque in the episode in which they snatch a pair of gold earrings belonging to Polemarchus' wife (Lys. 12.19–20). Toward the conclusion of his speech, Lysias explicitly reminds the jurors that the Thirty accumulated wealth by taking advantage of public affairs (Lys. 12.93).[51] From the other side of the political spectrum, Xenophon

---

50. Danzig, for example, suggests that Plato's concern with distinguishing himself and his own positions from Critias may be reflected in the opposition between the tyrant and the wise king in the *Republic*: Danzig 2013, p. 501n32.

51. On the greed of the Thirty and of the oligarchs in general, see also Lys. 25.16–17 and Lys. 34.4–5.

suggests that the more moderate Theramenes' disgrace in front of Critias and his death sentence (Xen. *Hell.* 2.3) resulted from his opposition to the killing of innocent people in order to confiscate their property. Moreover, in the *Memorabilia*, Xenophon portrays Critias as greedy, selfish, bloodthirsty, and lacking the self-restraint and moderation displayed by his former friend, Socrates (Xen. *Mem.* 1.2.12).

While this hypothesis may appear attractive at first sight, given Critias' reputation for greed and violence, at closer look some relevant problems emerge concerning both the historical appraisal of Critias' political profile and Plato's own portrait of his infamous relative in *Charmides, Protagoras, Timaeus,* and *Critias.*

The figure of Critias has undergone a revaluation in recent years. His traditional depiction as a greedy tyrant is mostly based on the account provided by Xenophon in the *Hellenica*, and partially in *Memorabilia*. In the *Hellenica*, Xenophon has Theramenes saying that Critias, once in power, turned from a hater of the demos into a hater of the rich (Xen. *Hell.* 2.3.47), the implication being that the motivation for this behavior was greed. The crux of the matter is not so much whether the oligarchs committed violent crimes and expropriated rich people but, rather, whether the motivation for these acts was greed, as claimed by Lysias and Xenophon. The *Seventh Letter*, for example, does mention the crimes committed by the Thirty, but it does not provide any explanation for these actions and does not make mention of greed (324c–325a). This problem is particularly relevant for the interpretation of Plato's tyrant, because violence alone would not be a sufficient criterion for identifying Critias as one of the Athenian politicians to whom Plato's tyrant alludes: the main motivation for this violence must be of appetitive nature and must have appetitive individual self-interest at its core.

A number of scholars have insisted on a different portrait of Critias' deeds and motivations, challenging the reliability of Xenophon's account, which—they claim—is biased.[52] On these accounts, while it is true that Critias was indeed a "hater of the rich," the Thirty's politics of exterminating and expropriating them was not motivated by greed but, rather, was part of a philo-Spartan doctrinal program and hence should be understood as an attack against plutocracy in the name of the ideal of laconizing Attica.[53] One could find a basis for this interpretation in two of Critias' fragments concerning wealth, fr. 8 and fr. 15 (D.-K. 88B8 and 88B15), which—taken together— indicate an opposition between the legitimate wealth typical of aristocratic families and the wealth of the *nouveaux riches*, the latter acquired through economic activities aimed at the accumulation of money. Moreover, we find there a dismissal of the pursuit of wealth in contrast to the pursuit of glory and to the possession of nobility of birth. Critias' policies against rich people would have been motivated by an ideal of radical sociopolitical reform, dispensing with the ethos of the accumulation of riches characterizing Athenian imperialism, rather than by greed, and would thus have very little in common with Plato's tyrant, except for the use of violence.

Perhaps the most detailed reconstruction of Critias' coherent political project is the one offered by Umberto Bultrighini, and based both on indirect sources and on Critias' fragments.[54] What emerges from this reconstruction is the portrait of a coherent anti-democrat, whose political project consisted in the rediscovery and re-elaboration of traditional aristocratic values, such as σωφροσύνη—reformulated as "doing one's own things"—in the insistence on the centrality of

---

52. According to Danzig 2014, Xenophon's would be biased by his rivalry with Plato, and his desire to put Plato in an embarrassing situation, given the *Charmides* rather sympathetic presentation of Critias, would be the motivation behind the decision to offer such a negative portrait of Critias in the *Hellenica*.

53. See, for example: Krentz 1982, pp. 64–68, 80–81; Dušanič 2000; Németh 2006; Tuozzo 2011, pp. 59–66; Canfora 2013; Danzig 2013, 2014.

54. Bultrighini 1999.

individual excellence as a prerequisite for participation in the political affairs of the city, in the opposition to the greed and corruption of democratic leaders (fr. 45 and fr. 52), and in the adoption of the Spartan constitution, considered to be the καλλίστη πολιτεία, in opposition both to democracy and to the mixed regime summarized by Theramenes' notion of πάτριος πολιτεία. In Bultrighini's interpretation, opportunism, lack of morality, and greed are features attributed to Critias in the *damnatio memoriae* subsequent to the fall of the Thirty, which contemporary interpreters have uncritically and all too quickly accepted.[55] This dismissal of Critias' political thought and of his actions, however, is an obstacle to the accurate historical understanding of the nature of Critias' project.

What we know of his life, beyond the role he played in the Thirty's government, not only seems to confirm the interpretation of Critias as a traditional philo-Spartan oligarchic thinker who intended to restore the government by the ἄριστοι in Athens but also runs against the possibility that Plato had his relative in mind when he described the rise of tyranny in the *Republic*. Critias, indeed, never participated in the political life of the city as a democratic leader or as a protector of the demos, and he never based his political career on the approval of the demos. On the contrary, all his activities in Athens link him to the oligarchic faction. In 415, he was accused of participating in the mutilation of the *hermai*, but was acquitted. He first appeared on the public scene in 411, after the fall of the first oligarchic government, as the proponent of a posthumous conviction for treason of Phrynichus, assassinated a few months earlier in the agora probably by other oligarchs. This act may have been motivated by the attempt to coopt Alcibiades to the oligarchic cause, for Phrynichus was Alcibiades' most vehement opponent.[56] Critias was exiled for a short

55. Bultrighini 1999, pp. 38–46.
56. Bultrighini 1999, pp. 218–219.

period to Thessaly, probably upon the impulse of the radical democratic leader, Cleophon. It is true that in the *Hellenica*, Theramenes suggests that Critias got involved in a democratic insurrection while in Thessaly, but this is the only reference we have to Critias' democratic entanglements during his exile, and it is likely that Theramenes' allusion was meant to question Critias' coherence and undermine his authority, and so had little or no factual basis (Xen. *Hell.* 2.3.36). In fact, Critias' involvement in a democratic insurrection runs against everything else we know of his political commitments and activities. A passage from Philostratus, moreover, contradicts Theramenes' statement, as it argues that in Thessaly, Critias worked to strengthen the oligarchies existing there and that he criticized Athenian democracy.[57]

This portrait of Critias helps us make more sense of Plato's sympathetic presentation of his relative. In none of the dialogues in which he appears is he portrayed either as a greedy, or as an opportunistic political leader, or as someone not in control of himself and enslaved to his appetites. In the *Protagoras*, he only intervenes shortly in order to criticize Alcibiades' excessively agonistic attitude and to serve as a mediator between Protagoras and Socrates, for the sake of continuing the discussion together (Plat. *Prot.* 336d–337a). The case of *Charmides* is particularly significant for our purpose, because it is entirely possible to read this dialogue as apologetic not of Socrates but of Critias. The first indication that this may be the case is the fact that Plato does not try to underplay the personal and intellectual connection between Socrates and Critias, which should, instead, be his first preoccupation if the intent were that of defending Socrates from his association with the infamous tyrant. On the contrary, at the beginning of *Charmides*, Socrates sits next to Critias, engages with him in a friendly conversation about the battle of Potidaea (Plat. *Charm.*

---

57. See Philostr. V S 1.16; see also Robinson 2011, p. 62.

153c), and subsequently comments upon the nobility of Critias' and Charmides' house, its connection with Solon, and its predisposition toward philosophy and poetry (*Charm.* 154e–155a). The tone of his conversation is that of a teasing friend who is having a discussion with a man in whom he recognizes culture and intelligence. Moreover, at some key passages, Critias shows to be a worthy interlocutor. Far from willing to win the contest at all costs, he is ready to withdraw some of his claims and to admit that he may have been mistaken in making them if they turn out to have inacceptable consequences, and he is in general open to honestly pursuing the inquiry together with Socrates.[58]

The dialogue also displays Critias' deep concern with σωφροσύνη—as he, for example, praises this virtue in Charmides as a proof of the young cousin's worthiness (*Charm.* 157d)—and moreover, attributes to him the formula "doing one's own things" (*Charm.* 161b and 162c). While it is true that in *Charmides*, Socrates challenges the obscurity of this formula and the dialogue ends in an *aporia*, we must also bear in mind that he will pick it up again in the *Republic* and transform it into his definition of justice. What interest would Plato have had in acknowledging Critias' paternity of a formula he himself would adopt in a key dialogue about justice, if his intent had *not* been that of offering a rather positive portrait of his relative and of rehabilitating his memory?[59] The fact that Critias is refuted in the dialogue and that there is no final definition

---

58. At *Charmides* 164c–165b, for example, Critias retracts his previous claim that temperance is doing good things, as it turned out that this definition had as a consequence that even a man ignorant of himself can be temperate if he does good things, a consequence Critias is not willing to accept, for he identifies temperance and self-knowledge. At 169c, Critias is embarrassed and ashamed of being caught in a difficulty, because he is accustomed to distinguish himself in analogous occasions. However, Critias' embarrassment does not prevent him from continuing the inquiry and does not lead him to adopt an aggressive attitude, as in the case, for example, of Thrasymachus and Callicles.

59. On the apologetic character of *Charmides*, see Dušanič 2000 and Danzig 2013. On Plato's positive evaluation of Critias' thought, see also Tuozzo 2011, pp. 57–58.

of temperance is clearly also meant to signal a significant difference between Plato and his older cousin. Plato adopts and rehabilitates some of Critias' slogans, his insistence on σωφροσύνη and self-knowledge, and the famous formula "doing one's own things," but he also re-elaborates them in a different direction, while showing that Critias' understanding of them was deficient. In the *Republic*, the formula "doing one's own things" not only becomes Socrates' definition of justice but it also acquires a much more complex and sophisticated meaning in light of the soul's tripartition. Moreover, the definition of moderation provided in this dialogue is alternative to the definitions offered by Critias in *Charmides*. Here, Plato's broadly sympathetic portrait of Critias coexists with a preoccupation with demonstrating Critias' mistaken understanding of both moderation and self-knowledge. Considering that the claim to σωφροσύνη—and contrasting characterization of the demos and its political leaders as lacking it—was an integral part of the oligarchic *hetaireiai*'s and the Thirty's self-legitimating discourse, it is significant that Socrates refutes Critias precisely on this point.[60] This reading of *Charmides* further helps make sense of Critias' appearance in *Timaeus-Critias*, where he is not only presented as a man versed in both politics and philosophy (Plat. *Tim.* 19e–20a) but also has the honor both of proposing the order of the discourses to be made and of speaking of the beautiful city in action, at war against Atlantis, by reporting Solon's story concerning the virtue of ancient Athens (*Tim.* 19d–27b). There are good reasons for identifying the mythical Atlantis of Solon's story with imperial democratic Athens: Atlantis is an island and it is organized around the sea, as attested by its link to Poseidon and its topography (*Criti.* 113c–d), and by the fact that it heavily relies on imports and exchange, it exploits a precious metal—*oreichalkos*—which clearly alludes to the silver exploited by Athens

---

60. On the centrality of the notion of σωφροσύνη for the oligarchic clubs, see McGlew 1999.

to fund its fleet (*Criti.* 114d–115a), and finally it lacks measure and moderation in its accumulation of riches, as well as in its architecture. Ancient Athens, on the contrary, presents several similarities with Kallipolis—in particular, the political and physical separation between the class of guardians and that of the producers,[61] the communal way of life of the guardians, the absence of silver and gold among them, the moderation characterizing the city as a whole, and its reliance on land rather than on the sea (*Criti.* 111e–112a). As noticed by Bultrighini, by portraying Athens at war with Atlantis, the myth actually describes Athens' war against itself: as Atlantis is nothing but the degeneration of an ancient, moderate, and nobler regime, we can take both the ancient Athens and the Atlantis of Critias' story as depicting two opposite evolutions of Athens.[62] The fact that Plato has Critias presenting these two alternatives and articulating in this way a critique of the appetitive nature of imperial Athens cannot be underestimated from the viewpoint of the appraisal of Plato's view of his relative. This is also the reason why a number of interpreters have implausibly argued that the Critias of these two dialogues is not the tyrant, but yet another Critias, grandfather of the tyrant.[63] The motivation for this interpretive choice is rooted in a biased understanding of the nature of Critias' political project and actions, and in the idea that Plato could have not possibly honored the memory of his relative in the way he does in these dialogues. However, the portrait of Critias in these two dialogues is

---

61. On the rationale for the separation between power and wealth in Kallipolis, see Arends 1988, pp. 18–25; Vegetti 1998c; Arruzza 2011.
62. Bultrighini 1999, p. 262.
63. See Taylor 1928, pp. 23ff.; Burnet 1950, vol. I, p. 338; Welliver 1977, pp. 50–57; Labarbe 1990; Morgan 1998. For a refutation of this thesis and possible solutions to the chronological puzzle on which it is based, see Rosenmeyer 1949; Bultrighini 1999, pp. 273–293; Iannucci 2002, pp. 3–11. For an accurate refutation of Labarbe's arguments, see Bultrighini 1999, pp. 294–297.

not that far from what we can gather of Critias' personality and political views in the *Charmides*.

It is certainly significant that ancient Athens does not perfectly match the description of Kallipolis. Most important, what is missing from ancient Athens is the rule by philosopher-kings, which signals a relevant difference between Critias' more traditional philo-Spartan and oligarchic project and Plato's more ambitious and decidedly more revolutionary project of a philosophical rule of the city. In conclusion, while showing his philosophical failings, in the dialogues Plato gives a positive and sympathetic portrait of Critias, a portrait in which there is no room for the greed attributed to him by other authors. On the contrary, Critias embodies a traditional aristocratic ideal and its values, as he displays an elitist attitude informed by the conviction that only the best men—those with real competence and moderation—should rule, and shows a dislike for manual labor and for the greed and appetitive inclinations of the demos and of its leaders. His philo-Spartan position, and his description of ancient Athens and its glory at war, qualify him as an example of timocratic character, which would also explain why he is unable to offer a proper definition of σωφροσύνη.[64] The ancient Athens described by Critias may also be taken as an example of timocratic city. An excess of θυμός can, of course, have tragic consequences, for it can lead to the attempt to take absolute power in order to radically transform the city without having real knowledge of the good and by exercising excessive violence. If this is the case, however, Critias can certainly be criticized, but he hardly meets the requirements for qualifying as Plato's licentious tyrant, and we should not take Adeimantus' reference to oligarchic clubs and conspiracies as denoting Critias specifically.

---

64. Along these lines, see Schmid 1998, p. 160.

2.5 POLITICAL OPPORTUNISTS, ASPIRING TYRANTS, AND CORRUPTING DEMOS

In order to identify the specific political phenomenon denoted by Plato's tyrannical ideal-type, we should attend to the transformation of the nature of democratic leadership during the last third of the fifth century. This transformation is exemplified by the very denomination of champion of the demos (προστάτης τοῦ δήμου), with which Plato designates the aspiring tyrant. While rare in fifth-century Greek, this appellation became much more frequently used in the last third of the fifth century, acquiring, at the same time, a technical meaning. In the 420s, it came to indicate a leader of the democratic faction, and it was adopted by a politician in order to present himself as the protector of the whole city or of the demos understood as the city's popular sector. The phrase was more frequently used as the relationship between the political leader and the citizen body ceased being mediated by the political leader's personal ties and friendships. As a protector and servant of the demos, the προστάτης established a privileged and direct relationship with the people.[65] According to Connor, this direct and systematic appeal to the demos marked a significant transformation in the nature and dynamic of democratic political leadership, in that it replaced the centrality of kinship and personal ties as the political leader's power base with the direct activation and organization of the poorest sector of the population.[66]

Several politicians from these years may have embodied aspects of Plato's description of the tyrant as a political opportunist who cultivates a direct relationship with the demos, does not refrain from using violence and deception in order to seize and maintain power, and uses power in order to advance his own personal agenda. Some

65. Connor 1971, pp. 110–117.
66. Connor 1971, pp. 90–91.

of the 411 oligarchs were former demagogues who supported the oligarchy after abandoning a successful political career as leaders of the demos. Peisander, the mastermind behind the oligarchic coup, was nominated in 415 to the committee inquiring into the mutilation of the herms; on this occasion, he displayed a particular anti-oligarchic ardor, and he went so far as to ask the Assembly to authorize the use of torture on Athenian citizens under the pretext of protecting democracy from oligarchic or tyrannical conspiracies. Only four years later, he would unite the *hetaireiai* in an oligarchic conspiracy, and he was most likely behind the terroristic strategy the clubs adopted.[67] Like Peisander, Phrynichus was probably a demagogue before adhering to Antiphon's radical faction among the 411 oligarchs. Thucydides attributes a certain capacity for strategic thinking to him, while offering a rather sinister portrait of his deeds. In particular, Thucydides' account of Phrynichus' competition with and enmity for Alcibiades reveals the extent to which the former's main concern was his own personal advantage, even at the costs of the city's common interests.[68]

The most notorious of these opportunistic political leaders who cultivated a direct relationship with the demos in order to acquire personal power, glory, and benefits was Alcibiades. As Jacqueline de Romilly writes, Alcibiades can be considered as an ideal-type for a politician whose personal ambitions had priority over the common interest, a flatterer of the people, and a man involved in conspiracies and intrigues that turned out to be disastrous for the collectivity. Moreover, he acted as the embodiment of Athenian imperialism, leading the city to its ruin. As such, he was a living lesson concerning

---

67. See Bearzot 2013, ch. 2.

68. In a letter sent to the Spartan Admiral Astyochus, where he denounced Alcibiades for promoting friendship between the Persian Tissaphernes and Athens at Sparta's expense, he justified his act of betrayal on the basis of his intention to get rid of an enemy even at the cost of some disadvantage to his own city: Thuc. 8.50.

the problems of democracy.[69] Some commentators have remarked that Socrates' discussion of the problem of the corruption of young men endowed with a philosophical nature and great talents in Book VI probably refers to Alcibiades.[70] Here Socrates argues that these philosophical natures, when corrupted, are the cause of the greatest evils for themselves and for the city as a whole (*Rep.* 495a10–b6). As, throughout the dialogue, the tyrant is referred to as the cause of the greatest collective and individual unhappiness, this claim can safely be taken as a reference to the danger posed by the degeneration of talented youths into tyrannical characters. Alcibiades was the most famous and most discussed example of a young man of excellent birth with great talent, beauty, courage, and wealth who, while interested in philosophy, was also characterized by excessive political ambition, lawless behavior, and, ultimately, was corrupted by the political and cultural climate of the city.[71] Not only did he do harm to the city but he also was suspected by his fellow citizens of having tyrannical aspirations.

Alcibiades' own political career was characterized by a strong, albeit instrumental, relationship with the demos. As Plutarch notes several centuries later, Alcibiades based most of his political career on his charisma and on his ability to speak persuasively in public (Plut. *Alc.* 10.3). But his special bond with the demos was not connected

---

69. De Romilly 1995, p. 11.
70. One of the most extensive and persuasive treatments of this point is in Larivée 2005 and 2012. See also Bearzot 1981, p. 28.
71. Alcibiades' father, Cleinias, belonged to the Eupatrids family, which counted Ajax as its ancestor and had been politically associated with Cleisthenes. Alcibiades' mother belonged to the Alcmeonids family, and her cousin, Pericles, became Alcibiades' guardian after the death of Cleinias. In addition to his nobility, Alcibiades was also significantly rich, both because of his inheritance from his family and because of the wealth he acquired through his marriage to Hipparete, the daughter of Hipponicos (a man famous for his wealth). Finally, he had undeniable political and military talent, a brilliant intelligence, much celebrated beauty, and insatiable ambition. See Hatzfeld 1951, pp. 1–26; and de Romilly 1995, pp. 22–33. This portrait resembles very closely the portrait of philosophically talented youth in Book VI of the *Republic*.

to a sincere democratic faith, as Alcibiades was able to rapidly switch positions according to his own advantage. Pseudo Andocides describes Alcibiades' relation to democracy in the following terms:

> after proving to the Greeks that they should not be surprised whenever he commits violence against one of them, for he does not treat his fellow citizens as his equals, but rather robs some of them, beats others, throws some into prison, and extorts money from others, he shows that democracy is worthless, by talking like a demagogue and acting as a tyrant, for he understood that what you worry about is just the name of tyranny, while the thing itself leaves you indifferent. (Ps.–Andoc. 4.27)

Alcibiades was the promoter of the most disastrous military enterprise of the Peloponnesian War, sharing and supporting the demos' and the radical democratic aspirations for conquest, and at the same time he was involved in the *hetaireiai* and in the scandal of the imitation of the Eleusinian Mysteries in 415. After being indicted with impiety, he did not hesitate to go into exile to Sparta, where he slandered Athenian democracy and offered strategic information to the Spartans, justifying himself as a betrayed lover of the city who is ready to do everything in order to regain his role within it.[72] The advice Alcibiades gave to Sparta was key to the joint Spartan and Syracusan victory over Athens in 413, to Sparta's strategically crucial conquest of the fort of Decelea in Attica, and to the erosion of Athens' hegemony among the colonies in Asia Minor: Alcibiades greatly harmed his city in the way a resentful lover could harm a former beloved.

In 411, while in exile, he plotted with the oligarchic conspirators, for the simple reason that he believed himself more likely to be

---

72. See Thuc. 6.92.2 and Isoc. 5.58.

recalled to Athens with full immunity by an oligarchic government, rather than by a democratic one.[73] And, indeed, both Theramenes and Critias were among the most strenuous supporters of the necessity of recalling Alcibiades to Athens.[74] Once the alliance with the oligarchs failed, Alcibiades, metamorphosed back into a democrat, galvanized the democratic fleet, and played an important role in the management of the democratic resistance in Samos.[75] After the fall of the oligarchic government and the restoration of democracy, Alcibiades' aspirations to autocratic power seemed to be realized when not only he was recalled to Athens with full immunity but he was also nominated ἡγεμὼν αὐτοκράτωρ (a commander with full powers).[76] The Athenian demos loved him again and trusted him with the outcome of the war. Plutarch goes as far as to say that the poor Athenian populace was so charmed by Alcibiades that they wanted him as their tyrant (Plut. *Alc.* 34.7).[77]

Alcibiades' strongly erotic character—attributed to him by a number of ancient Greek authors—is a further element suggesting his identity with the figure of the corrupt philosophical youth. In the *Symposium*, Plato refers to Alcibiades' inner conflict, split as he is between his attraction to Socrates and philosophy and his political ambition (*Sym.* 216a–b). Moreover, the ancient sources insist on Alcibiades' *anti-isonomic* attitude, egocentrism and arrogance,

---

73. See Thuc. 8.48.4. Here Thucydides says that Phrynichus believed that Alcibiades did not care for oligarchy more than he cared for democracy, and that his only concern was to come back to Athens, even at the cost of changing political order. Thucydides writes that Phrynichus was right in believing this: this passage is one of the rare instances in which Thucydides takes an explicit position in the first person.

74. See Plut. *Alc.* 33.1.

75. See Thuc. 8.81.1–2 and 86.4–5.

76. See Xen. *Hell.* 1.4.20. See Plato, *Rep.* 566e8–9, where Socrates says that the tyrant wages constant wars so that the demos will always be in need of a ἡγεμών.

77. According to Bultrighini, Plutarch is here mistaken, as it is much more likely that it was Critias and his oligarchic circle who tried to persuade Alcibiades to suspend democratic freedoms: Bultrighini 1999, p. 207.

which led him to interpret freedom as the freedom to do whatever he pleased.[78] These, for example, are the terms in which Lysias addresses the jury in his first oration *Against Alcibiades*, where he warns the jurors that if men are allowed to do whatever they please, then codes of laws and elections of generals become useless (Lys. 14.11). In other words, this kind of freedom, which resembles the license Socrates parodies in Book VIII of the *Republic*, had an eminently anti-isonomic and lawless character, and was a danger to the political institutions of the democratic city. Thucydides also connects Alcibiades' lawless behavior and the suspicion of his tyrannical ambitions (Thuc. 6.15). Alcibiades' negative freedom is often exemplified by references to his unrestrained eros and to his sexual license, with accents that remind us of Plato's description of the tyrant's unbounded pursuit of desires and erotic madness.[79]

The responsibility for Alcibiades' moral corruption was a debated topic in the fourth century. From both Xenophon (Xen. *Mem.* 1.2.12–16) and Isocrates (Isoc. 11.4–6), we learn that his association with Alcibiades was probably used as a slander against Socrates, deemed responsible for Alcibiades' political exploits and lack of self-restraint. Xenophon's and Isocrates' accounts attempt to distance Socrates from responsibility for Alcibiades' character: the first insists that Alcibiades did not learn anything from Socrates' embodiment of the virtue of moderation; and the second argues both that Socrates never really taught Alcibiades and that Alcibiades was in any case an excellent politician. Plato is more adamant in indicting the democratic city for Alcibiades' corruption. In Book VI, Socrates discusses the reason why philosophical youths run the risk of going seriously astray. One of these reasons lies in the very goods belonging to such

---

78. Among the anecdotes that display Alcibiades' arrogance from a young age, see Plut., *Alc.* 2.3–4.

79. See, for example, Ps.-Andoc. 4.10. For a discussion of the sources concerning Alcibiades' sexual license, see de Romilly 1995, pp. 42–44.

natures: their intelligence, courage, moderation, beauty, nobility of birth, and material possessions (*Rep.* 491b7–c4). The reason why these various qualities and goods will in the end most likely destroy the philosophical nature is twofold. First, a young man with talent and goods of such a rare kind will be the privileged object of flattery for the politicians and fellow citizens who want to use his talent for their own purposes. They will resort to persuasion and, whenever necessary, to compulsion (*Rep.* 494b8–e7). Second, a young man who has such a rare nature, good family connections, and wealth, and is flattered by corruptors, will tend to become ambitious and to overestimate his own capabilities (*Rep.* 494c7–d1). In an extremely significant passage, Socrates addresses the question of the presumed corruption of the youths by the sophists who sell them a private education. The passage is particularly relevant in the light of the accusation addressed to Socrates of corrupting the youth, and of the fact that the distinction between Socrates and the sophists was anything but clear to the Athenian public, as it appears evident from Aristophanes' parody in the *Clouds*. Moreover, the passage reveals that the belief that the sophists corrupted young people was one shared by the many:

> Or do you too agree with the many that there are some young people who are corrupted by sophists, that there are sophists who corrupt young people in private, which is worth mentioning? Don't you think, however, that those who say this are the greatest sophists, and that they educate most completely and transform young and old, men and women into the kind of people they want them to be? (*Rep.* 492a5–b3)

While it is true that some lines later Socrates will also accuse the sophists of contributing to the corruption of young people, in that they teach nothing but what the demos believes and desires (*Rep.*

493a6–8), this should be taken only as a symptom of a disease, the real cause of which lies elsewhere: in the incapacity of the demos and of its politicians to be real educators, and in their action of corruption of the entire city. The first sophists are then precisely those many who accused Socrates of corrupting the youth, and their force of corruption lies in their capacity to assimilate everybody to their own ethos, to make everybody into a demotic person. This observation introduces us to the conceptual relationship between tyranny and democracy established by Plato in the dialogue, which will be addressed in the next chapter.

Chapter 3

Tyrannical Democracy

In no city is the best element friendly to the demos, in each city it is
rather the worst element that is friendly to the demos.

Pseudo Xenophon, The Constitution of the Athenians

3.1 PLATO AND ATHENIAN DEMOCRACY

Since the appearance of Karl Popper's indictment of Plato as a proto-
totalitarian thinker in *The Open Society and its Enemies*,[1] the *Republic*'s
political argument has been a source of embarrassment for sympathetic readers of Plato. Popper's reading of the dialogue was deeply
flawed and rested on conceptual anachronisms, ungrounded historical claims, and gross mistranslations of the Greek text. However,
while Popper's criticism ceased to be taken seriously by Plato
scholars rather soon after its publication,[2] the effects of his indictment have lingered in the debate about the *Republic*. While almost
all of Popper's specific interpretive claims have been refuted, these
refutations have failed to challenge his major assumption—namely,
that modern liberalism is the definitive political doctrine with which
to measure the thinkers of the past, who are therefore required to live

---

1. Popper 1945.
2. Among the negative reviews that received the book, see Field 1946, pp. 271–276; Hackforth
   1947, pp. 55–57; and later Tate 1958, pp. 241–242. An extensive and detailed rebuttal of
   Popper's interpretation was offered in Levinson 1953. See also Banbrough 1967.

up to the ideal of liberal democracy.[3] In this sense, Popper's defense of liberal democracy against its enemies has indeed set the framework within which the political argument of the dialogue is often read.

The lingering effects of Popper's denunciation of Plato are manifest in two interpretive tendencies that take divergent approaches to meet a common goal—namely, saving Plato from suspicions of proto-totalitarianism. The first is the de-politicization of the *Republic*, with the consequent privileging of its moral psychology at the expense of its political argument. The second includes the various attempts at qualifying, softening, and denying Plato's critique of democracy.[4] Some have claimed that both the relatively inoffensive description of the democratic regime in Book VIII and the recognition of its openness would contradict its ranking as the worst regime after tyranny.[5] Others have held that the dialogical form of Plato's writings and the democratic features of Socrates' character—playing multiple roles and voicing different positions in the *Republic* as an Athenian democrat would do, being primarily concerned with individual liberty or perfection, or being open to self-criticism and incorporating democratic practices into his own philosophical method—would performatively challenge the anti-democratic argument of the

---

3. See Fronterotta 2010, p. 129; and Vegetti 2009b, p. 121.

4. Among the most prominent depoliticizing readings of the dialogue, see Annas 1981, 1997, 2000. For a critique of Annas' position, see Fronterotta 2010, p. 133; and Arruzza 2012, pp. 261–262. For a discussion of the phenomenon of depoliticizing readings of the dialogue, see Vegetti 2009b, pp. 108ff. Santas also remarks on this phenomenon and argues that the increasing tendency to ignore Plato's political theory is due to the fact that it is considered antidemocratic: Santas 2007, p. 70. Instead of following this path, Santas prefers to show that by decoupling Plato's theory from his metaphysics, we end up with a set of political points that—if taken more moderately than the extreme form in which they are presented, and with the exception of the principle of specialization and of the criticism of democratic free choice of occupation—are perfectly compatible with some forms of liberal democracy, the principle of separation of power and wealth and scholocracy, in particular.

5. Saxonhouse 1996; Monoson 2000, pp. 115–118; Wallach 2001, p. 293. Marshall and Bilsborough 2010 argue that this controversy is unsolvable, as there are sufficient indications in the text to conclude that democracy is both worse and better than oligarchy.

Republic.[6] Still others, observing that Plato's writings are entangled with Athenian democracy and that some key democratic practices and concepts, such as *parrhesia*, are consistently accepted and employed by Plato,[7] have interpreted Plato's critique of democracy as a serious, but not entirely unsympathetic, engagement with the limitations of democratic politics rather than as a simplistic and oppositional rejection,[8] or have claimed that Plato changed his mind and softened his critique of Athenian democracy in the *Statesman* and the *Laws*.[9]

Some of these rebuttals of the anti-democratic character of the *Republic* insist that the dialogic form and the description of the democratic regime suggest a fundamental affinity between philosophical practice and democratic practices, in that the first—as understood by Plato—would not be possible without diversity, common inquiry, openness, and freedom, characteristics they associate with democracy.[10] While this argument has the merit of rejecting views of Plato's philosophy as a closed theoretical system in which disputation is irrelevant and the dialogic form is nothing but a literary device, it nevertheless incorrectly appraises the theoretical grounds of Plato's hostility to Athenian democracy. This line of argumentation rests on taking liberalism as the evaluative criterion with which one should judge the political argument of the dialogue and on confusing democracy with liberalism. The insistence on diversity, openness, freedom, and common inquiry reveals a concern for the compatibility of Plato's philosophy with liberalism, but this concern does not license any inference about Plato's attitude toward democracy. While

6. Griswold 1995; Euben 1996; Saxonhouse 2009.
7. Monoson 2000.
8. Wallach 2001.
9. See, for example, Bobonich 2002. Rowe, on the contrary, insists on the continuity between the *Republic* and the *Laws*, arguing that underlying both there is a "single preferred model for constitutions," the essential features of which have more in common with democracy than with autocratic constitutions: Rowe 1998.
10. See, for example, Roochnik 2003 and Recco 2009.

commonly conjoined as liberal democracies, liberalism and democracy should not be conflated. Liberalism, a political theory born in the seventeenth century and asserting the centrality of liberty and the protection of individuals' equal rights, is not necessarily democratic, and its values are compatible with constitutional forms that ignore the basic principle of democracy—namely, popular rule. Democracy, on the other hand, is a form and theory of government predating liberal political theory. In its Greek, and specifically Athenian, version, it had as its main tenet the citizens' self-government, but it was not accompanied by either a practice or a theory of human rights, protection of minorities, or separation of legal powers and religious authority. While failing to acknowledge political and civic rights of women and slaves, the Athenian political system was still a democratic one, in that it recognized the political equality of those who were granted citizenship status and had as its core tenet the notion that the citizens have the capacity to govern themselves, without the need of a superior political authority.[11]

Because it misidentifies democracy with liberalism, the democratic reading of the *Republic* also mistakes the ideal of agreement (ὁμόνοια) and unity of the city pursued by Kallipolis as the key problem for a democratic interpretation of *The Republic*.[12] Agreement,

---

11. On the difference between liberalism and democracy and on the nonliberal nature of Athenian democracy, see Ober 2017.

12. See, for example, Saxonhouse 2009, which instead insists on the contradiction between the multiplicity of points of view and perspectives embodied by Socrates and the unidimensional man of Kallipolis. Saxonhouse's reading in this essay is problematic on two counts: first, it presumes that the key issue for democratic interpretations of the *Republic* is the plurality of forms of life and viewpoints, neglecting that this is not the core aspect of Athenian democracy (or of democratic government in general) but, rather, of liberalism; and second, it misreads Kallipolis' men as unidimensional, neglecting how Kallipolis' goal is, rather, that of creating a unity comprehensive of differences, through institutional devices and forms of life capable of satisfying the desires of the different parts of the soul in a normatively optimal way. On the relation between unity and difference in the notion of justice articulated in the *Republic*, see Kosman 2007.

however, was a properly democratic ideal in fifth- and fourth-century Athens, and ensuring the unity of the city was a democratic concern, as shown most exemplarily by the restored democracy's decision to pass a general amnesty for the supporters of the oligarchic coup of 404. Kallipolis' ideal of unity and agreement was not at odds with Greek democracy, for the latter did not have liberal pluralism as its core; it is, rather, the means for achieving this agreement and unity suggested by Plato's argument that entail a critique of democratic practices and principles.

More specifically, notwithstanding the openness of philosophical practice presented in the dialogue, democratic self-understanding in Athens emphasized a set of core tenets straightforwardly at odds with the political argument of the *Republic*. The first, popular rule through majority voting, was based on a strong notion of political equality for all adult male citizens. Popular rule entailed the rejection of any political authority superior to the demos gathered in the Assembly. Freedom was in this sense understood as freedom from a master. The second tenet was the notion of collective wisdom and the educational role of the demos' deliberations, which collapsed the distinction between objective truth and subjective political opinions. What "appeared right" to the demos in its political deliberations had truth-value, insofar as collective opinion was the key criterion of truth, and the demos' collective decisions were supposed to educate the city as a whole.[13]

Plato's claim that tyranny is the natural offspring of democracy jeopardizes both these key tenets of democratic self-understanding. In contrast with readings of Plato's position suggesting a rather benevolent view of the democratic regime as characterized by pluralism and softness, this chapter unpacks the argumentative logic at the basis of Plato's claim that tyranny naturally derives from democracy.

13. See Ober 1989, pp. 159–165; Ober 1998, pp. 34–35.

It will become evident that there are two strands of critique involved in Plato's claim that the demos is the tyrant's father. The first strand refers to democratic institutional mechanisms as they developed especially in the last third of the fifth century. The second concerns what Plato takes to be the democratic ethos and the relationship between a certain kind of political practice and moral education. The outcome of this analysis will be a much more somber picture of Athenian democracy than the apparently inoffensive democracy of Book VIII.

3.2 TYRANNY EVERYWHERE

As mentioned in chapter 1, Aristophanes ridiculed the Athenian obsession with tyranny, arguing that accusations of tyranny had become more common and cheaper than salt-fish. Plato would probably not have escaped Aristophanes' derision, for the *Republic* is haunted from start to finish by the problem of tyranny and the opposing figures of the happy and unhappy tyrants. Far from simply being one among the several forms of government analyzed in Book VIII, throughout the dialogue tyranny embodies complete injustice by combining the behavior, pathologies, and motivations most opposed to the beautiful city and the philosopher-king. The problem appears to be so pressing that the discussion of the tyrannical regime and of the tyrannical man in Books VIII and IX (563c–580c) occupies the same number of Stephanus pages as those devoted to timocracy, oligarchy, and democracy taken together. It would perhaps be excessive to claim that the critique of tyranny is the heart of the dialogue. However, taking into account the inherent polysemy of the text, it is reasonable to claim that Plato's analysis of the internal dynamics and genesis of tyranny, together with his refutation of the idealization of the tyrant, constitutes one of its main threads. A survey of the various explicit discussions of and implicit hints at the problem of tyranny throughout the dialogue will give a better sense of the relevance of the topic to the dialogue's general argument, and will provide a better understanding of Plato's claim that tyranny is a natural offspring of democracy.

Tyrants are evoked for the first time in Book I, toward the end of the conversation between Socrates and Polemarchus. Having refuted Polemarchus' various attempts at defining justice as harming enemies and benefiting friends, Socrates attributes this view of justice to tyrants or notorious kings such as Periander, Perdiccas, or Xerxes (*Rep.* 336a5–6). It is at this point that Thrasymachus breaks into the conversation, preventing Socrates and Polemarchus from proceeding from their refutation of this fallacious definition of justice to an inquiry into a better one. Thrasymachus displays several traits traditionally characterizing tyrannical behavior. Like a wild beast, he is ready to jump on Socrates and Polemarchus and tear his frightened interlocutors into pieces (336b1–6). Like the tyrannical Oedipus and the Creon of Sophocles' tragedies, he consistently refuses dialogue, is unwilling to listen to other people's arguments, sarcastically fakes agreement, and is prone to unrestrained anger (336d8). These antisocial features make Thrasymachus look like an untamed beast or, more specifically, like a wolf (an animal often associated with tyrants).[14]

The thesis Thrasymachus opposes to Socrates' "childish" attempts to defend justice is as tyrannical as his behavior. His long tirades on justice combine different arguments in a seemingly incoherent way.[15] On the one hand, justice is defined as obedience to the laws or to the orders of the rulers, a position close to legal conventionalism, which views justice as an effect rather than the source of law. From this

---

14. *Rep.* 336d5–7; Socrates refers here to a legend according to which a man who does not stare at the wolf before the wolf stares at him would be struck dumb. See Adam 1963, *ad loc.*
15. See for example, Vegetti 1998b, pp. 239–242; Annas 1981, pp. 35–49.

perspective, justice is imposed and defined by the law independently of its content, and the just man is simply the one who obeys the law (338e1–6). On the other hand, justice is also defined as the advantage of the stronger (338c1–2). This definition seems at odds with legal conventionalism, in that it identifies justice with a specific positive outcome of the laws—namely, the benefit of those who establish them. The two arguments can be held consistently if one assumes that the self-interest of those in power stands for the hidden rationale of every law: in this case, obeying the laws is identical to doing something that benefits those in power. However, this only holds if the rulers are infallible, a tenet that Thrasymachus is anxious to defend.[16] Justice, in this view, is nothing more than an institutional device contrived by the strong to dominate the weak.

The view that the ruler's interest is the true content of any law entails that there is no significant difference in the foundations of democratic and tyrannical laws, as the only distinction is the kind of ruler establishing them: "And each makes laws to its own advantage. Democracy makes democratic laws, tyranny makes tyrannical laws, and so on with the others" (338e1–3).[17] The suggestion that democracy is the form of regime that inherently pursues the interests of the demos (understood as the poorest sector of the population rather than as the totality of the citizen body) is a typical trope of antidemocratic literature already found in the Old Oligarch's *Athenian*

---

16. Socrates immediately notes the tension between the conventionalist and the political realist sides of Thrasymachus' definition, and hence pushes Thrasymachus to argue that a ruler is actually the stronger only insofar as he does not make evaluative mistakes in identifying what laws and orders are to his advantage and what his advantage in general is. This is a crucial step that will compel Thrasymachus to admit that ruling is a τέχνη and that the ruler can be assimilated to a craftsman: *Rep.* 339c–341a.

17. Contrast this with the conventionalist and formal account of laws given by Pericles to Alcibiades in Xenophon's *Memorabilia*: laws are whatsoever the sovereign power in a city enacts, whether the majority under democracy, a minority under oligarchy, or a tyrant. The only criterion, in addition to sovereignty, is persuasion; only the laws enacted through persuasion, and not through force, count as laws (Xen. *Mem.* 1.40–46).

Constitution.[18] This trope challenged democratic discourse by pointing out the classist character of the democratic regime and questioning the tenet that only the citizens' self-rule can fulfill the interests of the city as a whole. Furthermore, Thrasymachus questions the democratic assumption that tyranny and democracy are polar opposites by suggesting that their difference is irrelevant, as the principle guiding both forms of political power is to make laws and rules for the benefit of those who are in power, whether that be the demos or the tyrant.

Some of the apparent contradictions in Thrasymachus' arguments depend on whether we interpret them as prescriptive or as descriptive. As argued by Chappell, if we assume that Thrasymachus' views on justice are prescriptive, it is obvious that his arguments are incoherent.[19] This interpretation, however, does not take account of the fact that Socrates will spend nine books of the dialogue answering his challenge. In fact, Thrasymachus does not hold any prescriptive thesis about justice; he denies that justice is a virtue (348c) while refusing to claim that it is a vice. Thus, his thesis on justice is better understood as merely descriptive. This does not necessarily entail that Thrasymachus holds a prescriptive view of injustice. While he does recommend acting unjustly, the prescriptive dimension of his argument is limited by considerations regarding accessory consequences, for in his view one should commit injustice only as long as one can avoid paying the penalty (348d).[20] Within this context, the tyrant

---

18. Ps.-Xen. *Ath. Pol.* 1.4–9. See also Isocrates' lamentation about the sad lot of rich people in Athens in the much later *Antidosis*: Isoc. 15.159–160.

19. Chappell 1993 argues that Thrasymachus' thesis about justice and injustice is only descriptive. According to him, Thrasymachus is not an immoralist but, rather, has an idea of human flourishing consisting in getting for oneself as many conventional goods as possible. This definition, however, does justify the attribute of "immoralist," as by the fifth century, πλεονεξία was commonly conceived of as the main source of the vices and political evils of the city: see Balot 2001.

20. As Roslyn Weiss notes, this does not mean that Thrasymachus holds that doing justice is, on occasion, more profitable, for example when one cannot escape punishment: Weiss 2007, p. 98.

is put forward as a sort of regulative ideal—that is, an inspirational model combining complete injustice with cunning and impunity: as a regulative ideal, the figure of the tyrant should guide our actions whenever circumstances allow it. This conception of tyranny is based on Thrasymachus' view that πλεονεξία (that is, getting more than one's share or acquiring as many conventional goods as possible at the expense of others) is what makes human life flourish.[21] His praise of tyranny, however, should not be understood as the expression of a political theory identifying tyranny as the best form of political regime, for there is no doubt that in his account tyranny is extremely bad for the ruled. Tyranny is good for the tyrant alone, and only he who manages to seize it is happy.[22]

This thesis is reformulated in a refined piece of dramaturgical art—the long monologue about shepherds and sheep in which Thrasymachus lays bare the brutality implied by every power relation, of which tyranny represents the most accomplished form (343b–344c). Like the ruler, the shepherd does not fatten and look after his sheep in order to benefit them, as the childish Socrates seems to think, but, rather, for his own or his master's good (343b1–c1). Here Thrasymachus redefines justice as the good of another. This should be understood descriptively, in the sense that justice does not make just people happy but, rather, benefits the rulers, while injustice—as we have already seen—will make unjust people happy so long as their crimes are not discovered and they are not punished. This redefinition of justice introduces the problematic relations between justice, injustice, and happiness, which are a guiding thread running through the dialogue. From the very beginning of the dialogue, therefore, the question of happiness and what makes a life worth living is shaped

---

21. On the notion of greed in Greek literature, see chapter 4, this volume.
22. Chappell 1993, p. 14: "In short Thrasymachus is neither a revolutionary nor a fascist; he's an opportunist."

by the problem of tyranny and the fascination exerted by the figure of the tyrant on those who identify πλεονεξία with flourishing. The tyrant is, indeed, the perfectly happy man, having the greatest power to outdo others (τὸν μεγάλα δυνάμενον πλεονεκτεῖν; 344a1) and being able to do whatever he wants without paying a penalty for his crimes. Tyranny is complete injustice (τελεωτάτην ἀδικίαν; 344a7), the enslavement of the citizens and the complete appropriation of all common and private goods. It is the combination of limitless greed (πλεονεξία) and violence:

> This is tyranny, which through treachery and violence appropriates the property of others—sacred and profane, public and private—not little by little, but all at once. When someone commits only one part of injustice, he is punished and falls into great disgrace. Those who commit these partial forms of injustice are called temple-robbers, kidnappers, burglars, cheats, and thieves. But when someone, in addition to appropriating the citizens' possessions, kidnaps and enslaves them as well, instead of these shameful appellations he is called happy and blessed, not only by the citizens but by all those who learn that he has committed the whole of injustice. (344a6–c2)

As Thrasymachus concludes, the fascination with the tyrant's happiness reveals that people do not want to act justly, but do so only because they fear punishment or loss of reputation. This observation is the leitmotiv of Glaucon's intervention in Book II. Unsatisfied with Socrates' refutation of Thrasymachus, Glaucon plays the devil's advocate with the help of his brother, Adeimantus. By doing so, he attempts to compel Socrates to formulate a better defense of justice that demonstrates that it is a good both for itself and for its consequences. Glaucon suggests that doing so necessitates an examination of both the life of the just man that abstracts from all possible external benefits deriving from acting justly (i.e., public recognition, a successful life, and even the mere absence of suffering) and the life of the unjust man that grants him license to do what he wants (ἐξουσία; 359c7) with impunity. Glaucon, indeed, points out the fact that human beings' natural πλεονεξία inclines them to always outdo others and can only be limited by the external boundaries of the law imposing equality (359c3–6). Glaucon tells a story concerning the Lydian Gyges[23] (whose magic ring makes him invisible, allowing him to commit all possible crimes without being noticed) as an exemplification of this diagnosis of human motivations. As a result of finding the magic ring, Gyges seduces the king's wife, kills the king, and takes his kingdom (359c7–360b2). The story is most likely a free re-elaboration of the story of the initiator of the Lydian dynasty of the Mermnadae and ancestor of Croesus, a variant of which can also be found in Herodotus (Hdt. 1.8–12). According to ancient authors, Gyges was the first monarch to be called τύραννος, a term that indeed was believed to have a Lydian origin.[24] Both in Herodotus and in Plato's account we can find elements that are typical of narrations of a tyrant's rise to power: the lack of a dynastic justification for the ascent to power, the seduction of the queen, and the murder of the legitimate ruler. Gyges' story provides a fictional image of what a man

---

23. *Rep.* 359d1–2. The text of the manuscripts may be corrupted, as the manuscripts report τῷ Γύγου τοῦ Λυδοῦ προγόνῳ, *to an ancestor of the Lydian Gyges*, while in 612b3, Socrates refers to the story by speaking of Gyges' ring. A story about an ancestor of Gyges taking power through the use of a magic ring would be incompatible with Herodotus' narration concerning Gyges' rise to power, as Gyges did not inherit the kingdom from his ancestors: Hdt. 1.8–12. Slings 2003 suggests that προγόνῳ may be a gloss. For a defense of the text reported by the manuscripts, see Laird 2001, who interprets the variation made by Glaucon as a part of Plato's reinvention of Herodotus' story aimed at emphasizing the fictional aspect of the manipulated version. See also Danzig 2008 for an interpretation of Plato's political reasons for transforming Herodotus' story, by introducing the ring and by putting the entire blame on Gyges. Finally, it is also possible that both Herodotus and Plato relied on older versions of the Gyges story.

24. See Archil. fr. 19 West, where the word first occurs.

would do if given the chance to suddenly enjoy the license and impunity typical of a tyrant. A few lines after telling the story, Glaucon further argues:

> Suppose there were two rings of this kind, one worn by a just and the other by an unjust man. Nobody would be so adamantine, it seems, that he would stick to justice and endure to stay away from other people's property instead of seizing it, when he could take with impunity whatever he wanted even from the marketplace, enter into private houses and have sex with whomever he wanted, kill or free from prison whomever he wanted, and act in all the other things as if he were equal to a god (ἰσόθεον) among humans. (360b4–c3)

Equal to a god: this is how Hecuba defines tyranny in Euripides' *Trojan Women*, in a verse that Socrates quotes in Book VIII (568b3). In the latter passage, Socrates both accuses Euripides of praising tyranny and further justifies the exclusion of tragic poets from Kallipolis on the basis of this affinity between tragedy and tyranny (568b5–8). Tragedy, he argues, drives a city's constitutions toward tyranny, and tragic poets customarily receive honors and funds from tyrants— perhaps an allusion to Euripides' stay in 408/7 at the court of the Macedonian king Archelaus, mentioned in the *Gorgias* as a cruel tyrant (*Gorg.* 470cff.). Hence, tragic poets should be banned from the beautiful city.

In his first treatment of poetry, in Books II and III, neither Socrates nor his interlocutors explicitly mentions tyranny. However, this appears to be an underlying concern throughout the discussion of the education of the guardians; here Socrates addresses some of the ways in which tyrannical characters are birthed in a city and he puts forward an alternative educational project to avoid this outcome. Toward the conclusion of Book III, after having examined the kind of physical training and musical education appropriate for creating a harmonious combination of spiritedness and reason in the young guardians, Socrates states that the most shameful thing for a shepherd is to train dogs who will end up attacking the sheep they were supposed to protect, becoming more similar to wolves than to watchdogs (416a2–7). We have already met the wolf in the admirer of tyrants, Thrasymachus, and we will meet him again in Book VIII, where the tyrant is compared to a werewolf (565d4–e1).[25] If we read the passage of Book III in light of these further references associating wolves with tyrants, it would appear that one of the main stakes of the educational program described in Books II and III is to avoid arousing tyrannical impulses in the guardians and to tame the aspects of their souls that may lead to such a degeneration. Further hints confirm this interpretation. For example, while addressing the kinds of musical rhythms that should be excluded from the beautiful city, Socrates refers to metrical feet that generate servility (ἀνελευθε ρία), arrogance (ὕβρις), and madness (μανία); servility and madness are attributes of the tyrannical man in Book IX, and all of his behavior can be considered as hubristic.[26] A passage from Book IV further hints that certain kinds of music and poetry allow lawlessness (παρανομία) to slowly creep into the soul until it becomes a character or way or life (424d3–e2). Lawlessness is again one of the main defining features of the tyrannical man, which differentiates him from the other two appetitive men discussed in Books VIII and IX, the oligarch and the democrat. Moreover, the tyrannical regime is the only regime in which laws have no meaning, as the tyrant's power is inherently arbitrary.

---

25. I will discuss at length the metaphor of the wolf and its connection to tyranny and to spirit in chapter 5, this volume.
26. For the combination of servility and madness, see *Rep.* 577d1–5.

This concern with παρανομία and μανία as possible outcomes of a flawed educational program reappears in the discussion of the study of dialectics in Book VII (537e–539d). Here, Socrates is preoccupied with determining the correct age to initiate pupils into dialectics, for, as he argues, the current practice of teaching it to young people decoupled from an educational process oriented to grasping the truth causes great evils. In this context, Socrates puts forward a telling analogy: a young person practicing dialectics and the art of refutation in such an inappropriate way would be in a condition analogous to an adopted son in a wealthy family who at some point discovers that his parents are not his real parents. He will be prone to abandon all his previous convictions and ways of life, and to endorse whatever opinions the flatterers surrounding him offer. He will abandon his old beliefs about what is shameful and what is fine, will question all the values he was raised with, and become lawless. The inappropriate teaching of dialectics, by stimulating a taste for the game of contradiction and refutation for its own sake, which Socrates defines as madness (μανία; 539c6), can easily generate moral relativism, which is a fertile soil for lawlessness (537e4 and 539a3).

The problem of the corruption of young elite men into what can plausibly be taken as tyrannical figures is discussed in some detail in the conversation about the characteristics of philosophical natures, in Book VI. Philosophical natures combine a number of talents and predispositions that allow them to excel in both political life and philosophy. They are a rare combination of natural gifts that require a careful education as well as an appropriate social and political context in order to properly develop in the direction of virtue, like a plant growing (αὐξανομένην) in adequate soil (492a1–3). When planted in the wrong soil, a philosophical nature may become the cause of the greatest evils, both for itself and for the rest of the city. Indeed, *only* great natures, such as the philosophical ones, can be the cause of great evils (491d7–e6 and 495b3–6). As tyranny, understood both as a psychological condition and a political regime, is the greatest evil in the dialogue, for both the individual soul and the city, these passages may be taken to be further hints at the danger of developing tyrannical characters owing to a combination of bad education and social conditions. Philosophical natures—that is, young members of the elite endowed with a rare array of internal and external gifts—are especially exposed to this danger.

On the basis of this short survey, it is possible to conclude that the extensive treatment of tyranny and of the tyrannical man in Books VIII and IX is carefully prepared through a number of anticipations and hints throughout the dialogue: Thrasymachus' praise of the tyrant as the happiest man and Glaucon's intervention with the story of Gyges' ring raise a problem that will find a solution only with the final demonstration of the unhappiness of the tyrant in Book IX and with the consideration of his fate in the afterlife in Book X.[27] References to the always-present danger of developing tyrannical impulses in the soul show that the treatment of education is concerned with the dangerous fascination that the idealized figure of the tyrant as presented in the opinions of Thrasymachus and Glaucon exerted on talented youth. Refuting Thrasymachus' argument and countering his fascination for tyranny will require Socrates to elaborate a city in thought, a moral psychology based on the theory of the soul's tripartition, and a figure of the philosopher as the alternative to the happy tyrant—the latter only accomplished through the articulation of a metaphysics of the Forms and of the Good, and of an epistemology devaluing opinions. It is important to notice that this refutation only targets two aspects of Thrasymachus' arguments: the idea that an unjust life is happier than a just one (and

---

27. See the reference to the punishment of the tyrant Ardiaeus (615c5–616a4) and the further references to the choice of the tyrannical life as the worst choice of all in the myth of Er: *Rep.* 619a3–4 and 619b7–c6.

hence the regulative ideal of the happy tyrant) and the notion that the intrinsic aim of political power is the interest and advantage of the ruler, which by definition entails the domination and exploitation of the ruled. This latter argument is refuted by imagining a city that realizes an ideal of political power understood as the art of taking care of the city as a whole by harmonizing it and making it as virtuous as possible. Socrates' refutation leaves the descriptive dimension of Thrasymachus' argument untouched, for by the end of the dialogue, we discover that perhaps all existing cities are indeed governed according to the brutal principle enunciated by Thrasymachus: the advantage of the stronger.

3.3 WHEN THE DEMOS IS THE TYRANT'S FATHER

Plato's description of the tyrannical regime is not entirely original (566b–569c). It combines and systematizes a number of traits already attributed to tyranny by democratic literature: Otanes' speech reported by Herodotus puts the accent on the corruptive effects that absolute power unavoidably has on the ruler and the incompatibility between the absolute rule of a single man and the rule of law (Hdt. 3.80). Depictions of tyrannical regimes in Herodotus and in tragedy often emphasize the inherent fragility and instability of tyranny, resulting from its illegitimate and arbitrary character. Along similar lines, Plato's tyranny displays illegitimacy, instability, and fragility; these aspects compel the tyrant to increasingly brutal and bloodthirsty actions, all aimed at preserving his fragile power. He demands a bodyguard, proceeds to eliminate internal enemies, and enacts a series of economic policies such as the elimination of debts and the redistribution of the lands expropriated from the rich. Then he continuously wages wars and establishes war taxes, increasingly impoverishing the people and forcing them to spend their time doing menial work instead of engaging in politics. Through war taxes, the tyrant partially reappropriates what he had given when he redistributed the land among the people. From this point onward, the tyrant becomes increasingly isolated, as he begins losing his former supporters and friends who had helped him take power. Not trusting anyone in the city, he exiles or kills all the most prominent people— those who are brave, smart, and large-minded—in this way showing himself an apt pupil of Periander and Thrasybulus (Hdt. 5.92.ζ). After the city is purged of these talented and good people, the tyrant, seeing the growing hatred against him, increases his bodyguards and surrounds himself with foreign mercenaries and newly freed slaves. In order to pay for them, he appropriates the common goods of the city, stealing the sacred treasuries, using the properties of the rich, and, finally, feeding off the people's estates.

Plato systematizes the existing tradition of criticizing tyranny into an account that emphasizes the constraints internal to the very logic of tyrannical power. On this level, his contribution to an existing debate would seem to lie in both his flamboyant style (which allows his narrative to compete on equal footing with tragic depictions of tyrannical characters) and his systematization of various tropes related to tyranny into a coherent narrative. However, the apparently conventional nature of Plato's treatment of tyranny should not lead the reader astray. As already argued, the democratic critique of tyranny represented it as the polar opposite of fundamental democratic principles and hence played a crucial role in democratic self-understanding. The role of this literary trope appears even more fundamental when taking into account that, in the absence of a democratic political theory in fifth- and fourth-century Athens, it was through orations, decrees, theater, poetry, and histories that the democratic citizens came to have an understanding of their political practices. Plato, however, appropriates the democratic critique of tyranny and turns it into a weapon against democratic principles.

Plato's subversion of democratic ideology through the appropriation of its conventional tropes is mirrored in the substantive content of his description of tyranny and account of its genesis. All the tyrannical acts and measures mentioned here take place within an ambiguous transitional space between tyranny and the democratic regime, undermining the purported opposition between the two.[28] This continuity is emphasized through precise linguistic choices evident by contrast with the descriptions of the genesis of the other regimes. In Book VIII, Socrates famously organizes the discussion of the main forms of corrupt regimes according to a narrative scheme probably borrowed from Hesiod, and he rearranges the moral and political elements of proximity between different kinds of regimes into relations of derivation in a story of progressive decline. Rather than articulating a philosophy of history and depicting a chronological progression from one regime to the next, the discussion of corrupt regimes should be better understood as the adoption of a diagnostic, medical stance and as a description of the symptomatic progression of a disease.[29] In this narrative scheme, the different forms of government are represented in such a way as to maintain sufficient similarities to the corresponding existent regimes, while at the same time exaggerating their respective guiding moral principles. The outcome is a sequence of ideal model states that are both

28. My reading has some similarities with Sylvain Roux's interpretation of the genesis of tyranny, which emphasizes this as Plato's original innovation, observing that this account insists on the derivation of tyranny from sociopolitical and economic dynamics inherent to democracy (Roux 2001). Roux, however, does not draw any particular conclusions concerning the role of the critique of tyranny in Plato's criticism of Athenian democracy, besides a reference to the continuity between tyranny and democracy and to the institutional mechanisms that the tyrant exploits to take power (2001, p. 152). Moreover, I would disagree that Plato's tyrant is an ordinary man (p. 154); on the contrary, as it will appear clear from my present analysis of the tyrannical man's soul and from the last chapter of this book, he is an exceptional character, although Plato deeply revises and reformulates this traditional theme.

29. For this insight, see Brill 2013, pp. 132–133. For an other nonhistoricist reading of the decline of the corrupt regimes, see Frede 1996.

similar and dissimilar to the corresponding forms of regimes historically experienced by the Greeks of the fifth and fourth centuries.
In addition to undergoing the same process of philosophical styli-
zation as the other forms of regimes, the depiction of democracy is
characterized by parodic exaggerations. This resemblance to a caricature, however, is an insufficient reason for ruling out Athenian
democracy as the main historical referent of this section of the dialogue. In fact, parodic exaggerations are a common part of political
polemics; for example, a similar caricature of democratic freedom
can be found in the later *Areopagiticus*, where Isocrates explicitly
refers to later Athenian democracy in contrast to that of Solon and
Cleisthenes (Isoc. 7.20).[30]

The regimes guided by reason and spirit and those guided by
the appetites are divided by the respective causes of their degeneration. In contrast to the timocratic and aristocratic regimes, which
fall due to their failure to uphold their corresponding virtues, the
oligarchic and democratic regimes fail because of the excessive application of their own guiding moral principles. Aristocracy falls because of the philosopher-king's miscalculation of the proper time for
breeding the guardians. It is the irreducibility of sensible reality to the
perfect grasp of reason—its resistance to perfect knowledge—that
introduces corruption into the ideal city. Thus, the problem lies in
the very nature of sensible reality, rather than in the guiding principle
of aristocracy. Aristocracy falls because of the opaque and contingent nature of sensible reality, which human beings can only grasp,
govern, and organize to a limited extent (546a–547a). As for timocracy, rather than the excessive desire for honor, power, and victory,
it is the timocrats' secret accumulation of wealth that leads to their
fall. Crucially, the accumulation of wealth is *not* the guiding principle

---

30. See also the attribution of license and equal right of speech (ἰσηγορία) to slaves in Ps.-Xen.
Ath. Pol. 1.10.

of timocracy; rather, it is the subordinate by-product of the rule of the spirited part of the city unsustained and untamed by reason. To a certain extent, this image reproduces a traditional understanding of heroic values in which the acquisition of material goods accompanies the pursuit of glory.[31] In fact, in Book III, Socrates blames Homer for impiously portraying Achilles as a bribable man interested in gifts, money, and ransoms (390e–391a). However, the whole passage remains quite puzzling, insofar as the timocrats honor wealth in secret and not in public, which seems to indicate that their desire for wealth is not driven by their passion for honor and glory. In any event, the accumulation of secret treasures is not the declared guiding principle of timocracy, hence the degeneration from timocracy into oligarchy is not caused by the excessive application of its guiding principle.

The situation changes in the case of oligarchy. Under the oligarchic regime, the insatiable desire for wealth produces a class of dangerous, impoverished drones, once belonging to the leisured elite of the city; moreover, it impoverishes the demos to the point of pushing it to rebellion. In this case, it is indeed the guiding principle of the oligarchic regime that contains the germ of its dissolution within itself. The same holds for the democratic regime, which degenerates into tyranny because of the insatiable desire for freedom that guides it. While both processes of degeneration are framed in a naturalistic perspective that marks the passage from a form of government to the other as "natural," Plato adopts a markedly more biological and botanical language to describe the genesis of tyranny. This linguistic choice stresses the natural continuity between tyranny and the democratic regime. Within the context of a civil conflict dividing the poor and the rich, the demos, deceived by the demagogic drones motivated by their desire for the goods and properties of rich people, comes

---

31. See the discussion of competitive traditional values in Adkins 1960 and my discussion of this theme in relation to greed in chapter 4, this volume.

to believe that an oligarchic conspiracy is taking place. In order to protect themselves and the democratic regime, the people choose a leader on whom they confer special powers as a champion of their interest. As we have already seen, the appellation προστάτης τοῦ δήμου became rather common in the last third of the fifth century and was used especially to indicate a leader of the democratic faction, who maintained a direct and unmediated relationship with the demos he championed.[32] In Aristophanes' comedies we can find traces of the fear that the demos' leader may use this privileged relationship with the people for his own advantage.[33] Plato transforms this fear into a diagnosis of the birth of tyranny:

This is clear . . . , that whenever a tyrant grows (φύηται), he sprouts from the roots of this leadership and from nothing else (ἐκ προστατικῆς ῥίζης καὶ οὐκ ἄλλοθεν ἐκβλαστάνει). (565d1–2)

The terms adopted in this passage—growing, root, sprouting (φύηται, ῥίζης, ἐκβλαστάνει)—all refer to the process of a plant's natural growth. Consistent with this view, Socrates describes the relationship between the demos and the tyrant in terms of direct generation—that is, the relationship between a father and a son. The demos is the parent (γεννήσας), the father, who is required by the tyrant to feed him and his companions;[34] it had generated the tyrant so that, like a good son, the latter could take care of his father (568e7–569a1); the tyrant, however, turns out to be an altogether different kind of creature (θρέμμα; 569b1). Like Oedipus, Plato's tyrant is a parricide (πα-τραλοίαν; 569b6), but in this re-elaboration, the themes of parricide

---

32. Connor 1971, pp. 110–117.
33. See Aristoph. *Kn.* 1121–1130 and *Peace* 680–681 on Cleon and Hyperbolus. A similar accusation of acquisitive and opportunist behavior is addressed against demagogues in the much later Isocrates' *On the Peace*: Isoc. 8.128.
34. The verb used, τρέφω, evokes parenthood and is often associated with nursing and rearing.

and illegitimate rule take on an altogether different meaning. The demos' full realization that the creature they have generated is not a loving son arrives only when the tyrant turns against the very people who gave him power. Until the very conclusion of this tragic story, the demos continues to consider the tyrant as its own loving son, and it is only when the tyrant begins dispossessing common people, at the conclusion of his ascent to power, that the demos finally recognizes that its son is a parricide (568e7–569c4). The reasons for the demos' misunderstanding lie in a combination of factors that help elucidate the sense in which the demos is the tyrant's father. The tyrant is a child of the demos by virtue of the institutional mechanisms proper to democratic government, which install the supreme authority in a demos incapable of correctly assessing both concrete situations and its own genuine interests, as well as the interests of the city as a whole. The demos' ignorance exposes it to the dangers of deception and of what we may anachronistically call the political charisma of ruthless and self-interested politicians. This institutional deficiency of democracy, however, specifically generates tyrants because of the moral continuity between the appetitive nature of the demos and that of the tyrant. The tyrant privately appropriates an ideal of appetitive enjoyment and freedom from authority and constraints that the demos collectively cultivates.[35] Indeed, the demos' misunderstanding of its champion's intentions is due to the fact that—until the very conclusion of the story—they seem to share exactly the same goal: the elimination of the rich and those who are called gentlemen (καλῶν κἀγαθῶν) (569a3–4), which appears as a condition for the realization of unconditional freedom and unrestrained appetitive enjoyment.

---

35. On this continuity between the democratic city's desire to be ruled by nothing outside itself and the tyrant's equivalent desire, as well as between the fragmented idle desires in the city and their crystallization and concentration in the tyrant, see Rosenstock 1994, p. 383.

3.4 TYRANNICAL ORATORS, TYRANNICAL ASSEMBLIES

An interesting passage in the *Gorgias* recounts what seems to be the only act Socrates accomplished in an official capacity within a democratic institution. After Socrates argues that acting unjustly is worse than suffering injustice, his young interlocutor Polus laughs at him and provocatively invites him to see whether any of those listening to their conversation agree with him. Socrates gives a strange answer in the form of what initially seems to be an innocent anecdote. He argues that he cannot do what Polus asks—namely, to call people for a vote—because he lacks the competence to do so as he is not a politician. To illustrate his point he recalls when he was a member of the Council and had to call for a vote in the Assembly; Socrates ended up as an object of laughter because he did not know how to do it (*Gorg.* 473e–474a). While this may look like a typical Socratic proclamation of ignorance and incompetence meant, in this case, to emphasize Socrates' lack of expertise in politics, the anecdote is far from innocent. Socrates' reminiscence contains a reference to one of the most dramatic events of the last years of the fifth century: the trial of the generals of the battle of the Arginusae in 406. The generals were accused of leaving shipwrecked Athenian sailors to drown after the battle. As this counted as a betrayal and impiety, the generals probably received an εἰσαγγελία trial, for we know that the trial took place in the Assembly and not in a court.[36]

In that year Socrates happened to be a member of the *boule*, and it fell to him to be the ἐπιστάτης (that is, to preside over the Assembly) on the day of the trial. Callixenus, bribed by Theramenes,[37] put

---

36. See Xen. *Hell.* 1.7.
37. The reason why Theramenes orchestrated the trial is open to discussion. One possibility is that he was afraid of being accused himself, for he was a trierarc during the battle of the

forward a motion to sentence the generals to death on the basis of a single vote, and the presiding committee (πρυτάνεις), faced with a crowd shouting that nobody should prevent the people from doing what they wanted to do, was willing to let the motion pass. However, on Xenophon's account, this proposed motion was illegal.[38] It may be the case that collectively sentencing a group of people to death with a single vote was a serious violation of procedure, and that this violation is what Xenophon refers to. However, it is also possible that the vote did not violate any procedure and was perfectly legal. In fact, it does not seem that the Athenians approved Callixenus' proposal because they wanted to unduly rush the trial, as the trial lasted several days, with two meetings of the Assembly, two of the Council, and multiple speeches and votes.[39] It may also be questioned to what extent the presidency of the Assembly was intimidated by the shouts of the crowds, as expressing approval and disapproval through clapping and shouts was the way Assemblies usually unfolded. Nonetheless, the purported reason why Socrates, in his function as the chair of the Assembly and against the advice of the other members of the presiding committee, did not call for the vote was not Socrates' ignorance of judiciary and political procedures, as the passage from the *Gorgias* would lead us believe. Rather, as is clear from the *Apology*, it was his unwillingness to call for a vote that—as he claims—entailed a blatant violation of those legal procedures:

Arginusae, and that he therefore directed the blame toward the generals. Another is that he wanted to eliminate capable democratic leaders and generals, in order to create space for his own political career and the conditions for a second oligarchic coup. This is Bearzot's interpretation: Bearzot 2013, ch. 3.

38. See Xen. *Hell.* 1.7.12–15; Xen. *Mem.* 1.1.18.

39. See, for example, Hamal 2015, pp. 89–90, who concludes that the trial was in fact legal and that the critical evaluation of the Athenian demos' decisions should only concern the content of the decision and not its form. The Athenian Assembly itself, as a matter of fact, came later to regret its own deliberation.

I have never held any other office in the city, Athenian men, but I served in the Council. It happened that our tribe Antiochis held the presidency of the Assembly the time you wanted to condemn by a single vote the ten generals who did not rescue the survivors of the naval battle. This was against the law, as you all acknowledged later. I was the only member of the presidency who objected to your doing something contrary to the laws, and I voted against it. Despite the fact that the orators were eager to prosecute me and take me away, and that you incited them with your shouts, I thought I should run any risk in defense of the law and justice, rather than side with you for fear of prison or death when you wanted to do something unjust. (*Apol.* 32a9–c3)

In their respective accounts of the episode, both Plato and Xenophon insist that orators and the crowd created an irrational climate of anger, suspicion, and resentment that led to a result that the Athenians would bitterly regret only a year later. The elimination of the generals of the Arginusae deprived the city in one blow of many of its most capable military experts and of its most prominent and loyal democratic leaders. This in turn would accelerate Athens' defeat in the Peloponnesian War and prepare the ground for the Thirty's oligarchic coup. In sum, on this account the many gathered in the Assembly passed an illegal vote detrimental to their own interests. By referring to this episode in both the *Apology* and the *Gorgias*, Socrates reveals the democratic notion of the demos' collective wisdom as an illusory form of self-deception. Moreover, by referring to this episode in the *Gorgias*, he indirectly answers Polus' objections, by opposing his own lived example to Polus' continuous appeal to tyrants, orators, and politicians as faithful witnesses to his point of view. In that circumstance, Socrates acted according to his own principle: he preferred to be laughed at and even risk prosecution rather than perform an unjust and illegal act. By recalling this episode in the context of these dialogues, Plato implicitly suggests that, at the end of the day, Socrates was right and the demos was tragically wrong.

The Assembly where the fate of the generals—and, ultimately, of the city—was sealed resembles the analogy between the ship and the city in Book VI of the *Republic* (488a7–489a6). While not explicitly called a democracy, it is only natural to interpret the simile as referring to Greek democracy in general and to Athenian democracy in particular. The large, deaf, shortsighted and ignorant shipowner evokes the demos as source of political power.[40] This figure for the demos should be identified with the many gathered together a few lines later (492b5–7), as well as with the large animal representing the majority when it gathers together and expresses its opinions at 493a–c. He is, more specifically, the demos gathered in Assembly and in law courts, where it embodies the supreme source of political authority, hence the competition among the sailors-politicians to gain its favor through persuasion and force in order to take possession of the wheel.[41] If interpreted as referring to democracy, the analogy appears to express very similar concerns to those we may find in the *Gorgias*: collective wisdom is nothing but an illusion, and the institutional mechanisms presiding over collective deliberation only offer ruthless and self-interested politicians the opportunity to deceive and take advantage of the people.

A similar critique of democracy undergirds Plato's description of the genesis of tyranny. As already seen, the demos confers power on the would-be tyrant because it misjudges the intentions of its presumed champion. This blindness characterizes the demos throughout the tyrant's ascent to power, as it is only his ultimate dispossession of the common people that finally opens its eyes to the truth of what it has wrought.

---

40. Aristotle interprets it as the demos in *Rh.* 1406b34–6.
41. See the compelling case for such an interpretation in Keyt 2006.

A restrictive reading of these passages of the *Republic* could provide aid and comfort to interpretations of Plato as sympathetic to democracy. Thus, *if* Plato's critique of democracy were merely confined to illustrating the inability of democratic institutional mechanisms and majority rule to reach well-informed rational decisions, this critique could still be plausibly interpreted as a sympathetic reflection on the insufficiency of democratic institutions alone. Such an interpretation would view Plato's argument as a limited critique of democratic institutions lacking the critical reason necessary to provide more stable and reliable criteria for discrimination, rather than as a general rejection of democracy *tout court*. Moreover, suggesting that democratic institutions need critical reason—and, by extension, philosophical criticism—to assess their founding values and find stable evaluative criteria is not inherently anti-democratic.[42] In fact, such an interpretation of Plato's engagement with democracy may suggest a complementary relationship between philosophical and democratic practices, or even one of necessary supplementation. In this light, the generative relation between tyranny and democracy would indicate that democracy provides the necessary institutional and moral conditions for the emergence of tyranny, but not by virtue of its specifically democratic character. In other words, tyrants would be not "men of the people" but, rather, ruthless politicians taking advantage of the deficiencies of democratic practices and institutions that are incapable of defending themselves from these external attacks because they lack the evaluative criteria necessary for critical self-reflection.[43]

As appealing as such an interpretation may appear, it ignores the specific terminological choices Plato makes in describing the relationship between tyranny and democracy; it neither harmonizes with Plato's terminological insistence on natural derivation nor

42. Along these lines, see Wallach 2001, pp. 295 and 300.
43. Wallach 2001, pp. 298–299.

elucidates why Plato would repeatedly describe the tyrant as the son of the demos if he were not, precisely, "a man of the people." It is also difficult to harmonize this interpretation with the corrupting effect Plato ascribes to democratic gatherings and practices per se. Plato's linguistic choices are mirrored in the content of his account, which demonstrates that tyrannical natures do not simply take advantage of institutional shortcomings and deficient competence in collective deliberation; they are literally *created* by the very unfolding of the gatherings of the many.

In Book VI, immediately after accusing the many of being the main corruptors of talented youth, Socrates directly refers to the institutional mechanisms and political style of the democratic Assembly and the popular courts (which were the two main sites of expression of popular rule):

> When many people are sitting together in assemblies, courts, theaters, army camps, or in some other public gathering of the crowd, they object to some of the things said or done and applaud others by making big noises, with excess in each case. When they shout and clap, even the rocks nearby and the place where they gather redouble with their echo the clamor of praise or blame. In this kind of circumstances, what do you think is the effect on the heart of a young man, as they say? What private teaching could hold out, without being washed away by that kind of praise or blame and carried away by the flood wherever it goes, so that he will call beautiful or ugly the same things the crowd does, will pursue the same things the crowd pursues, and will be such as the crowd is? (*Rep.* 492b5–c8)

This passage emphasizes the corrupting effects of the practice of collective approval and disapproval expressed by the many when gathered together, and by the specific style in which it is expressed: shouting and clapping. These practices encourage conformity by forcing participants to anticipate the whims of the many, and to adjust to them regardless of their factual validity or moral value. One could say that Plato here recognizes the educational dimension of public democratic practices, while simultaneously suggesting that this "education" results in general moral corruption.

Plato's reference to the style of discussion in assemblies and courts recalls the shift in the manner of political communication in the last third of the fifth century discussed in the previous chapter. Once a political leader's exclusive allegiance to the demos or to the city took the place of the reliance on a network of personal friendships and family ties characteristic of previous generations of Athenian politicians, orators and generals became increasingly dependent on securing the continuous approval of the people. A successful political career could end in sudden ruin, which included the risk of judicial indictment for having supported policies that turned out to be detrimental or even for arguing for an unpopular policy before the Assembly. The orator addressing the Assembly had to take the ideas and moral principles of the ideology of the masses into account while somehow combining them with pragmatic proposals for workable policies.[44] This new, unmediated relationship was also reflected in a shift in the political vocabulary, as terms previously reserved to indicate interpersonal relationships between individuals came to be used to illustrate a new kind of personal relationship between the politician and the demos; friendship, and even erotic love, came to characterize his attachment and loyalty to the people while declaring oneself the most sincere friend and protector of the people became a trope of political oratory.[45] This shift in vocabulary was accompanied by a new style of communication, characterized by the frequent resort to flamboyant

44. Ober 1989, pp. 121–124.
45. Connor 1971, p. 100. On political eros, see chapter 4, this volume.

language; appeals to passion, anger, laughter, and even erotic desire; and evincing a certain taste for theatricality and exaggerations both in the orator's posture and his tone of voice.[46]

Socrates' observation about the corrupting power of public gatherings points out the problem of this unmediated relationship between the leader and the demos, in which the demos has the supreme political authority and acts as the educator of both the whole city and its political leaders, despite lacking the necessary moral and political competence for this task. In the *Gorgias*, Socrates addresses this problem in his conversations with both Polus and Callicles. He points out that Callicles—in spite of his bombastic conceptions of what superior men are, should, and can do—is, in the last instance, a lover subordinated to the demos (*Gorg.* 481d–e and 513c). As a matter of fact, Callicles always tells the Athenian Assembly what this wants to hear.[47] The exchange with Polus tightens the bond between tyranny and the moral corruption of the city caused by popular rule. In response to Socrates' characterization of oratory as similar to pastry baking, in that they both have flattery as a goal, Polus counters with an analogy between orators and tyrants: like tyrants, orators can put whomever they want to death, confiscate their property, or banish them from cities, which shows that orators are the most powerful men (*Gorg.* 466b–c). Socrates contests Polus' characterization by pointing out that both orators and tyrants have the least power to do what they really want. The main point of this rebuttal is that neither of them actually knows what he really wants, as they neither know what is good for them nor what they naturally aspire to; both the orator and the tyrant rely on appearances—that is, on what merely seems fitting to them. But where do their ideas about what is

---

46. Connor 1971, pp. 139–143.
47. See chapter 4, this volume, for a more detailed analysis of these passages.

good for them come from? What are the appearances they rely on? When trying to refute Socrates' claim that a tyrant cannot be happy if he knows nothing about justice, Polus, instead of using arguments, can only cite examples: Archelaus, the king of Macedonia, and the Persian King. Polus' rebuttal is based merely on appearances: he does not know the rulers he is evoking, hence he knows nothing about their actual happiness or unhappiness. As he knows nothing, he just mentions these names and gives a survey of Archelaus' criminal deeds, as if the mere mention of these rulers' infamy could act as a witness to his point and would be sufficient to prove his claims true. Socrates notices that what Polus is doing is perfectly consistent with the oratorical style used in assemblies and law courts and, in particular, with the method of presenting an array of false witnesses to refute the defendant. But if Polus wishes to appeal to the authority of such witnesses as an argument, he may well have the whole city at his disposal, for nearly all Athenians would agree with his claim. Socrates continues by arguing that some of the most prominent Athenian politicians would agree with Polus as well: people like Aristocrates son of Scellias (one of the Four Hundred), Nicias and his brothers, and the whole house of Pericles (*Gorg.* 471e–472c). Polus is simply parroting the city's common beliefs, which is also the source of the orators' and tyrants' beliefs about what is good for them.

The passages from the *Republic* and the *Gorgias* examined here convey a somber diagnosis of the corruptive effects of democratic institutional mechanisms on its citizens and leaders. The rationale for this diagnosis lies in the combination of the logic of majority rule, the lack of political and moral competence in the demos, and its appetitive nature. The tyrannical figures the demos generates are, indeed, "men of the people," insofar as they share ignorance and an ideal of freedom as appetitive enjoyment in common with their father.

3.5 THE DECEIVING GENTLENESS
OF TYRANNICAL DEMOCRACY

The passage from Book VI of the *Republic* on the corrupting effect of public gatherings (492b5–7), as well as the comparison between the Assembly and a large beast (493a–c), depicts what Plato takes to be a process of assimilation between the many, the corrupted youth, and private teachers or sophists: the common denominator in both of these discussions is the opinions of the many gathered in the Assembly. In the analogy of the ship, while the sailor-politicians persuade the shipowner by inebriating him with wine and drugs, they themselves are not exempt from this inebriation for, once they take possession of the wheel, they revel in feasting and drinking, using up the ship's resources for the sake of their own appetitive enjoyment. Becoming as appetitive as the demos is the condition for a successful political career under democracy—a point Socrates illustrates for Callicles in the *Gorgias*: the hedonistic ideal does not differentiate Callicles' aspiring tyrant or successful politician from the demos for it is, rather, what they share in common.

The same insight undergirds Book VIII's description of the genesis of tyranny. Here Socrates unambiguously claims that tyranny is derived from the *freedom* characterizing the democratic regime (*Rep.* 562c4–6; 564a3–4). This characterization of democracy as a disordered form of freedom is common in the fourth-century anti-democratic tradition.[48] Socrates resorts to outrageous exaggerations in order to stress the anarchic character of this freedom, which is extended to everybody and everything— women, slaves, and animals— to the point that even dogs, donkeys, and horses roam freely along the streets and without a master (563b4–d1). This pursuit of freedom

---

48. See, for example, Isoc. 7.20 and 15. 286. See also Bearzot 1981, pp. 84–85.

is characterized by ἀπληστία (an insatiable, almost obsessive desire) such that freedom becomes the only concern and the only criterion for making judgments and deliberating about both the practical affairs of the city and the private concerns of the households. Life under this democratic regime appears colorful and sweet.

It may be tempting to read this presentation as indicating that this regime represents a more a tolerant society than the Athenian democracy that put Socrates to death. Arlene Saxonhouse, for example, reads it as a depoliticized society characterized by gentleness and based on indifference, a refusal to make decisions and to participate, and an incapacity for determining exclusion and inclusion. In this reading, this portrait of democracy is constructed to show the logical endpoint of the democratic principle of freedom, understood as indifference; fallen into apathy, this society would not be able to be governed politically.[49]

This reading of the democracy of Book VIII as a gentle regime, however, does not withstand close scrutiny of the nature and content of the freedom at stake in these pages. This freedom has two interrelated aspects. The first lies in its identity with anarchy and license, ἀναρχία (560e5) and ἐξουσία (563e8–9), entailing that the free subject has the authority to entirely determine his own course of action and does not recognize any authority outside and above him. Conceived in this manner, freedom is incompatible with any notion of law and control; rather than corresponding to apathy,[50] it expresses the viewpoint of a sovereign position that does not recognize or tolerate any superior authority. At 562c–d, for example, Socrates notes that, unless they comply with this desire for unrestrained freedom,

---

49. Saxonhouse 1996, pp. 101–114. For her reading of Book VIII, see also Saxonhouse 1998. Along similar lines, Nichols comments that, in contrast to the Athenian democracy that put Socrates to death, the democracy of Book VIII does not seem to be a regime at all, for it lacks any principle of cohesion: Nichols 1987, p. 131.

50. *Contra* Saxonhouse 1996, p. 109.

political rulers are *punished by the city*. And at 563d–e, he insists that nobody in such a city takes notice of laws and that people become extremely irritated at the least hint of slavery. These two passages alone are sufficient to refute the notion that such a city would be unable to discriminate or make decisions. On the contrary, such a city does make relevant decisions precisely in order to defend its insatiable love for freedom.

This anarchic notion of freedom is based on a specific conception of the sovereignty of the demos as a collective body and a corresponding understanding of its collective decision-making processes, which is echoed in the identification of the demos as a tyrant discussed in chapter 1. In his treatment of the democratic city, Plato transfers this collective freedom to the individual citizen and then, by extension, to every inhabitant, with no distinctions between women, foreigners, slaves, and animals. One may obviously question the validity of this reasoning; it seems fallacious to mechanically apply a principle that characterizes a collective body to all its single components, as a collective body may well have its own prerogatives and rights *qua* collective. But Plato's reasoning takes seriously the Athenian citizenry's attribution of a moral and educational aspect to their collective decision-making processes. If in such processes the demos arrogates to itself—as a collective body—this supreme authority that elevates it above the law, as in the infamous trial of the generals of Arginusae, the consequence is that the demos' collective action corrupts *individuals* by teaching them that there is nothing above such freedom and by suggesting that they are entitled to it.

As argued by McGlew, collective democratic freedom resembled, in a sense, the passionate and personalized freedom of the tyrant. In the democratic city, this sovereign freedom belonged to the demos as a collective body gathered in assemblies and law courts. According to Plato's diagnosis, tyranny is the natural offspring of the democratic freedom because the tyrant simply expropriates for himself at the expense of everybody else the tyrannical privilege of the demos—the tyrant's overthrow of democracy is simply the individual appropriation of the ideal of sovereignty enshrined in democratic liberty. As McGlew argues, Plato's grasp of this point comes at the cost of abstracting from all concerns of political form.[51] However, such abstraction may be justified in Plato's eyes, given that his concern in these pages is not with political forms per se but, rather, with political forms seen from the consequences of their moral and educational dimensions. The tyrant can privately appropriate this freedom, because the demos practiced it, elevated it to a supreme principle, and inculcated it in the whole city through their democratic "education." Plato's point is that this so-called education imparted by the demos creates tyrannical individuals.

The second aspect of this freedom relates to its positive content and refers to the appetitive nature of the demos. The demos—and by extension, individual citizens—interprets sovereign freedom as the indiscriminate satisfaction of all of their desires. Moreover, this interpretation of freedom is motivated primarily by the satisfaction of unnecessary desires. Their desires may sometimes include nonappetitive ones (such as the desire to practice philosophy or for conversation), but it is primarily the appetitive kind that is viewed as their life's goal.[52] The democratic citizens want to be free agents in the sense of being hedonistic agents.[53] While it is true that their desires are not lawless, this may be because the demos enjoys sovereign freedom only insofar as it acts as a collective body, and the individual citizens are free only insofar as they are parts of a political collectivity—that is, *qua* citizens. As such, their πλεονεξία is limited

---

51. McGlew 1993, p. 211.
52. For a discussion of the appetitive nature of the democratic man, see chapter 4, this volume, and in particular, note 1.
53. I will address the issue of hedonism and appetitive enjoyment in greater detail in chapter 4, this volume.

externally by the other citizens' desire for appetitive enjoyment and freedom, and is therefore constrained within the boundaries of laws. This internalization of other people's claims disappears in the case of the tyrant, for the tyrant expropriates everybody else's claim to freedom and enjoyment.

The interrelation of these two aspects of freedom explains the political and institutional dynamic that, according to Socrates, leads to the tyrant's rise. The demagogic drones, who manipulate assemblies by organizing cliques and intimidating the opposition, do not recognize any laws and have the expropriation of rich people for the sake of their own appetitive enjoyment as their single purpose. The demos takes part in assemblies only when there is the possibility of extracting some honey from the rich. Thus both drones and the demos gathered in the Assembly, albeit dissimilar in other respects, share a common hedonistic and acquisitive ethos (564d–565a). In the social and political conflict that arises from the expropriation of wealthy people, the demos confers full powers on a προστάτης in order to defend its prerogatives against what the people, deceived by the demagogic drones, interpret as an oligarchic attempt to limit both their political freedom and their license to appetitive enjoyment. *Pace* the gentle reading of Plato's democracy, while performing this political act they are neither affected by apathy nor indifferent nor tolerant. Tyranny does not arise from an absence of communal action, as the demos deliberately transfers its power to its presumed champion who incarnates the demos' appetites and collective freedom within a single individual.[54] The people, therefore, make a communal decision to defend what they take to be what is good for them; Plato's point is that this decision is both a disastrous mistake *and* the logical outcome of the practices, institutions, and motivations that constitute Athenian democracy. Thus, it is precisely the freedom defended by

54. *Contra* Saxonhouse 1996, p. 111.

the demos—understood in its double dimension, as freedom from authority and license of appetitive enjoyment—that is the fertile soil and seed for the growth of greedy and lawless tyrannical characters and, ultimately, for the political rise of a tyrant.

PART II

THE TYRANT'S SOUL

The theory of the tripartite soul articulated in the Republic states that there are three fundamental psychic elements, which Socrates calls either "parts" or "forms" of the soul: τὸ ἐπιθυμητικόν (the appetitive "part"), responsible for hunger, thirst, sexual arousal, and desire for money; τὸ θυμοειδές (spirit), responsible for the desire for victory, power, and self-esteem, and the feeling of anger; and τὸ λογιστικόν (reason), which desires learning, wisdom, truth, and the good. Socrates infers the existence of these psychic elements by analyzing cases of psychic conflicts. While conflicts vary in degree, the three forms of the soul struggle with each other in every individual. Philosophers are the exception to this rule, as they are the only ones who manage to achieve psychic harmony.

While most readers of Plato take no issue with this basic summary of the theory of tripartition, as soon as one begins analyzing its details, an array of problems, seeming inconsistencies, and unclear points emerge. First, there is no agreement among commentators about what we should understand by "parts" of the soul, whether we should take them to be real and distinct parts (realist reading), or to be a mere figure of speech indicating forms of motivation (deflationist reading). Moreover, there is no agreement concerning whether the picture provided by Socrates in Book IV should be taken as a provisional one that does not exclude the existence of further parts. It is equally an object of controversy whether the partition of the soul provided in Book X is consistent with that in Book IV, for in the last book of *the* Republic, *Socrates speaks of only two parts of the soul. The rationale for the analogy of the three parts of the city and the three parts of the soul has appeared incoherent to some. Further problems concern the nature of each part. It is controversial whether each part is endowed with rational cognitive abilities or whether the capacity for means–end reasoning belongs to the rational part alone; whether there is a sufficient rationale for the distinction of the spirited part from the other parts and what the spirit's exact nature and form of motivation is; and whether the appetitive part should be understood as further divided into subparts, considering that passages of the dialogue seem to suggest the presence of a conflict among appetitive desires. Finally, further controversies concern the dynamics of psychic conflict, especially as exemplified in the treatment of the different kinds of men corresponding to the different corrupt regimes presented in Books VIII and IX, as well as the transaction between individual souls and the city.*

A detailed analysis of the three parts of the tyrant's soul and their reciprocal interactions requires addressing at least some of these controversies. The interpretation of the theory of tripartition that is adopted for this analysis relies on a realist reading of the soul's parts. While I do not exclude the possibility that the Republic *provides us with only a partial view of the nature of the soul, I do hold that this partial view is consistent through the dialogue (including Book X) and is based on a sound rationale. This view consists of considering the soul divided into no less and no more than three distinct parts, based on the observation of the existence of a specific kind of conflict, which we may summarize as a conflict between desire and aversion toward the same object at the same time and in the same respect (Rep. 436b8–9). All the soul's three parts are bearers of different forms of desire, but they are distinguished insofar as reason alone is endowed with rational cognitive capacities, while the other two parts should be taken—as the text explicitly indicates—as nonrational. The appetitive and spirited parts certainly have cognitive capacities and therefore can grasp reason's orders and have nonrational beliefs, but they do not have a capacity for means–end reasoning. Reason calculates and elaborates plans for the whole soul, even when it is motivationally and normatively enslaved to one of the other two parts. As I will illustrate in chapter 6, in cases of moral corruption, in addition to forcing reason to calculate on their behalf (that is, to satisfy their desires), the nonrational parts of the soul can pervert reason's own desire. Similarly, in cases of the moral enslavement of spirit to the appetitive part of the soul, both its motivational power (its capacity to fight on behalf of what is perceived as good or just) and its conative side (the form of its desire) are corrupted.*

Fully appraising the tyrant's nature demands we focus not only on its dominant part (i.e., the appetites) but also on its two enslaved parts, in order to assess both the way in which the dominant appetites impact those parts and the ancillary role they play in making a man into a tyrant. As it will emerge from my analysis, Plato's tyrant shares in the exceptionality belonging to philosophical natures. He should actually be better understood as a philosophical nature gone astray. Therefore, his soul's uncontrolled appetitive part puts his particularly strong spirited and rational parts at the service of the satisfaction of its desires.

The tyrant obviously provides an exceptional case study of the effects and dynamics characteristic of the moral corruption of the soul. As Socrates gathers information about the nature of the three parts from his observation of psychic conflicts, a detailed study of the most conflicted and unhappy of all souls—the tyrannical one—will yield interesting insights into the nature of the soul in general. But there is a further reason why the study of the tyrannical soul is a promising endeavor. One of the tenets of Plato's investigation throughout the dialogue is that individual souls and the city shape each other. Thus it would be impossible to understand fully moral corruption (or moral perfection) in the Republic while abstracting the social and political conditions in which souls are embodied, the educational processes they undergo, and the effects that society and its institutions have on them. Plato's treatment of the nature of the tyrannical soul's corruption is, by the same token, a political diagnosis of what is wrong with democracy; if, as argued in part I, the tyrant is nothing but the natural offspring of the demos, it is in the tyrant's interaction with the democratic city that we have to look for the causes of his moral corruption.

The analysis of the tyrant's soul that follows will take into account and analyze both aspects of the moral corruption of the tyrant: the interactions between the three parts of his soul, including the ancillary role played by spirit and reason; and the dynamic transactions between the three parts of his soul and the democratic city.

Chapter 4

The Tyranny of Eros and the Tyrannical Man's Appetites

Tyranny is shot from all sides by the arrows of terrible erotic desires;
one must guard it against them.

Euripides, fr. 850N

Plato's treatment of tyranny differentiates between the tyrannical man (who lives a private life and acts upon his tyrannical impulses in his everyday relationships with his family and fellow citizens) and the political tyrant (a tyrannical man who finds propitious circumstances to take power). This distinction suggests the presence of tyrannical impulses and characters in the city, regardless of whether the men who have them happen to hold political power. As in the case of the oligarchic and the democratic man, the tyrannical man's soul is dominated by the appetitive part.[1] However, while the oligarchic man

---

1. For a critique of the standard reading of the psyche of the democratic man as dominated by the appetitive part, see Scott 2000 and Johnstone 2013. Scott argues that the desires of the democratic man are not appetitive but quasi-appetitive, in the sense that while the democratic man is also driven by spirited and rational desires, these desires are not properly directed toward the good and therefore work along the lines of appetitive desires. It is unclear, however, what the interpretive advantage is in considering these rational and spirited desires as quasi-appetitive rather than arguing more simply that the domination of appetitive desires in the democratic man influences and shapes the desires of the rational and of the spirited part of the soul, as Socrates explicitly suggests in the case of the oligarchic man (*Rep.* 553d1–7). Johnstone argues that the democratic man is temporarily ruled by whatever

focuses on money, and the democratic man is driven by unnecessary yet lawful objects of desire, the tyrannical man's appetites are specifically attracted to unlawful objects of desire. The tyrannical man is like a somnambulist, for he is a prisoner of his beastly dreams—of incest, murder, and paraphilic sexual desires for animals and gods alike—that the majority of people have only while asleep, but which he indulges in waking life (*Rep.* 571c3–d3). A second major distinction between the tyrannical man and the other two types of men dominated by their appetites is the role eros and madness play in unleashing those appetites:[2] it is eros that, with the help of madness, unshackles his appetites from the restraints of traditional beliefs, social bonds, or mere shame. Eros is installed by the "tyrant-makers" (that is, corruptors in the city) as a great winged drone in the soul of the tyrannical man in order to remove the restraining effect of his democratic father and of the rest of the household. By acting as a

desires arise in him and that these are neither necessarily nor primarily of an appetitive nature. I consider this reading incompatible with both the architecture of Book VIII, which describes different degrees of moral corruption dependent on the part that is ruling the soul at each time, and some rather clear textual indications. That the corruption of regimes and corresponding kinds of men are organized according to the part of the soul in charge appears clear from a passage in Book IX, 586e–587c. Here, Socrates first discusses the consequence of one of the nonrational parts of the soul taking control, then suggests that there are degrees of corruption according to which part of the soul has taken power, with the tyrant being the most distant from reason. Then he addresses the distinction among pleasures, identifying three kinds of pleasure, one legitimate (the rational) and two illegitimate (those related to spirit and the appetitive part). The tyrant is third from the oligarch at the bottom end of the illegitimate ones, while the democratic man is between them. Pleasures are here ordered on a ladder that is obvious to interpret as corresponding to the three parts of the soul, with the second kind of illegitimate pleasure—the appetitive one—having three main forms, corresponding to the oligarchic, the democratic, and the tyrannical man. This is confirmed by the fact that, at 581c, the three forms of pleasure are explicitly related to the three parts of the soul. Moreover, Socrates argues that there are three primary kinds of people—philosophic, victory-loving, and profit-loving (where profit-loving, φιλοκερδές, is metonymic for appetitive). The democratic man must be one of the "main types" of man because in Book IV, at 445c5–7, Socrates had claimed that, while there are many forms of vices, only four of them are worth mentioning, corresponding to four types of constitutions and four types of men.

2. This will be discussed further in chapters 5 and 6, this volume.

leader (προστάτης) of his appetites, eros makes sure that the tyrannical man will indulge in them and pursue them without restraint. Moreover, eros adopts madness as its bodyguard, so that it becomes frenzied. Madness indeed annihilates the beneficial influence that good beliefs and desires might have on the soul of the tyrannical man (572d8–573b4).

This process reveals the supposed absolute freedom of the tyrannical man to be absolute slavery—that is, having a radical incapacity for self-mastery or self-determination, which incites him to perform the most execrable acts and throws his soul into a state of disorder and misery. This condition is exacerbated within the political tyrant: isolation, paranoia, and the inability to satisfy basic desires and enjoy simple pleasures characterize his whole life (579b3–c2). The tyrant's absolute lack of self-mastery contrasts him to the kingly man, for whom self-mastery is the condition for government over others (586e4–587e4). The miserable slavery of the tyrant—who, being a slave to his own eros, enslaves the whole city—contrasts with the happy harmony of the soul of the kingly man.

As already argued in chapter 3, the apparent freedom of the tyrant corresponds to the private appropriation of that absence of superior authority and license of appetitive enjoyment that, according to Plato, characterizes democratic life. Plato includes the tyrannical man with those character types dominated by their appetites and, moreover, makes him the exemplification of the consequences of the appetites' and eros' unrestrained tyranny within a soul. While the tyrannical man is both brutal and power-seeking, his inclination to violence and will to power are not the main cause of his behavior and deeds but, rather, a consequence of his eros and unlawful appetites and only an ancillary cause of his behavior.[3] As I will discuss further in chapter 5, the tyrant's attachment to power and propensity

3. This, however, does not entail that the spirited part of the soul has no role to play.

to violence are very different from those of the timocratic man. The timocratic man values honor and power above everything else. His greed is subordinated to his love of honor (φιλοτιμία), for his spirit rules over the two other parts of the soul. From this viewpoint, the timocratic man more closely reflects a traditional heroic ethos, where the accumulation and acquisition of wealth is part of the path to social status and recognition. The tyrant, on the contrary, is the figure for a new ethos that emerged during the Peloponnesian War and the oligarchic revolutions at the end of the fifth century. In Plato's reading, this ethos cherished absolute and unaccountable power as an instrument for the acquisition of material goods and the gratification of appetites, in the name of a selfish and highly individualistic conception of the good.

Classical depictions of tyrants included narratives of hedonistic excesses and sexual paraphilia, which were common tropes indicating the tyrant's transgressive and exceptional character. Both greed (understood as an excessive desire for the acquisition of money, goods, and power at the expenses of others)[4] and eros (understood not just as a private passion but also as a proper political category)[5] played a key role in classical debates on the nature and purpose of political power, Athenian imperialism, and Athenian democracy. These classical debates set the framework for Plato's treatment of the tyrant and offered him the "raw material" upon which he elaborates in his diagnosis of the tyrannical man's pathology.

Plato's treatment of the tyrannical man's appetites and eros aims to address the corrupting effects of the new hedonistic interpretation of the traditional competitive Greek virtues adopted by sections of the Athenian elite involved with Athenian democracy. Greed and political eros are two key concepts that originate in the political and public debates of democratic Athens that shape Plato's depiction of the tyrannical man. Contextualizing Plato's arguments will throw further light on the sense in which tyranny should be considered as the natural child of democracy. The originality and conceptual strength of Plato's contribution to these debates lies in the articulation of his diagnosis of the nature and origin of tyrannical impulses within an innovative moral psychology based on dynamic relationships between the three parts of the soul and between the soul and the city. Plato opposes precisely this complex moral psychology to the fascination exerted by the happy figure of the greedy and hedonistic tyrant on a portion of the Athenian elite.

4.1 GREEDY DEMOS, GREEDY LEADERS, GREEDY TYRANTS

Greed—or the desire to have a greater and better share than one ought to (πλεονεξία and its cognate verb πλεονεκτεῖν)—is central to the political discourse in fifth-century Athens.[6] In Greek literature, the notion of greed is connected to the problem of distributive justice in a community, where it describes an excessive propensity for acquisition at the expense of others and without regard for fairness. It is a divisive attitude vis-à-vis the community, as it prioritizes individual self-interest over the interests of the community, divorcing individual and collective well-being.[7] While this excessive acquisitiveness

---

6. On the notion of greed in Greek literature and thought, see the excellent Balot 2001.

7. On the Athenian demos' suspicion that wealthy people may pursue interests opposite to those of the community, including harboring treasonous designs, see Ober 1989, ch. 5. As stressed by Ober, while the Athenian demos never endorsed an ideal of economic equality and never used its political power to systematically expropriate wealthy people, excessive wealth was a matter of concern to them for several reasons, including the fear that wealthy

generally refers to the appropriation of material goods, it may sometimes refer to excessive desire for power.

The archaic heroic ethos expressed in the Homeric poems, in which the display of material wealth is a symbol for its possessor's greatness, already associates power, social status, and the acquisition of material goods. The Homeric system is based on competitive virtues, which had more weight than the still underdeveloped cooperative virtues. Thus, the heroic code encourages the accumulation of material goods through pillage, conquest, raids, and ransoms by associating it with social prestige and honor.[8]

According to the heroic code, the accumulation of wealth through dispossession of others has a positive value insofar as it is subordinated to the pursuit of honor. As noticed by Adkins, the Homeric society is a "shame-culture," where the maintenance of honor (τιμή) is the chief goal. The ἀγαθός (that is, the man who possesses the skills and qualities of an effective chief in war and in peace) and ἀρετή (understood as the ἀγαθός' excellence in performing this function) are valued only insofar as one's reputation is attached to them: if this reputation happened to be withdrawn, they would cease to be valued.[9] The seizure of material goods would reveal a disgraceful and excessive acquisitiveness when turned inward against the community of allies and soldiers with whom the distribution of the spoils ought to be based on the criteria of merit and fairness. In such a case, exemplified in the *Iliad* by Agamemnon's robbery of Achilles' spoils (Hom. *Il.* 1.130–240), the instrumentalization of power for the sake

people may display a sense of superiority and entitlement incompatible with democratic principles. Envy of the rich, moreover, was a common feeling.

8. The distinction between "competitive" and "cooperative" or "quiet" virtues is the core of Adkins' reconstruction of the transformation of ethical standards from the archaic to the classical period: Adkins 1960. While Adkins' reconstruction of this development has several limitations, I take his distinction between competitive and cooperative virtues to be quite useful to grasp some fundamental tensions in the ethos of fifth-century Athens.

9. Adkins 1960, pp. 48, 63, 154–155.

of accumulating wealth at the expense of one's allies and in disregard for criteria of fairness inverts the relationships between power, prestige, and acquisition of material goods.[10]

The notion of greed and of its relation to power in the classical period is key to the Greek understanding and interpretation of both Athens' internal conflicts and her conflicts with the other Greek cities. In particular, the conceptualization of greed shifts during the Peloponnesian War from a feature mainly characterizing the behavior of the Athenian elite at the community's expense to a description of the collective character of the city as such. Greed is a key notion in both Herodotus' and Thucydides' historical analyses. In Herodotus, the Athenian elite's greedy impulses are foreshadowed as the primary cause of Athens' imperialism,[11] while the combined greed of the demos and of its leaders is explicitly indicted by Thucydides as the driving force behind Athens' imperialistic enterprise and as the cause of its fall.[12] By dominating other cities and appropriating their goods, Athens channeled its constitutive greed outward, thus preventing it from undermining its internal unity.

Ryan Balot stresses a significant difference between Thucydides' portrait of Pericles' attitude toward Athenian imperialism and his analysis of the unrestrained desire for gain found in the demos and Pericles' successors. Pericles' democratic idealism subordinated the desire to acquire wealth to the interests of the community as a

10. Balot 2001, pp. 59–70.
11. See Hdt. 5.97, 6.132–133; on Themistocles' greed, see Hdt. 8.112.
12. See Thuc. 1.42, 1.70. On Alcibiades' greed, see Thuc. 6.12, 6.15. On the greed of the demos, see Thuc. 2.65, 4.21.2, 4.65.4. On the way in which Alcibiades' and the collective Athenians' aims, desires, and ambitions mirrored each other in Thucydides' account of the Sicilian expedition, see Kallet 2001, pp. 36–37. According to Kallet, Thucydides' intention is to denounce the irrationality of the Athenians, who emulated Alcibiades' tyrannical mode: excessive expenditure and display of wealth, and passionate desire for the expedition motivated by greed. The tyrant's greed is associated with that of the Athenian demos: Kallet 2001, p. 81. See also Smith 2009 for an excellent argument in support of this view, based on a literary analysis of Thucydides' style, particularly his adoption of epinician allusions.

whole—that is, to an ideal of greatness and glory: πλεονεξία was sub-ordinated to φιλοτιμία.[13] In this regard, Pericles' view of the Athenian empire was based on that traditional heroic ethos for which the acquisition of goods was part of the pursuit and display of social status. In this view, power was not an instrumental good pursued for a greater share of material goods but, rather, had glory as its ultimate goal. Pericles' attitude exploited a Greek moral tradition valuing competitive virtues. Some concepts typical of aristocratic ideology (such as the sense of ancestral worth, a code of behavior based on loyalty to friends and bravery in battle), together with a set of distinctively aristocratic practices (e.g., athletic training, homoeroticism, hunting, horse raising, symposia), were deeply embedded in Athenian culture, albeit in tension with the emerging democratic ideology.[14] At the same time, some of these concepts also underwent processes of transformation. For example, the ἀγαθός came to be identified with the good citizen (ἀγαθὸς πολίτης), valued for his commitment to benefiting the city, his contribution to the advancement of Athens, and thus, for his courage, daring, resourcefulness, and willingness to take risks for the sake of the city.[15] Even the concept of nobility of birth (εὐγένεια) was appropriated by democratic ideology and made common property of all citizens, becoming a general characterization of the possession of Athenian citizenship. Thus, by being an Athenian citizen, a man immediately shared in the glorious deeds of all his Athenian ancestors.[16]

The relationship between the pursuit of glory and greed is inverted with Pericles' successors, who, in Thucydides' analysis, were

13. See Thuc. 2.44.4. Ludwig stresses that, in Pericles' eyes, the reason why, in contrast with Spartans, Athenians can be trusted with pleasures and acquisitiveness is that their acquisitiveness is, first of all, that of honor and of the pleasure deriving from it, rather than material gain: Ludwig 2002, p. 328.
14. See Ober 1989, pp. 250–251.
15. Adkins 1960, pp. 197–225.
16. Ober 1989, 261–263.

more straightforwardly motivated by desire for gain and therefore ended up further nourishing the demos' own greed. For Cleon, Alcibiades, and even the more moderate Nicias, material individual self-interest took priority over the city's interest. Thus, Athens' imperialistic enterprise took on a different meaning, being motivated not by φιλοτιμία but, rather, by the desire to acquire more.[17] Nicias' speech against the Sicilian expedition (Thuc. 6.9–14), although apparently supporting a more moderate and reasonable stance, already shows an inversion of the Periclean definition of the good citizen. While in Pericles' Funeral Oration individual citizens will only flourish by putting the interests of the city first, for Nicias a good citizen puts his private interests first and acts on behalf of the polis in order to protect his own prosperity.[18] Alcibiades' speech in support of the Sicilian expedition (Thuc. 6.15–18), in addition to blurring the line between his individual power and the power of the polis, suggests the idea of an unlimited and uncontrolled expansion of Athens' power, driven by necessity and oriented toward the acquisition of wealth.[19]

The progressive transformation of political power into an instrumental good for the accumulation of wealth, as exemplified in Thucydides by the democratic leaders' (and especially by Alcibiades') unrestrained greed for profitable enterprises, marks a shift in the ethos of (at least a portion of) the Athenian elite.[20] The

17. Balot 2001, pp. 142–172. On Cleon's greed at the expense of the demos, see Aristophanes' accusations in the *Knights*, 801–808. The Old Oligarch, on the contrary, indicts the demos' own desire to distribute the wealth of the allied cities among Athenian citizens and refers to this desire as one of the main causes of the Athenian mistreatment of its allies: Ps.-Xen. *Ath. Pol.* 1.14.

18. See Kallet 2001, p. 32.

19. See Kallet 2001, pp. 37–41.

20. In his presentation of the immoralists' position, Adkins tends to emphasize the elements of continuity with the traditional competitive values, as their commendation of πλεονεξία is coherent with the traditional belief that the ἀγαθός has a right to a greater share: Adkins 1960, pp. 236–238. While these traditional elements are clearly present in the immoralists' position, I follow Balot in thinking that the subordination of φιλοτιμία to πλεονεξία represents a decisive shift with regard to the traditional competitive ethos.

tyrannical figures and the discourses of the supporters of tyranny discussed by Plato in the *Republic* and in the *Gorgias* are figures that exemplify this new ethos. Consideration of the moral decay of the political elite of Athens illuminates the central role given to the notion of greed in the *Republic*. Greed is explicitly connected with the problem of tyranny, and its political resonance within Athenian ideology is crucial to understanding Plato's choice to depict the tyrannical man as an appetitive individual. The first explicit reference to πλεονεκτεῖν occurs in Thrasymachus' powerful speech on shepherds and sheep in Book I, which directly relates outdoing others to holding power (*Rep.* 343e7–344a1). As discussed in chapter 3, the tyrant is introduced as the embodiment of the ideal of holding absolute and unaccountable power for the sake of complete injustice— that is, of outdoing (πλεονεκτεῖν) everybody else. The tyrant pushes the principle of rulership for the ruler's advantage to its extreme consequences: he is fundamentally an appropriator whose only regulative ideal is acquisitiveness and who, in addition to appropriating the private possessions of his subjects, goes so far as to turn all citizens into his private possessions. He is de facto a temple robber, a house breaker, a kidnapper, and would be openly identified as such were he not granted immunity and the more pompous name of a tyrant owing to his power. Tyranny is the appropriation of the property of others—of the common as well as of the private, and even of the sacred as well as the profane (344a6–b1); everything and everyone is a tyrant's property.

In Book II, Glaucon draws a significant opposition between, on the one hand, desire, nature, greed, and injustice, and on the other hand, law, respect for equality, and justice:

> We can see most clearly that those who practice justice do it only because they don't have the possibility of committing injustice and that they do it unwillingly, if we make a thought

experiment: let's grant both to a just and to an unjust man the license to do whatever he wants, and then let's follow both of them
closely and observe where their desires lead them; we'll catch the
just man red-handed following out of greed (διὰ τὴν πλεονεξίαν)
the same path as the unjust man. This is what everybody's nature naturally pursues as good (πᾶσα φύσις διώκειν πέφυκεν ὡς
ἀγαθόν), but the law forces it to go astray into honoring equality
(νόμῳ δὲ βίᾳ παράγεται ἐπὶ τὴν τοῦ ἴσου τιμήν). (*Rep.* 359b6–c6)

Here Glaucon establishes a causal link between πλεονεξία and injustice insofar as injustice is the consequence of the greed naturally
present in everyone. Moreover, he indicates that the only limit to
the proliferation of both greed and injustice is the law, which is, in
Glaucon's words, both nonnatural and externally imposed. Thus, according to this view, the desire to get the better or get more has no
internal limits of its own. Glaucon's observation echoes the hedonistic and philo-tyrannical position voiced by Callicles in the *Gorgias*,
as well as his belief in the opposition between nature and law.[21]
Callicles' view is an incoherent combination of traditional heroic
ethos (according to which those who are stronger and superior have
a legitimate claim to a greater share of the available goods, πλεονεκτεῖν, as a consequence of manifest excellence) and the new hedonism
of the Athenian elite (for whom positions of power and prestige are
instruments to the satisfaction of appetites).[22] In this view, the law,
as an instrument used by natural inferiors to protect themselves
and grant themselves an equal share, is opposed to nature (*Gorg.*

21. While Glaucon apparently means to restate Thrasymachus' argument, he actually voices a
position more similar to Callicles': the laws are a tool of the weak (not of the stronger) and
they end up controlling the strong on behalf of the weak. See Weiss 2007, pp. 100–101.
22. On the contradiction between the two sets of values cherished by Callicles—that is, between his abiding by traditional standards of excellence and the leveling tendencies of the
hedonism he endorses—see Kahn 1983, pp. 107–108.

483b–484c). In both his words and behavior during his conversation with Socrates, Callicles embodies a traditional culture of manliness that values intelligence, force, courage, and political competence as grounds for a claim, purportedly legitimated by nature, to a greater share of the city's goods. This self-assertive and competitive attitude leads Callicles to accuse repeatedly Socrates—in a similar manner to Thrasymachus in the *Republic*—of behaving like an inexperienced boy—that is, of being an adult man who indulges in the childish game of philosophy while failing to live up to ideals of maturity, manliness, and political involvement (484c–d). When Socrates suggests that the pleasure of the catamite should also be included among the pleasures available to the Calliclean superior man, he is able to shame Callicles precisely because the latter still holds these traditional values (494d–e).[23] The image of the passive partner in a homoerotic relationship—in addition to running against Callicles' ideals of activity, force, and bravery—evokes the possibility of exclusion from both public offices and the right to speak in front of the Assembly, an unacceptable proposition for the politically ambitious Callicles.[24]

---

23. According to Irwin, in the *Gorgias*, Socrates sets aside shame as a part of his eristic tactics because he relies on the idea that his moral argument will have sufficient persuasive force for rational interlocutors: Irwin 1995, 122–124. This reading is based on Callicles' accusation that Socrates pushed Polus to agree to false conclusions out of shame, and on the frankness characterizing the exchange between him and Socrates. It overlooks, however, Socrates' complex strategy in the use of the feeling of shame with his interlocutors. For more persuasive readings of Socrates' use of shame within his conversation with Callicles, see Kahn 1983; Moss 2005; and Tarnopolsky 2010. Renaut analyzes the different kinds of shame at play in the dialogue and concludes that it is a shame related to admitting failure that prevents Callicles from accepting to be refuted and therefore persuaded by Socrates. From this viewpoint, Callicles would be a somewhat philotimotic character: Renaut 2014, pp. 102–116. In fact, as I will show, it is eros for the demos that prevents Callicles from being persuaded, not shame. The same applies to Alicibiades in the *Symposium*, which Renaut mentions as another instance of the negative role played by shame.
24. On the privation of political rights inflicted on boys and men who have been either raped, or prostituted themselves, or have sexually submitted to their lovers, see Aeschin. 1.13–14 and 1.19–20.

Callicles' superior man, however, fails to qualify as a sincere honor-lover. Opposing Socrates' suggestion that the stronger and the better are those who, first of all, are capable of self-mastery and of ruling themselves, Callicles reveals that a fantasy of unlimited enjoyment and maximization of pleasures lies behind his praise for power, force, and courage. From Callicles' perspective, ruling is good for the ruler because it allows him to satisfy all his appetites:

> How could a man who is enslaved to anybody be happy? Rather, what is fine and just by nature is what I'm now going to tell you with all frankness: the man who'll live correctly should allow his own appetites (τὰς μὲν ἐπιθυμίας) to be as strong as possible and should not repress them (μὴ κολάζειν). And when they are as strong as possible, he should be capable of servicing them by virtue of his courage and intelligence (δι'ἀνδρείαν καὶ φρόνησιν), and of satisfying them with what each appetite desires every time. (*Gorg.* 491e5–492a3)

Temperance (σωφροσύνη) is not a necessary virtue for the ruler, who does not need to be capable of governing himself in order to be entitled to govern others. On the contrary, temperance is indicative of slavery, stupidity, and cowardice. Callicles, contrary to Polus, is not ashamed to stress the contradiction between the competitive and cooperative sets of virtues that coexisted in fifth-century Athenian society, nor does he hesitate to take the side of the competitive ones.[25] Moderation is for him only a slave morality aimed at taming the metaphorical "lion cubs" in the city (that is, those individuals with exceptional capabilities who are forced to abide by the criteria of equality and fairness imposed by the demos). Force and superiority are not exemplified by the capacity of restraining oneself but, rather, by the

25. On this point, see Kahn 1983, p. 97.

capacity to ensure oneself the absolute freedom of an endless gratification of appetites. For a tyrant, nothing would be more shameful
than submitting himself to self-control and justice—that is, to the
scrutiny of the many—as this would equate to becoming a slave of
the people (*Gorg.* 492b).

Callicles' superior man is, therefore, characterized not only by the
competitiveness and acquisitiveness of the traditional ethical background of the Athenian elite but also by a new conceptualization of
the relationship between power and greed that subordinated the first
to the second (488b; 490a; 491c–d). In Callicles' view, power, social
recognition, courage, and intelligence are all means to acquire more
in order to enlarge and gratify one's appetites. Socrates challenges
Callicles' hedonism, forcing him to recognize that not all appetites
are worthy of being gratified and not all pleasures are conducive to
happiness. He opposes Callicles' superior man with praise of temperance and self-control as the authentic features of a strong man.
Callicles, however, has no ears for Socrates' arguments and is anything but persuaded at the end of the dialogue. Socrates' refutation of
Callicles' position in the *Gorgias* does not contain an explicit discussion of the kind of moral psychology based on the soul's tripartition
that we find in later dialogues. In the *Republic*, on the contrary, the
problem of greed, combined with an identically hedonistic and instrumental view of political power supported now by Thrasymachus,
is addressed by following a different path, combining political theory,
metaphysics, and moral psychology.[26] As we will see, the tripartite
theory of the soul and the identification of the ἐπιθυμητικόν as the
part of the soul responsible for lawless appetites are both key to
Socrates' refutation of the happy and greedy tyrant, which is by the
same token an indictment of the moral bankruptcy of Athenian political leadership.

---

26. See Socrates' conclusive words on the problem of greed in Book IX, 586a1–b4.

4.2 POLITICAL EROS AND EROTIC LEADERS

The eroticization of political discourse and of the relationship between political leaders and the demos in fifth-century Athens is crucial to understanding the Platonic tyrant's erotic character and, more generally, Plato's intervention in the problem of political leadership in the *Republic*.[27] Consideration of this ideological and discursive context will reveal the associations between excessive desire and political strife that motivate Plato's psycho-political response to the threat of tyranny.

Aristophanes' *Knights*, in which the Sausage-Seller and Paphlagon (who represents the demagogic and war-loving leader Cleon) compete to gain the benevolence of their master, Demos, a gullible old man, is a perfect example of this eroticization. The Sausage-Seller and Paphlagon present themselves as rival lovers (ἀντ-ερασταί) struggling for the favors of their beloved: they both declare themselves in love with him (ἐρασταί), of having only his well-being in mind, and of being his generous benefactor. The reference to the typical erotic contest among the adult lovers of a boy is explicitly made by the Sausage-Seller, who reproaches Demos for behaving like a flattered youth courted by many lovers who ends up choosing the least worthy suitors instead of conceding his favors to the real gentlemen (Aristoph. *Kn.* 733–748). This passage from *Knights* is only one of a number of texts that adopt erotic language in a political context and attribute intense erotic desires to political leaders (in this case, for the Athenian demos). This erotic desire with a political

---

27. Larivée has correctly remarked that, after the publication of an array of studies on the political usages of the notion of eros and the links between eros, tyranny, and democracy, Plato scholars are less justified than ever either in adopting anachronistic interpretations of the tyrant—comparing him to a modern dictator—or in insisting on the obscurity of the reasons why Plato portrayed the tyrant as an erotic man: Larivée 2012, pp. 2–3. See Annas 1981, p. 304, as an example of anachronistic comparisons between ancient tyrants and modern dictators.

content is, as in *Knights*, often depicted in terms that explicitly recall pederastic love.

In the classical Greek conceptualizations of pederastic relationships, the position of the lover (ἐραστής) and of the beloved (ἐρώμενος) corresponded, respectively, to the active and passive poles of the bond. The ἐραστής was usually an adult male belonging to the Athenian elite who actively took part in the political life of the city and its frequent military campaigns. As an active citizen, he was meant to educate the young beloved in the most important civic virtues and obligations, embodying in his eyes a model of civic commitment and competence and preparing him to contribute actively to the community. The legitimacy of the pederastic relationship depended on its educational function and the role it played in initiating the Athenian youth into active political life in the community of aristocratic gentlemen. This educational aspect was also meant to counterbalance a more problematic dimension of pederastic love—namely, the opposition between passivity and activity entailed in all erotic relationships as they were conceptualized in classical Greece.[28]

Metaphors of hunting and conquest associated with the lover are sometimes employed in Greek literature: to be seized by eros is compared to falling into a hunter's trap, and the work of seduction is represented as a hunt where the beloved is the prey.[29] Eros was indeed generally understood in terms of a particularly intense desire to possess a beautiful object.[30] This strong and obsessive desire for possession was frequently linked with ὕβρις—that is, with the desire

28. On this problematic aspect of homoerotic love and on the kind of behavior expected from the beloved boy, see Dover 1989, pp. 81–91; Foucault 1990, pp. 187–225. For a critique of interpretations of eros in antiquity influenced by Foucault's *History of Sexuality*, see Sissa 2008.

29. See Ibyc. fr. 287; Xen. *Mem.* 2.1.4; Plat. *Charm.* 155d; *Lysis* 206a; *Phaedrus* 241d. On hunting metaphors associated with homoerotic pursuit, see Dover 1989, pp. 87–88; on the association of eros more generally with images of hunting, see Thornton 1997, pp. 40–41.

30. In Xen. *Mem.* 3.9.7, in the context of the discussion of the definition of madness, Socrates makes an analogy concerning the way people call a great delusion "madness" and the

to shame another for the sake of rising above him in a perverse sense of honor. It is not by chance that in some contexts, especially when its victim is a woman or a boy, the verb ὑβρίζειν indicates sexual assault, for rape is a possible way of shaming a victim, and being the perpetrator of a rape can be a form of self-aggrandizement.[31] Ancient sources evince anxious preoccupation with the possibility that a boy could be subject to the ὕβρις of an adult lover or assume a passive position in a homoerotic relationship. Aeschines' speech *Against Timarchus* provides evidence of the existence of specific laws in Athens meant to protect young male citizens from this kind of assault or temptation by regulating the opening and closing times of schools and forbidding adult men access to schoolrooms (Aeschin. 1.9–12).[32] A position of passivity was highly dangerous for a boy, in that it could entirely discredit him by revealing a character flaw, making him unfit for political participation. A boy who submitted sexually to another man, whether willingly or unwillingly, was considered incapable of self-restraint and of autonomous judgment and, consequently, irremediably damaged.[33] Thus, reciprocal positions between

way they call a strong desire (τὴν ἰσχυρὰν ἐπιθυμίαν) "eros." Eros is also defined as "desire doubled" (ἐπιθυμίαν μὲν διπλασιασθεῖσαν) by Prodicus, DK 84 fr. 7. The acquisitive aspect of erotic desire is emphasized in the *Symposium*, where Diotima asks Socrates what a lover of beautiful things desires, and Socrates answers that he desires that they become his own: Plat, *Sym.* 204d5–7. There has been some debate about whether this desire ought to be understood as always sexual in nature: see Ludwig 2002, pp. 7–9. Against Dover's excessive emphasis on the sexual aspect of eros (in Dover 1989), Ludwig argues that sexual reductionism neglects the complexity of the experience of eros in classical Greece. Eros was certainly related to sexual arousal, but was not identical to it, and in some of its manifestations it did not have sexual connotations at all, or it did not have them in a primary way. At the same time, Ludwig criticizes attempts to underplay the dangerous, aggressive, and acquisitive aspects of eros, arguing that including romantic love within the ancient experience of eros should not entail forgetting that in its full range of manifestations, eros may include aggression. On the dangerous and violent aspects of eros, see Thornton 1997, ch. 1.

31. Ludwig 2002, pp. 173–173.
32. For an analysis of this speech, see Dover 1989, ch. 2.
33. It must be noted that the boy was deprived of political rights even in cases in which he submitted unwillingly—for example, by being forced into prostitution by an adult member

the adult man and the boy in an erotic relationship were subject to a constant negotiation aimed at establishing bonds of affection and gratitude while preserving the honor of the boy as a future active member of the political community. The standard answer to this conundrum was the lack of reciprocity in erotic desire. The boy was not supposed to show sexual passion or reciprocate the erotic attraction of his lover but, rather, to carefully evaluate the virtues of his suitors and to concede his favors only to the one who displayed the necessary civic virtues. Rather than on the reciprocity of desire, the pederastic relationship was based on a morally respectable exchange of favors: the lover was supposed to educate the boy and motivate him to improve himself, while the boy was supposed to show gratitude for the lover's benevolence in terms of affection (φιλία), not eros.[34]

Aristophanes' comic representation of the two leaders competing for the favors of Demos as two rival lovers competing for the favors of a boy is apt, given that in classical Athens the boundaries between private erotic passions (in particular, pederastic ones) and political discourse and behavior were anything but neat. Among other things, eros was believed to be the underlying origin of an array of different passions ranging from ambition to patriotism.[35] In the *Symposium*, this

of his family: see Aeschin. 1.14. In terms of the consequences for the boy, the boundaries between being a victim of rape and willingly adopting a passive sexual role were rather blurred.

34. In Xenophon's *Symposium* we find a differentiation between a boy and a woman with regard to sexual intercourse: while women do share in the pleasures of sex, a boy maintains his sobriety while looking on the inebriated lover, Xen. *Sym.* 8.21. See Dover 1989, pp. 52 and 67.

35. Ludwig 2002, p. 2. Ludwig, however, also notes that Diotima's observation in the *Symposium* that people usually refer the term ἔρως to erotic passion alone and do not define, for example, people who love money as erotic (*Sym.* 205d4–6), may be an indication that in prose and in spoken language the term tended to be used only in its specific sense: Ludwig 2002, p. 146. Diotima's remark, however, can hardly apply to poetry, where both the use of a generic sense of eros, understood simply as intense desire, and the use of a transferred sense of eros, understood as intense erotic desire, to nonerotic objects of desire is well attested: see, for example, Hom. *Il.* 13.636–639, 24.226–7; Archil. fr. 19.3 West, on the eros for tyranny; Sappho fr. 16 LP, in which a transferred specific sense of eros is applied to the intense desire

entanglement between erotic attachment and patriotism is manifested in Phaedrus' speech, which describes the habit of exploiting homoeroticism in order to strengthen civic and military bonds by means of placing lovers side by side on the battlefield (Plat. *Sym.* 178e3–179a4). This political dimension of pederasty is further articulated by Pausanias' speech, where we find a taxonomy of the differing treatments of homoeroticism in cities under different rules. In particular, both the Persian Empire and its subject Ionian cities discouraged or even forbad homoeroticism owing to the danger posed to the rulers by strong bonds of friendship among people (*Sym.* 182c1–3). As an example, Pausanias mentions the two Athenian civic heroes, the tyrant-slayers Harmodius and Aristogeiton, whose homoerotic bond was the source of their opposition to the Athenian tyrants.[36]

There are numerous examples of the politicization of eros outside the Platonic corpus as well. In Thucydides, the notion of eros is used to explain key events of the Peloponnesian War. Pericles' funeral oration reconceptualizes the bond between Athens and its citizens in terms of eros by encouraging the Athenian citizen to see himself as an ἐραστής of the polis. In this definition, Athens becomes the beautiful object of the citizens' intense desire, and patriotism is transformed into the erotic admiration of the city's power (Thuc. 2.43.1).[37] Pericles' definition—which replaces the more familiar metaphor of the motherland and fatherland, as well as the notion of friendship among

---

for armies; Pind. *P.* 3.20, on the eros for far away things. These uses of eros abound in tragedy, especially in Euripides: see Aesch. *Ag.* 540 and Eur. *Phoen.* 359, where eros indicates patriotism; Aesch. *Ag.* 341–347, on eros for plunder and gain; Eur. *IA* 808–809, on the intense desire to conquer Troy (also indicated as Aphrodite, at 1264–1266); Eur. *Her.* 65–66, on eros for tyranny; Eur. *Heraclid.* 377–378, where Euripides applies the rather specific term ἐραστής to the lovers of war; and Soph. *OT* 601, where Creon says that he has never been an ἐραστής of the idea of tyranny. In prose, apart from Thucydides, the transferred use of eros is attested, for example, in Hdt. 3.53.4: "tyranny is a dangerous affair, but it has many lovers (τυραννὶς χρῆμα σφαλερόν, πολλοὶ δὲ αὐτῆς ἐρασταί εἰσι)"; Xen. *Hell.* 5.2.28; Isoc. 10.52.1).

36. On the civic cult reserved to the two "tyrant-slayers," see Monoson 2000, ch. 1.

37. See Balot 2001, p. 145.

citizens, aims at stimulating intense desire for the power and beauty of Athens so that the citizens will become as active and daring as the suitors courting a beloved boy. However, this definition also entails a number of dangers, including excessive competition between citizens, who are now put in the position of being rival lovers, and the transformation of the city into a potentially passive object of erotic desire.

Moreover, the eroticization of the citizen's bond with the city opens the possibility of citizens acting as jealous lovers who wish to reclaim possession of the city *qua* their object of love. The Aristophanic depiction of Cleon as a lover of Demos varies from the Periclean understanding of patriotism as erotic attachment to the city, for it eroticizes not the civic bond uniting all citizens to the city but, rather, the political relationship between a leader and the people. Eros between a leader and the demos, however, is an even more dangerous affair, because it risks turning the city and its demos into a passive object of love; moreover, because this eros can be associated with jealousy and possessiveness, it can thus transform the city and the demos into the prey of a leader who plays the role of a hunter/seducer. This eroticization of the exchange between demos and leaders is exemplified in the case of Alcibiades.[38] In our sources, Alcibiades' eros is twofold: on the one hand, it is the wild and jealous passion of an ambitious young political leader for the demos of his city, while on the other, it is a sexual love linked to the *aphrodisia* that Alcibiades reportedly indulged in. The young Alcibiades is depicted as a δημεραστής—that is, as a passionate lover of the people, in the (pseudo?-)Platonic *Alcibiades* (*Alc. I*, 132a1–4).[39] Further references

---

38. For a good collection of ancient sources on Alcibiades' eros, see Wohl 1999.

39. The controversial question of the *Alcibiades'* authenticity is irrelevant to the point I am making here: whether the dialogue was actually written by Plato or by later members of the Academy, this passage shows the persistence of an association of Alcibiades with political eros (in this case, eros for the Athenian people) within the traditional presentation of his character.

to Alcibiades' political eros can be found in two important passages from Thucydides' *Peloponnesian War*.

In the first scene, while debating with Alcibiades about the Sicilian expedition, Nicias warns the older men present to beware of younger men's intense desire for far-away things: eros, according to Nicias, is driving Alcibiades' imperialistic expedition to Sicily (Thuc. 6.13.1). Thucydides transfers a specific sense of eros—as not just a generic desire for something but also as an erotic passion—to the motives animating both Alcibiades and the Athenian demos. This appears clear from the four features that characterize the Athenians' decision to conquer Sicily: the fantasy inherent in the scheme, with its irrational hopes, expectations, and mental imagery; the sudden increase of daring; the surprising resourcefulness and liberal expenditure in preparing for the expedition; and the gratuitousness of the attempt.[40] Thucydides' explanation of the motivations of the Sicilian expedition combines the topics of political eros and greed. The intensity, obsessive character, and irresistibility of the desire for personal gain driving both Alcibiades and the Athenian demos resembles an erotic passion whose object is Sicily, set against the background of a fantasy of unlimited expansion and appropriation of resources for the Athenian empire.[41]

In the second passage from the *Peloponnesian War*, Alcibiades justifies himself before the Spartans—after having fled Athens— by describing himself as a lover of his city (Thuc. 6.92.2). His love, however, is the vengeful passion of the rejected lover, who attacks the object of his love, willing to win his beloved back by any means. Although the word used by Thucydides is φιλόπολις, Alcibiades' love for the city features the brutal and possessive erotic passion that does

40. See Ludwig 2002, pp. 165–166.
41. A further instance of the use of a specific sense of eros within a political context is to be found in Thuc. 3.45.5, where the combination of eros and hope—that is, false illusions or expectations—is indicated as the cause of the greatest ruin.

not disdain the use of violence in order to retake possession of its lost object or to force the city to recognize that she needs his love.[42]

Further references to Alcibiades' political eros can be found in the much later *Life of Alcibiades*, where Plutarch stresses the complexity of his personality—a contradictory mixture of political cleverness, bravery, and luxurious self-indulgence—that causes the noble men of the city to despise his tyrant-like character and lawlessness, and simultaneously the Athenian demos to desire, love, and hate him. In the same passage, Plutarch reports that Alcibiades' shield was emblazoned with a thunder-bearing Eros, an image evidently combining erotic love and political and military power (Plut. *Alc.* 16.1–2). Alcibiades' political eros, moreover, is only one aspect of his strongly erotic personality. As mentioned in chapter 2, Alcibiades' sexual license and propensity to libertinage—along with his anti-isonomic attitude, egocentricism, extravagance, and arrogance—are aspects of his character that attracted suspicions of tyrannical aspirations.[43]

In Plato's dialogues, Callicles is the exemplification of the dangers entailed by political eros in general and the eroticization of the relationship between politicians and the Athenian demos in particular. At the beginning of his conversation with Callicles, Socrates tries to establish a common ground for dialogue by referring to their shared experience of being in love with two different objects of desire: Socrates is the ἐραστής of both Alcibiades and of philosophy, while Callicles is in love with a young boy named Demos and with the Athenian demos

42. See McGlew's commentary on this point: McGlew 1993, pp. 188–189. A much more benevolent description of Alcibiades' love and dedication to Athens and a defense against the accusation that he had tyrannical aspirations is offered by his son in Isocrates' speech *On the Team of Horses*: Isoc. 16.

43. Thucydides connects Alcibiades' lawless behavior with the demos' and his adversaries' suspicions about his tyrannical intentions. According to Thucydides, the Athenian people feared him because of the extravagance of his habits, and this fear led the Athenians to disaster during the Sicilian expedition, because it made them prefer to commit military command to inferior men than him: Thuc. 6.15.

(Plat. *Gorg.* 481d–e). In spite of this commonality, however, Socrates' and Callicles' experiences of erotic attachment are quite different, as the former always follows what philosophy dictates rather than the volatile Alcibiades, while the latter always tells the young Demos and the Athenian people what they want to hear and changes his views and statements according to their whims. Put simply, in contrast to Socrates, Callicles is a flatterer. According to Lysias' speech in the *Phaedrus*, flattering the beloved boy is a standard pattern of behavior for the ἐραστής, who is always ready to please his boy with words and deeds (Plat. *Phaedrus*, 231c). In the *Lysis*, this type of flattering lover is exemplified by Hippothales, who spends much of his time writing eulogizing poems and prose pieces in the hope of seducing his beloved Lysis (Plat. *Lysis* 204c–206a).

Callicles' arrogant answer to Socrates, however, shows no sign of love for the Athenian people. In Callicles' view, the many are weak and make laws to compensate for their weakness by forcing superior men to abide by their notions of the shameful and unjust. When Socrates suggests that the Athenian demos *is* the stronger and the better in the city because it holds political power, Callicles retorts by aristocratically dismissing the idea that the statements of a bunch of uncultivated and worthless menial laborers have validity and authority:

> It's not cobblers or cooks that I call superior, but those who are intelligent about the affairs of the city, about the good way to govern, and not just intelligent, but also brave, able to accomplish whatever they devise, without flinching out of softness of the soul. (*Gorg.* 491a7–b4).

Yet, Socrates' depiction of Callicles gives us precious information about his political activity: in spite of his elitist contempt for the common people, Callicles is a typical example of an elite citizen actively taking part in the political life of the city by attending and speaking at the meetings of the Assembly. Socrates' characterization is consistent with Callicles' training in philosophy and rhetoric, his strong political ambitions, and his identification of superiority with intelligence and competence in public affairs. Socrates interprets as a display of eros Callicles' habit of flattering the Athenian people by accommodating himself to their views and wishes in the Assembly. This remark about Callicles' erotic character should be taken seriously, for later on in the conversation Socrates further argues that the reason Callicles is not persuaded by his arguments, in spite of rationally seeing that they are correct, is his eros for the demos (*Gorg.* 513c7–8).[44] Given that Callicles seems to both desire and despise the Athenian people, it is necessary to specify what kind of eros Socrates attributes to him.

Socrates' first speech in the *Phaedrus* provides a picture of a bad lover that accords with his characterization of Callicles in the *Gorgias*: a man ruled by appetites who uses his desired boy as a means for pleasure and self-gratification (*Phaedrus*, 238e); who, for this reason, always wants to keep his beloved in a condition of inferiority, ignorance, and dependence (239a–b) and is envious of his beloved's wealth (240a); and a jealous lover who clings to his boy as long as his erotic attraction is still alive, but who is ready to forget him as soon as desire fades away (240c–241a). This lover is like someone with a hunger that he wants to satisfy by possessing and consuming his beloved: "The way wolves love (ἀγαπῶσιν) lambs, this is how lovers befriend (φιλοῦσιν) a boy" (241d1). To extend this metaphorical characterization of the bad lover given in the *Phaedrus* to Socrates' characterization of Callicles, the Athenian demos is Callicles' lamb, while Callicles is a would-be tyrannical wolf. Socrates explicitly reveals the underlying motivation of Callicles' eros for the

---

44. Contrast this key passage with Renaut's claim that it is the feeling of shame and his excessive love of honor that makes it impossible to persuade Callicles: Renaut 2014, p. 113.

demos: endearing himself to the Athenian people is merely a means to the great power he cherishes (*Gorg.* 513a1–4). In both the *Gorgias* and his second speech in the *Phaedrus*, Socrates opposes a different notion of loving and caring for someone to this flattering kind of intense desire, one whose goal is to make the beloved as good as possible (513e5–7). This caring attitude is missing in Callicles' erotic relationship to the demos, for his eros is founded on pleasure and not the good.[45]

The criticism of the eroticization of political power informs the *Republic* as well. Here, one of Socrates' main concerns is to conceive of an ideal philosophical leader who is not motivated to rule by his attraction to political power. In Book VII, Socrates argues that a well-governed city is not possible if those who go into public life are motivated by the desire to acquire private goods, as this appetitive acquisitiveness is a major source of internal conflict. In this context, he adopts an erotic language that echoes Aristophanes' verses from the *Knights* presenting

45. The puzzling contradiction between Callicles' frankly stated contempt for the Athenian demos and Socrates' insistence on his love for it has drawn the attention of various readers. Irwin interprets it as a contradiction between Callicles' desire for honor and recognition and his contempt for the very same people from whom he desires to be admired: Irwin 1979, pp. 179–180. This reading, on the one hand, correctly grasps the tension within Callicles' personality I mentioned earlier, as Callicles abides by traditional competitive values but, on the other hand, underplays the fact that Callicles' desire for recognition is ultimately subordinated to his hedonism and is instrumental to the acquisition of power for the sake of the gratification of appetitive desires. See Kamtekar 2005, pp. 322–323, for a discussion of Irwin's reading. Ober 1998, pp. 199–203, argues that Socrates' aim in using an erotic language is to show to Callicles that, in spite of his professions of superiority and his stated contempt for the masses, he is actually dependent on them and subordinated to their power, hence subject to the democratic ideological hegemony. Kamtekar 2005 develops this point in a slightly different direction by arguing that Callicles' love for the people indicates the assimilation of his character to that of the people, in the sense of valuing as good the same things as the people. Callicles is dependent on the people because he has unreflectively endorsed their conception of the good as pleasure. I do not deny Callicles' dependency on the demos and its centrality in Socrates' refutation of his position, but I do claim that this dependency does not exclude the negative and aggressive aspects of Callicles' eros I stressed earlier. Precisely because of his commitment to pleasure as the good, Callicles' eros is similar to that of the bad lover in the *Phaedrus*.

Paphlagon and the Sausage-Seller as rival lovers: "But men who aren't lovers of ruling (ἐραστάς τοῦ ἄρχειν) must go to it; otherwise rival lovers (ἀντερασταί) will fight" (*Rep.* 521b4–5). The word ἀντεραστής is not frequent in our ancient sources before Plato; as a matter of fact, we find it only in Aristophanes' *Knights* (*Kn.* 733).[46] Plato's passage combines the topics of political eros and greed. This intense desire for rulership, which creates the conditions for civil war and unhealthy competition among the elite, views power as a means to gratify their appetites and acquire private goods rather than as an ultimate object of desire. As we will see, the tyrant embodies these two aspects—acquisitiveness and eros—in their extreme form. With regard to this classical debate, beyond illustrating the danger of conceptualizing the relationships between rulers, demos, and power in erotic and competitive terms, Plato offers a moral psychology that connects appetites and this kind of eros to a specific part of the soul and he reveals their combined dominance as a source of disease and unhappiness.

4.3 THE TYRANNICAL MAN'S APPETITES

The appetitive part (ἐπιθυμητικόν) is the strongest motivational source within the soul. It is said to be the largest part of the soul (ὃ δὴ πλεῖστον τῆς ψυχῆς) in each individual (*Rep.* 442a6), which should include philosophical natures as well. In Book IX, Socrates resorts to suggestive metaphorical language to further describe the soul's composite nature (588c–589a): the appetitive part is compared to a multicolored beast with many heads—a mythical monstrosity such as the Chimera, Scylla, and Cerberus—and it is the largest in size; the spirited part is a lion, which is medium in size; and the

---

46. The term is to be found also in Xenophon's *Cynegeticus* 1.7.2, and becomes more frequent in the literature after Plato. The cognate verb ἀντερᾶν, which can mean both to love someone in return and to be someone's rival in love, is more frequent.

rational part is a human being (or, rather, a *homunculus*, owing to its small dimensions). The metaphor of size conveys the idea that the ἐπιθυμητικόν is characterized by both a multiplicity of appetites and its capacity, as the most powerful motivational source, to enslave the other two parts.[47]

The dangers implied by the appetitive part's strong potential for dominance appear more clearly if we consider that the desires belonging to each of the three parts of the soul are potentially in conflict with the desires proper to the other parts. In particular, Plato views the desires of the appetitive part as naturally opposed to those of reason. But what exactly does the appetitive part strive for? Throughout the dialogue, the words ἐπιθυμία and ἐπιθυμεῖν do not specifically refer to the appetites of the lowest part of the soul but, rather, are loosely employed to refer to all kinds of desire.[48] Specifying the nature of appetitive desires requires, therefore, attention to the context in which more articulated discussions of the different kinds of desire take place and the privileging of those passages in which Socrates specifically discusses the ἐπιθυμητικόν as a distinct part of the soul.

When he first introduces the notion of tripartition in Book IV, Socrates attributes to the ἐπιθυμητικόν basic biological urges that do not entail any participation of reason, such as hunger, thirst, and sexual arousal (436a10–b1; 439d6–8). However, at other points in the dialogue, the appetitive part is considered responsible for both a larger variety and more complex appetites. Moreover, the

47. Size recurs in the description of the black horse in *Phaedrus* 353e1. The bad horse, indeed, is πολύς, large. The multiplicity and lack of inner unity of desires are indicated by the depiction of the horse as a malformed jumble.

48. Even before the passage in Book IX where Socrates attributes three kinds of ἐπιθυμία to the three parts of the soul (580d7–8), these terms are employed to indicate an array of various desires that are not appetitive in nature—for example, desire for conversation or for philosophy (*Rep.* 328d2–4 and 561d2) and desire for recognition (338a5–7). See also the use of the term within the discussion about intense desire in reference to honor lovers and wisdom lovers at 475b4–6. For a discussion of this point, see Lorenz 2006, pp. 45–46.

dialogue constantly associates the appetitive part and the desire for money. At 442a6, Socrates says that the ἐπιθυμητικόν is the largest part of the soul and it is by nature insatiable for money (χρημάτων φύσει ἀπληστότατον). The oligarchic man is a miser and hoarder of wealth, and his dominant appetitive part is also called money-loving (φιλοχρήματον; 553c5). The appetitive part is called φιλοχρήματον and φιλοκερδές (profit-loving) at 581a6–7, and φιλοκερδές again at 581c4. At 580e5–581a1, Socrates argues that the appetitive part is appropriately called a money-lover because appetites are most easily satisfied by means of money. Finally, the third class of Kallipolis, whose members have souls dominated by the appetitive part, is composed of χρηματισταί (money-makers).

Some commentators have taken Plato's insistence on appetite for money and consideration of complex appetites as indicating that the appetitive part must be endowed with rational cognitive resources, including a capacity for means–end reasoning or cognitive access to the rational part's reasoning about means–end relationships.[49] On this view, the ἐπιθυμητικόν would have the capacity to recognize that money is an effective means to the satisfaction of appetites and would develop a desire for it as a consequence. More radical versions of this view have held that means–end reasoning does not amount to a genuine exercise of reason, for it is an activity in which the nonrational parts of the soul are able to participate. On a more plausible view, however, the appetitive part's attachment to money can be explained through habituation and acculturation without entailing the attribution of rational capacities to it. As noted by Anna Schriefl, the fact

49. See, for example, Moline 1978 (who speaks of a minimal cognitive capacity to discern means to ends and of awareness of means–end relationships); Annas 1981, pp. 129–130; Cooper 1984, p. 128; Kahn 1987, p. 85; Lesses 1987; Price 1995, pp. 60–61; Burnyeat 1997, p. 227; Bobonich 2002, p. 244. Irwin 1977, p. 282, does not attribute means–ends reasoning to the appetitive part, but argues that it must have access to reason's grasp of means–ends relationships and that its attachment to the means is a consequence of this.

that the desire for money is universally present in the appetitive part of human beings is connected to the fact that, for Plato, all human societies that exchange goods use money. For example, a marketplace and currency are introduced in the City of Pigs as soon as Socrates speaks of exchange of goods in the city or with other cities, even though the City of Pigs is characterized by a minimal division of labor and by the satisfaction of needs (*Rep.* 371b7–9).[50] In societies that exchange goods, human beings constantly associate money and the satisfaction of appetites. As Hendrik Lorenz persuasively argues, the repeated practical experience of this association establishes, reinforces, and sustains patterns of attention, response, and attachment.[51] This habituation through practical association accounts for the appetitive part's strong affective attachment to things like money. Moreover, the variety and complexity of human appetites also depends on the fact of acculturation: the greater the division of labor in a society and the greater the variety of goods produced in it, the more inflated the appetitive part becomes and with it its increasingly multicolored and complex appetites. This conceptualization of the tripartite division of the soul as socially malleable preserves the view of means–end reasoning as a genuine exercise of reason beyond the basic cognitive capacities of the nonrational parts of the soul. As I will explain in chapter 6, this observation is extremely relevant for understanding the tyrannical man's reason.[52]

The influence of familial relationships, political and social context, and education on the preferences of the appetitive part is

---

50. Schriefl 2013, pp. 179–180. For the relationship between ἐπιθυμητικόν and love for money more in general, see Schriefl 2013, pp. 174–194.

51. Lorenz 2006, p. 48.

52. Lorenz 2006, part I, provides a persuasive and textually grounded discussion of this issue. I defer to it for the main arguments against the attribution of rational capabilities to the nonrational parts of the soul and in favor of what he calls "the simple picture" or "simple interpretation" of tripartition, according to which the three parts of the soul are distinct *parts*, and not just three kinds of desire or motivation, and their conflict does not need to be

evidenced in the contrast between the different appetites and consequent patterns of behavior characterizing the oligarchic, democratic, and tyrannical man. In the case of the oligarchic man, the accumulation of wealth becomes the focus of his attachment at the expense of other appetites, which the oligarchic man has to control through his reason and his spirited part so as not to jeopardize his main goal. This capacity for self-restraint is the reason why, at 559d1–2, Socrates says that the oligarchic man is ruled by necessary appetites: satisfying idle appetites entails spending money. For the oligarchic man, then, the accumulation of money itself becomes an object of insatiable desire and a source of pleasure in its own right, rather than an instrument to gratify his other appetites.[53] The oligarchic man's obsessive desire for money is the outcome of complex processes involving his relationship to his father, his experience during childhood, and the social and political conditions of his city. Because of turmoil in the city, his timocratic father has fallen into disgrace, been brought to court by false witnesses, disenfranchised, and either put to death or exiled. The experience of poverty and fear for his life produce a shift in the oligarchic man's soul, establishing the appetitive and money-making part as its ruler. This new master enslaves the two other parts of the soul, forcing the rational part to reason about nothing except how to make more money and the spirited part to value and honor nothing but wealth and wealthy people. Crucially, the relevance attached by the oligarch to money is the outcome of a specific practical experience, in which the possession of money is associated throughout

interpreted as a conflict between competing first-order and second-order desires. Given the limited scope of my work, I will also need to leave aside the problems raised by this reading concerning the immortality of the soul and its incompatibility with its composition, or concerning the coherence on this point across various Platonic dialogues, in particular *Phaedo*, *Republic*, *Phaedrus*, and *Timaeus*.

53. See Schofield 2006, p. 255.

with security and safety, and the loss of money and property with disgrace, persecution, and mortal danger (553a–553d).

In contrast to his oligarchic father, the democratic man is ruled by unnecessary appetites and pleasures. He is not thrifty and his appetites do not have money as their main focus: rather, he lives day to day, gratifying the appetites at hand as if they were chosen by lot (561c–d).[54] Moreover, he does not care about spending money. In this case as well, his lack of focus and indulgence of unnecessary appetites and pleasures are the outcome of a complex dynamic involving his relation with his father, the bad upbringing he received, and the temptations coming from the city. Having been brought up in a miserly and uneducated manner by his father, the democratic man lacks psychic defenses against the diverse opportunities of pleasure offered by the idle "drones" (that is, demagogic leaders, their followers, and criminals) populating the democratic city (559d–560e). In other words, the democratic man has been educated in rigid self-control, but without the kind of musical and intellectual education that could sustain and motivate such an austere way of life. He has no compelling motivation to continue living like his father, and the experience of formerly unknown pleasures, made possible by the multicolored character of the democratic city and its way of

---

54. Sometimes he even gratifies the desires of reason for, as Socrates says, at times the democratic man enjoys practicing what he takes to be philosophy (*Rep.* 561d2). Contrary to Cooper (1984, p. 11), I take his practicing "philosophy" as an activity that gratifies his reason's desire and not his appetitive desires. The democratic man is governed by his appetites, but he may well be open from time to time to pleasures deriving from the gratification of the desires of the two other parts of the soul (*Rep.* 561b–c). After all, he has a multicolored character. Old Cephalus' desire to have Socrates over more often, in order to enjoy conversations with him, may well be an example of this. As the reason of the democratic man is not well trained and directed to the correct objects, its desires are probably volatile and weak, which explains why practicing a bit of philosophy is nothing more than a momentary whim. Generally speaking, the domination of a part of the soul does not necessarily entail the complete disappearance of the desires proper to the two other parts— but, rather, their perversion—and does not necessarily require the agent not to act on them: each type of man still has three parts in his soul, hence three forms of desire.

life, increasingly stimulates all sorts of appetites in him. As in the case of the oligarchic man, lived experience plays a crucial role. The more either man experiences a certain kind of pleasure, the more their respective appetitive part becomes attached to the objects that can elicit that kind of pleasure.

Plato clearly distinguishes between two different forms of control of the appetites: one consists in mere repression, which is incapable of harmonizing and unifying the soul, and the other consists in persuading or taming the appetitive part.[55] Both the oligarchic and the democratic man are characterized by the absence of the inner harmony derived from the successful persuasion of the appetites by reason (aided by the spirited part). In both of them, on the contrary, certain kinds of appetites are rather forcibly kept under control. The oligarchic man is said to be twofold, διπλοῦς (554d10), for his reason and his spirited part hold the unnecessary appetites in check by force, compulsion, and fear (554d1–3), while the democratic man who tries to resist the corruption of the drones is said to have a civil war and a counterrevolution within his soul (559e9–560a2). This forcible repression, however, is an ineffective means to prevent appetites from proliferating. In the case of the democratic man, for example, Socrates argues that the forcible expulsion of appetites through

---

55. See, for example, Gavrielides 2010. The fact that reason can communicate its orders or intimations to the appetitive part and that Socrates speaks of persuasion through discourses and of the appetitive part as having beliefs, may lead one to think that the appetitive part must be endowed with some minimal rational capacities in order to be able to access reason's order or to form these beliefs. Lorenz 2006 has, in my view, persuasively argued that in the *Republic*, Plato does not operate with a notion of belief as a rational capacity, that his terminology with regard to beliefs and language is rather loose, and that the problem of how reason can communicate with appetites is neither fully articulated nor solved in the dialogue. Having a *doxa* for the appetitive part may well be just being in a representational state and accepting it. Moreover, the problem of how reason communicates with the appetitive part is solved in later dialogues, *Timaeus* and *Philebus* in particular, from which a theory emerges according to which certain kinds of thoughts are accompanied by exercises of sensory imagination which, as such, can be grasped by the nonrational parts of the soul: Lorenz 2006, ch. 7.

shame and under the pressure of his father and his household does not prevent other appetites akin to the exiled ones from secretly proliferating and growing strong (560a9–b2). When the democratic man is drawn back to the same bad company, these desires breed and multiply in secret, until they finally take over his soul, overcoming any resistance (560b4–10).[56]

The return of these repressed and secretly multiplied appetites is clearly represented in the description of the genesis of the tyrannical man and the nature of his appetites. While the oligarchic man seeks to satisfy necessary appetites, and the democratic man seeks to satisfy unnecessary but lawful appetites, the tyrannical man seeks to satisfy unlawful (παράνομοι) unnecessary appetites. These criminal appetites are present in everyone's soul, even apparently moderate ones, but are usually kept under control and are only unleashed in dreams (571c–572b). As examples of these dreams, Socrates mentions incest with the mother, paraphilic sex, cannibalism, and murder; all these acts were traditionally attributed to tyrants and autocratic rulers.[57] As if he were living his dreams, the tyrannical man does not abstain from any food or act (574e4). The definition of these appetites as παράνομοι puts them in direct relation with the notion of law, both human and divine: the tyrant's beastly nature should not be understood as the outcome of an absence of acculturation and law but, rather, as a violation of established law and social customs. The character of the tyrannical man's appetites is a product of civilization. For the tyrant, having sex, eating, and drinking are not just

---

56. See Solinas 2008, ch. 2, for a discussion of the similarities and differences between this description and Freud's notion of the return of the repressed. According to Solinas, for both Plato and Freud the merely repressive modality does not destroy the repressed desires but only keeps them in chains, leaving open the possibility of their further proliferation. He further compares Plato's notion of persuading and taming appetites to Freud's notion of inhibition, as a strategy of control which is midway between repression and sublimation: Solinas 2008, p. 42.

57. See chapter 1, this volume.

the satisfaction of bodily urges but specifically also their satisfaction through forbidden objects.[58] And indeed, Socrates explains the tyrannical man's possession of these appetites by referring once again to the combination of bad upbringing, the relationship between the would-be tyrannical man and his household, and the corruptors in the city (572c–573b). Once so transformed, these appetites are anarchic, devoid of moderation, and uncontrolled by shame. Moreover, the more the tyrannical man indulges in parties, luxuries, sex—that is, in all possible bodily pleasures—the more his appetites multiply and compel him to search for more.

The figure of the tyrannical man combines two aspects of the oligarchic and democratic man: greed and licentious enjoyment. The object of their appetites is not the only difference between the oligarchic and the democratic man, for they also have an opposite relationship to money and wealth. The oligarchic man is a typical figure of greed and acquisitiveness, but not of expenditure;[59] the democratic man, on the contrary, is intent on spending what he has and ruining himself for the sake of enjoyment.

By contrast, the tyrannical man, similarly to the Calliclean superior man, wants to acquire more in order to be able to enjoy more. Like the democratic man, he spends all his income and wealth in the pursuit of pleasures. But unlike the democratic man—who is said to

---

58. Johnstone 2015 argues that the tyrannical man seeks to satisfy his desire for bodily pleasures and that this should be read in connection with the hedonistic ideal voiced by Callicles in the *Gorgias*. This reading seems more persuasive and textually grounded than readings pointing, for example, at the tyrannical man's lust for power. However, the lawless dimension of the tyrannical man's appetites and the way this qualifies the desire for bodily pleasure are underdeveloped in Johnstone's treatment.

59. On the greed of the oligarchic man, see *Rep.* 554c4–9, where the oligarchic man reveals his greedy nature when he happens to be in charge of orphans and can act with impunity; and 555c1–d5, where the oligarchs are criticized for impoverishing young people through loans. It is their greed that gives birth to the drones within the city—that is, impoverished and disenfranchised people of no low birth. These drones will then be responsible for the corruption of the son of the oligarchic man and for the creation of the tyrant.

be better than that of the drones and his corrupters, for he has some sense of measure, and his life is neither criminal nor slavish (572c8–d3)—the obsessive character of his appetites and his contempt for the law push him to greedily appropriate the goods of others for the sake of the continuous gratification of an ever-growing mob of appetites (573e–575b). As in Callicles' depiction of the superior man, the tyrannical man's πλεονεξία is motivated by both the sting of his many appetites and his supposed entitlement to an absolute freedom of enjoyment.[60]

The term πλεονεξία does not appear in this description of the tyrannical man's appetites, but Socrates explicitly refers to it later on, in Book IX, in his discussion of the differences between appetitive pleasures, the pleasures of spirit, and those of reason. This discussion offers the conclusive response to Thrasymachus' challenge in Book I by showing that, in spite of appearances, the tyrant's life is the least pleasurable of all because fleeing reason's normative guidance leaves him entirely devoted to slavish pleasures that, owing to their own nature, can never bring happiness. In this context, Socrates describes the life of the people who have no experience of virtue and prudence and never taste the true pleasure of reason:

> Rather, always looking down like cattle and bending over the ground and dinner tables, they feed, fatten, and copulate. Out of greed (πλεονεξίας) for these things, kicking and butting each other with iron horns and hooves, they kill each other, because of their insatiability (δι' ἀπληστίαν). For they are trying to fill

---

60. In this analysis of tyrannical appetites I am momentarily abstracting from the role of the spirited and the rational part of the soul in this process. In my interpretation, the corruption of spirit is responsible for the tyrannical man's absence of shame and for his violent character, while that of the rational part is responsible for the madness that protects the tyrannical man's appetites. On this, see chapters 5 and 6, this volume.

with things that are not real that part of themselves that is not real and that is like a pierced vessel. (*Rep.* 586a6–b4)

Insatiability of the appetitive part and unrestrained greed are combined in the tyrannical man.[61] At the end of his process of moral corruption, the tyrannical man's appetites are characterized by two main features: their intensity, insatiability, and quantity appear to have multiplied to the extreme; and they have become specifically and obsessively attached to forbidden objects of desire. While, as already mentioned, this is the outcome of a combination of familial relationships, the ethos of the democratic city praising freedom of enjoyment above everything else, and the corruptive activity of the drones, the transformation of his appetites could not be completed and could not be psychologically understood without the intervention of eros.

4.4 EROS AND APPETITES

In Plato's account of the genesis of the tyrannical man, eros plays a crucial role in overcoming the inner resistance of the would-be tyrannical man to complete lawlessness:

> Suppose, moreover, that those same things that happened to his father happen to him. When he is led to complete lawlessness, which those who are leading him call complete freedom, his father and the rest of the household come to the aid of the middle desires, while the others come to aid in the opposite direction. When those clever wizards and tyrant-makers don't manage to gain control of

---

61. For a discussion of the connection between insatiability and the tyrant's unhappiness, see Gastaldi 2005a.

the young man in any other way, they contrive to instill in him a certain eros (ἔρωτά τινα αὐτῷ μηχανωμένους ἐμποιῆσαι) as the leader (προστάτην) of idle and wasteful appetites, like a big winged drone (ὑπόπτερον καὶ μέγαν κηφῆνά τινα). Or do you think that the eros of such people is anything different? (*Rep.* 572d7–573a2)

From this passage we learn that this newly implanted eros will act as the leader of unnecessary appetites. The language employed is carefully chosen: in the description of the genesis of the tyrannical regime, the people, deceived and encouraged by the demagogic drones, choose a προστάτης, a leader to protect themselves from the oligarchs, and this προστάτης will then turn from protector of the people into a tyrant (565c–566a). Plato clearly establishes some sort of parallelism between the tyrant's rise to power in the city and the establishment of eros' tyrannical power in the soul. But the parallelism between the political προστάτης and eros also echoes the eroticization of political leadership in classical ideology and political discourse already examined.

The sting of this winged drone acts as an intensifier of appetites: it multiplies them, making them uncontrolled, increases their intensity and obsessive character, and attaches them to unlawful objects.[62] Since, as already discussed, in Greek literature eros was often conceptualized as a particularly intense and obsessive ἐπιθυμία, it would seem that the implantation of eros in the tyrannical man's soul eroticizes *all* his appetites. Grasping this effect necessitates an elucidation of the nature of his eros. This is not an easy task, for Plato does not give much information to help specify the object of this eros, and it is not immediately clear whether this eros should be understood as sexual in nature or whether it has broader connotations.

---

62. See along similar lines Larivée 2012, p. 4.

Several commentators have argued that the *Republic* conveys an idea of eros rather different from the *Phaedrus'* enthusiastic praise of the god Eros, where the philosopher is possessed by both eros and madness, or the *Symposium*'s depiction of eros as a love for the beautiful and the good.[63] Indeed, in the *Republic*, eros is presented as so politically dangerous that it needs to be controlled through the extremely rigid set of rules prescribing the proper breeding of the guardians in Book V. Moreover, far from being described as a god or as a half-god, it is associated with the appetitive part in Book IV (439d4–8), a remark that could sound impious were we to maintain the consideration of eros as a divinity. In light of these aspects, the strong association between eros and tyranny is unsurprising, as the whole project of the beautiful city seems to be aimed at neutralizing eros' dangerously paranomic and antisocial power.[64] However, in point of fact, eros has many different manifestations throughout the dialogue, some of which are akin to the positive appraisal of it we find in the *Symposium* and *Phaedrus*. There is mention of political eros in the form of erotic desire for power (*Rep.* 521b4–5) or erotic desire for revolutions (555e1); of eros as sexual desire belonging to the appetitive part of the soul (443d6–7 and probably 458d5); of erotic love, particularly in reference to boys (368a3, 395e2, 402e2–3, 468c, 474c8–475b9); and of love for poetry (607e4–608a5).[65] Finally,

---

63. See, for example, Rosen 1965; Cornford 1971; Nussbaum 1986; McNeill 2001.
64. It is precisely on the basis of this apparent radical abstraction from eros that Leo Strauss judged the entire project of the beautiful city as against nature, and therefore unfeasible and in the last instance ironical: Strauss 1978, pp. 111–112 and 138. This is a reading supported also by Allan Bloom, who, while commenting on the eugenic rules in Book V, insists that in the *Republic* Plato abstracts both from the body and from eros: Bloom 1991, pp. 379–389.
65. In *Sym.* 205b4–d8, Diotima distinguishes between a generic and a specific sense of the term ἔρως. In its generic sense, eros indicates all desire for good things and being happy (πᾶσα ἡ τῶν ἀγαθῶν ἐπιθυμία καὶ τοῦ εὐδαιμονεῖν ὁ μέγιστός τε καὶ δολερὸς ἔρως παντί; Plat. *Sym.* 205d2–3), but the term is more often employed to indicate sexual eros or being in love. To further explain the point to Socrates, Diotima argues that even those who pursue good things and *eudaimonia* through money-making, sport, or philosophy are in love, ἐρασταί, although people do not call them that way (205d4–6).

as in the *Symposium* and *Phaedrus*, we find eros for philosophy at
490a8–b7, where, within the discussion of philosophical natures,
eros denotes the philosopher's love of learning. Socrates resorts here
to the language of sexual union (πλησιάσας, μιγείς; 490b5), sexual
generation (γεννήσας; 490b5), and birth pangs (ὠδῖνος; 490b7) in
order to describe the way truth and intellection are generated by
the encounter between love for learning and what really is. This love
for philosophy and for learning does have something in common
with the other kinds of eros. In Book V, the desire that those naturally inclined to philosophy have for wisdom is described through an
analogy with the desires that erotically inclined men have for beautiful boys (474d3–475c8). The analogy between erotically inclined
men and philosophers emphasizes some shared traits: erotically inclined people are those who desire not one part of their love-object
without another but, rather, their love-object in its entirety. This is
true for the lovers of boys (474d5), as well as for the lovers of honor
(475a9) and the lovers of learning and wisdom (475c2).[66] Moreover,
the lovers of sights (475d2) and the lovers of sounds (475d3), while
they are not philosophers, are *like* philosophers (475e2). The similarity among these different erotic desires lies in their intensity, insatiability, and focus on a specific object or content that partakes in
beauty (476b–d).

Several commentators sharply distinguish between the kinds of
eros found in different dialogues, challenging the idea that eros is a
single drive that can be oriented in different directions and toward
different objects. In particular, they argue that while philosophical eros is a rational desire for the good, appetitive, sexual eros is

---

66. The terminology employed by Plato in this passage is rather loose: φιλεῖν, ἐρᾶν, and
ἐπιθυμεῖν are used interchangeably to indicate an intense desire for a specific object. The
term ἐρωτικός has a specific meaning, in that it indicates the man who has a propensity to
fall in love with boys, but his erotic love is compared in the passage to φιλεῖν and ἐπιθυμεῖν,
in the sense of intensively desiring an object as a whole and in all of its aspects.

not.[67] The *Republic*, however, does not seem to offer persuasive textual grounds for this distinction. On the contrary, as we have seen, Socrates insists on the similarities among the various manifestations of erotic desire, and the terminology he employs is rather loose. On a minimal definition, eros appears rather to be a particularly intense and insatiable beauty-oriented desire, specifically and obsessively focused on an individual object or class of objects, which does not belong to a particular part of the soul but can, rather, get attached to one of the three parts and be oriented toward different kinds of objects.

Eros also affects the other desires. Employing an analogy of the channeling of a stream, Socrates argues that when someone's desire strongly inclines toward a specific object, the other desires become weaker (485d6–8). This is the case for the lover of learning, who thereby abandons the pleasures of the body.[68] As we have seen, the

---

67. On the rational dimension of eros, see Hyland 1968; Irwin 1995, pp. 303–306; Sheffield 2012. Cummins 1981 has provided compelling textual evidence against Hyland's conceptual distinctions between ἔρως, ἐπιθυμία, and φιλία based on the different degrees of rationality present in each of them, insisting that Plato's terminology is too flexible to allow such rigid technical distinctions. In particular, he has rejected Hyland's thesis that the reference to βούλεσθαι in *Sym.* 200b-d entails deliberation. For the view that all forms of eros are actually one, in that eros has different manifestations, including sexual desire, which all reveal a love for the good, see Ferrari 1992. Halperin draws a distinction between appetites and eros based on the fact that appetitive desires are content-generic and aim-oriented, while eros is content-specific and object-oriented, but he also takes sexual desire to be a genuine species and manifestation of eros, and insists that sexual desire is identical with respect to the nature of desire to the philosopher's desire for being and truth: Halperin 1985. Nucci also takes the tyrant's eros not to be different in nature from that of the philosopher and stresses that eros has no specific position within the soul but rather belongs to the soul as a whole: Nucci 2001.

68. On this "hydraulic" metaphor and its similarity to Freud's account of "psychic energy," see Santas 1988, pp. 76–79. Dominic Scott discusses the channel analogy at length: Scott 2007. According to his interpretation, philosophical eros makes the philosopher fundamentally *asocial*, by channeling all his attention and interest toward philosophy and the search for truth. However, it does not make him *antisocial*. As a consequence, while he will not be interested in engaging in the competition for material goods and honors, the philosopher will nevertheless willingly obey the laws of the city. While I do agree with Scott that the philosopher will be the least concerned with material goods and honors, I do not share his conclusion that this makes the philosopher asocial. The philosopher's interest in the city is

tyrannical man's appetites are not weakened by his eros but, rather, eroticized—that is, intensified, multiplied, and pushed beyond the boundaries of law. Eros lends its intensity and insatiability to the appetitive part's desires, giving them the obsessive character that describes many lovers. Understanding these effects constrains us to view the tyrannical man's eros as channeling his entire soul toward gratifying the desires of the appetitive part it has become attached to, at the expense of the desires of the spirited and of the rational part.[69] By becoming their leader, eros reinforces the domination of the appetites within the tyrannical man's soul.

At 573c9, Socrates says that once eros becomes the leader of the unruly mob of appetites, the tyrannical man becomes drunken, erotic (ἐρωτικός), and melancholic. Socrates had employed the term ἐρωτικός earlier, in Book V, specifically in order to denote the men driven by sexual love, particularly the lovers of boys. Moreover, at 574b12–c5, he attributes the brutal rebellion of the tyrannical son against his parents to his attachment to a newly found concubine or boy. While the object of the tyrannical man's eros is not specified,

only motivationally modified, not eliminated. I will address this issue in the conclusion of this volume.

69. Nucci argues that, as the tyrant's eros impacts the entire soul and reorients it, this orientation lends the tyrannical man's soul a coherence missing in the other epithumetic types of men. His conclusion is, then, that the tyrannical man's personality is more solid and organized, and less divided, than that of the oligarchic and of the democratic man: Nucci 2001. While I do agree with Nucci that the eros of the tyrannical man reorients his entire soul, his conclusion runs against Plato's normative notion of the soul's unity. A soul is more unified when it is normatively ruled by reason, which is the only part of the soul that can reshape and reorient the desires of the other two parts in such a way as to eliminate conflict and establish harmony within the soul. The "coherence" of the tyrannical man's soul is comparable to the apparent lack of opposition within a tyrannical regime. The other two parts of the soul are violently enslaved, not harmoniously ruled. From this viewpoint the tyrannical man's personality is even more conflicted than that of the democratic and of the oligarchic man. On this topic, see also Pappas 2013, pp. 191–192, who suggests that it would be obvious to think that, being dominated by a single desire, the tyrannical soul is unified rather than lacking unity; and Johnstone 2015 for a rebuttal of this reading along lines similar to mine.

it would seem reasonable to think that his eros is of a sexual kind.[70] Sexual eros, however, should be distinguished from mere sexual appetite or arousal. As suggested by Halperin, in contrast to sexual appetite, sexual eros is characterized by intensity, exclusivity, and ultimately futility. Contrary to an appetite, it does not merely aim at the gratification of a bodily need.[71] It is important to maintain this distinction in order to understand why it is specifically eros that drives the tyrannical man mad and makes him insatiable for all possible appetitive pleasures, in particular those deriving from forbidden objects of desire.[72] In conclusion, while this sexual eros is attached to the appetitive part of the soul, it is not identical with a mere appetite.

The sexual nature of this eros and its connection to the appetites would seem to undermine the connection I have established between Plato's attribution of a strong erotic character to the tyrannical man and the politicization of eros in classical political discourse that I have discussed earlier. Indeed, the text never describes the tyrant as a lover of the demos or of the city, and his erotic desire does not seem to have any political content per se. However, as we have seen in chapter 1, in classical depictions, unrestrained sexual eros was one of the most common characterizations of tyrants. Alcibiades' sexual license was strongly emphasized by his critics and was one of the main reasons for the suspicions of his contemporaries, in whose eyes his sexual license appeared as a clear symptom of his tyrannical aspirations. As unrestrained and violent erotic desire had a strong connection with hubristic attitudes and with the drive to humiliate and lessen others, erotic

---

70. It is interpreted as such, for example, by White 1979, p. 222. White, however, reduces it to simple "sexual craving."

71. Halperin 1985, p. 170. On the nature of eros see also Halperin 1986.

72. Johnstone 2015, on the contrary, interprets eros here as a specific appetite—that for bodily pleasure. On this account, however, it remains rather unclear why eros has such a devastating effect and manages to push the tyrannical man into complete lawlessness.

license and the dangerous aspects of political eros were combined in a conceptual continuum that Plato exploits in his description of the tyrannical man by presenting him as the most extreme embodiment of erotic license.[73] Moreover, political eros was conceptualized primarily as an extension of pederastic eros, where the lover's sexual attraction to the physical beauty of the boy played a key role.

Socrates himself suggests the connection between the two concepts when in the *Gorgias* he says of Callicles that he has two objects of love: the young Demos and the Athenian demos. As in the case of Callicles, the tyrannical man's eros is strongly related to an ideal of endless and unlimited appetitive *jouissance*. In the *Gorgias*, Socrates' attribution of an erotic character to Callicles sheds light on two of its main aspects: the specific kind of erotic attraction, dangerous for the beloved, in which the object of eros is just a means to appetitive enjoyment; and the effects of this appetitive eros on the lover, who paradoxically ends up becoming the slave of the loved object he wanted to exploit for the sake of his appetitive enjoyment. This kind of eros thus has strongly negative effects on both the lover and the beloved. Socrates tries without success to show Callicles that, in spite of his grandiloquent claims about superior men, he falls short of his own ideal of activity and superiority because he must flatter the very demos he simultaneously loves and despises. By describing and analyzing the effects of this kind of eros on the tyrannical man's soul in the *Republic*, Socrates effectively deconstructs Callicles' ideal of the superior man by turning him into a slave—that is, into a subject of the tyranny of eros and appetites. This is suggestively expressed through the image of eros' tyranny within the soul:

> Rather, living like a tyrant within him in complete anarchy and lawlessness so as to be his sole ruler, eros will drive him, as if he

---

73. On the continuum between private erotic license and tyrannizing in classical Athens and in the figure of Alcibiades, see Davidson 1997, p. 293.

were a city, to complete recklessness, from which it will feed itself and the noisy mob around it. (575a1–4)[74]

A few lines later, Socrates explicitly establishes a connection between eros' tyranny within the soul and political tyranny. The rise to power of a tyrant is to some extent the outcome of some specific external circumstances, such as the number of tyrannical men living in a city. But in addition to these external circumstances, an inner, psychological, condition is also mentioned:

> For, when such people become many and other people follow them along, once they become aware of their number, it is they who—helped by the foolishness of the demos—make into a tyrant the one among them who has the greatest and largest tyrant in his soul. (*Rep.* 575c4–d1)

Since only a few lines earlier Socrates had defined eros as the tyrant in the soul of the tyrannical man, this passage can be safely understood as indicating that the man who will be chosen to play the role of the political tyrant is the one driven by the most powerful and unrestrained eros. As we will see in the next two chapters, eros' tyranny has decisive effects on the tyrannical man's reason and spirited part, which are crucial to understanding his relationship to political power. For the moment, it suffices to notice that Plato's ruthless diagnosis of the relationship between sexual eros and political power established by our fifth- and fourth-century sources consists in showing that this relationship leads to slavery on both the side of the lover-leader and that of the people ruled by him. The tyrant is incapable of governing himself, and hence is a slavish figure, because he is driven by his eroticized appetites rather than by the autonomous judgments of

---

74. On eros as a tyrant, see Eur. *Hipp.* 538.

his rational part. His relationship to political power is instrumental to the futile attempt to satisfy his insatiable appetites, as ruling others is taken as the ultimate means to unlimited enjoyment. And precisely for this reason, his subjects are turned into his slaves and instruments of enjoyment. Thus, Plato's moral psychology provides a powerful response to the subordination of political power to hedonistic appetites figured in Thrasymachus and Callicles. This form of political hedonism rested on the identification of the tyrannical life with absolute freedom. Plato's introduction of the tripartite theory of the soul and his conceptualization of eros overturns this fantastic ideal by providing a psychological framework capable of exploiting the anxieties about passivity and activity that underpin this hedonistic discourse. Thus, Plato's response to the fantasy that only the tyrant, like Zeus, is free, is that under the tyranny of eros conjoined with appetites, nobody is free.

Chapter 5

The Lion and the Wolf

The Tyrant's Spirit

One should not rear a lion cub in the city.

Aristophanes, *Frogs*

In Greek literature, tyrants were regularly characterized by their attachment to power, to anger, and to excessive violence.[1] Stories of murders, collective punishments, and outbursts against enemies, friends, and relatives alike were often littered with comparisons between tyrants and savage beasts. This trope signaled the tyrant's distinctive tendency—owing to the fragility of his power—to fall into an endless spiral of violence and, moreover, to morbidly enjoy this bloodshed. However, in his diagnosis of the tyrannical man and re-elaboration of previous sources on the topic, Plato privileges another traditional trope—that of the tyrant's licentiousness and unlimited desires—by including the tyrannical soul among those ruled by its appetitive part. Hitherto, analyses of Plato's depiction of the tyrannical man's psyche have tended to focus on the role

1. See, for example, Alc. fr. 70 about Pittacus; Hdt. 5.92.ε11–ζ1 about Cipselus; Hdt. 5.92.ζ and Hdt. 3.49ff. about Periander; Hdt. 3.44–45 about Polycrates; Aesch. (?) *PB*. 12–14, 34–35, 163–164, 221–223, 323–324 about the tyrant, Zeus. See also the characterization of Critias' tyrannical policy in Xen. *Hell.* 2.3.15, and of the Thirty Tyrants in Lys. 12.19, 12.21, 12.44, 12.51, 12.78.

played by eros and its relation both to the tyrant's appetitive soul and to madness. While noting his violent and bloodthirsty aspect and its possible connection to spirit, they have not offered a detailed discussion of the condition of the tyrant's thumoeidic part.[2] The aim of this chapter is to provide such an analysis, both for the sake of better understanding the tyrannical man's psychology and of throwing light on the nature of the soul's spirited part as presented in the *Republic*.[3]

A major difficulty for this analysis is that, despite the fact that one of the main themes of Plato's description of the tyrant is attachment to power and propensity to anger and violence, spirit is explicitly mentioned only once in the treatment of the tyrannical man. However, one cannot make sense of the tyrannical soul, and its relationship to political power, anger, and violence, without taking into account the particular role that its spirited part plays. The scant explicit discussion of spirit is a consequence of Plato's argumentative and rhetorical strategy of treating the corrupt regimes with their corresponding types of man by focusing on the dominant part of their souls and its motives. However, as all nonvirtuous souls are conflicted and poorly unified, a consideration of all the participants in these inner conflicts is essential for a more complete understanding of the specific psychic dynamic of each type of man.

---

2. On the tyrant's eros, see, for example, Larivée 2005; Parry 2007; Scott 2007. Frère 2004 mentions the role of the spirited part in the tyrant's soul, but does not offer any sustained discussion of this psychic dynamic in the light of the theory of tripartition (p. 129). Solinas 2005 discusses the issue in a more systematic way, but fails to give a coherent account. Solinas 2008 returns on the issue of the role of spirit in criminal dreams in Book IX, and gives an account that has some similarities to mine, but is not fully developed (p. 36). Renaut 2014 correctly insists on the fact that spirit does play an important role in the tyrant's soul, but his discussion of this point is cursory (p. 273). A partial exception is Ludwig 2007, who examines the relationship between eros and spirit in the tyrant's soul and ascribes to the synergy between the two the possessiveness and acquisitiveness of the tyrant's eros, as well as its orientation toward objects that are against the law.

3. I will use "spirit," "spirited part," and "thumoeidic part" interchangeably throughout the chapter.

Confronted with the limited reference to spirit in the treatment of the tyrannical man's psyche, we may be tempted to conclude that spirit is significantly weakened in the tyrant's psyche, as shown by the fact that it does not play any role in controlling his lawless appetites.[4] On the contrary, as I will show, a hardened and corrupt spirit does play a significant role in the tyrant's psyche, because the latter's condition is determined in part by the spirited part's lawlessness *as inflamed by the appetitive part*. The tyrant's hardened and stimulated spirit, although enslaved to the appetitive part, *does* play an important role in determining his attachment to power, anger, and violent behavior. While the main causal explanation of lawlessness is rooted in appetite and eros, and not in spirit, and while the role of spirit is ancillary to that of the appetites, we cannot fully understand the tyrant's specific psychopathology without taking into account this auxiliary yet important causal role. Once inflamed by eros, the appetites, and madness, spirit further motivates the tyrannical man to seize power and do anything, no matter how brutal and monstrous the required deeds may be, in order to hold and defend his rule against his enemies, both presumed and actual.

5.1 WHAT IS SPIRIT?

Throughout the *Republic*, spirit is said to be responsible for propensity to anger,[5] savagery, violence, harshness, and perpetual war,[6] desire for victory and power,[7] and arrogance and stubbornness,[8] but

---

4. This is the interpretation put forward by Singpurwalla 2013, p. 64.

5. *Rep.* 440a5–6, 440c7–8 (*contra* Adam 1963, *ad loc.*, I take spirit, and not τῶν γενναίων at 440d1, to be the subject of the sentence). The connection between θυμός and anger is given in *Cra.* 419e, as Socrates derives the word θυμός from θύσις, the raging of the soul.

6. *Rep.* 375b11, 375c2–3, 410d1–2, 410d6–9, 411a3, 411a5–b3, 411d7–e2, 416a2–7e, 416b1–3, 547e1–548a3.

7. *Rep.* 548d8–9 and 581b2.

8. See the description of the timocratic man: 548e4–549b7.

also courage, desire for honor, sensitivity to what appears just, rebellion against perceived injustice, and alliance with reason in the conflict with the appetitive part.[9] Faced with the difficulty of identifying the unity at the basis of these various manifestations of spirit, some readers have suggested that, insofar as no decisive argument for a distinction of spirit from reason is provided, only a dual partition of the soul holds.[10] Others, without reaching this strong conclusion, have expressed some perplexities about the validity of Plato's argument[11] or have suggested that the only function of the thumoeidic part is to address the warrior-like characters of Kallipolis' guardians.[12] The validity of Plato's arguments for the existence of a spirited part as a distinct source of motivation has been defended on various, and sometimes diverging, grounds by several other readers, especially in more recent years.[13] The difficulty faced by the interpreters who have argued in favor of spirit's decisive and distinct motivational role lies, first of all, in the identification of the unity at the basis of the various manifestations of spirit in the dialogue, and second, in the clarification of the grounds on which the thumoeidic part is said to be the natural ally of reason in Book IV, while at the same time being distinct from the rational part.[14] The difficulties raised by the complex

9. On courage: *Rep.* 357a11–b7, 442b11–c3, 442b5–9. On honor: *Rep.* 581d5–8, 548c5–7, 581b2. On the alliance with reason and spirit's sensitiveness to issues of perceived justice and injustice: *Rep.* 440c1–5 and 440c7–d3, 440e2–6, 441a1–3.
10. Hardie 1936, p. 142; Penner 1971. Wilson 1995 offers a brilliant solution to this problem by suggesting that a conflict between spirit and reason is displayed in Thrasymachus' behavior in his exchange with Socrates in Book I, in particular at 342c–d, 342e, 346c, and especially 350c–d, in which Thrasymachus, accepting Socrates' arguments only after trouble, toil, and a large quantity of sweat, finally blushes at his defeat. To accept Socrates' arguments equates to defeat for Thrasymachus' spirit, but his reason is forced to accept them.
11. Shorey 1979, p. 224; Annas 1981, pp. 126–128.
12. Williams [1973] 2006.
13. See, for example, Tait 1949; Cooper 1984; Kahn 1987; Hobbs 2000; Frère 2004; Moss 2005; Boeri 2010; Brennan 2012; Singpurwalla 2013; Renaut 2014.
14. Another difficulty lies in the clarification of the role played by spirit for the virtue of courage. Indeed, according to the definition provided in Book IV, 429b8–c3 and 442b11–c3, courage is the capacity to preserve learned doctrine concerning what is and is not to be

character of spirit's various manifestations are exacerbated by Plato's underdeveloped account of the details of the interaction between the rational and the nonrational parts of the soul. This lacuna leaves the interpreter with the task of sorting out this inner-psychic dynamic.

In light of these complications, the first problem that needs to be addressed is the unity underlying these various and seemingly contradictory manifestations of spirit.[15] Various interpreters have

feared and remain immune to the pressures deriving from pleasures and sufferings. This definition, however, seems to be in tension with the remark in Book II, 357a11–b7, that the guardians need to be thumoeidic if they need to be courageous, because spirit makes the entire soul fearless (ἄφοβος) and unconquerable (ἀήττητος) in front of everything.

15. Readers who have defended the consistency of Plato's notion of a thumoeidic part have offered different solutions to this matter. The most common is that spirit expresses self-assertion in its various forms. According to Tait, for example, self-assertion combined with self-consciousness can lead to apparently diverging patterns of action, behavior, and disposition, from children's and animals' anger to righteous indignation, self-respect, or ambition (Tait 1949, pp. 209–210). Similarly, Kahn suggests that spirit is self-assertive and directed toward competition with others, which has affinities with the love for power and the desire to be first (Kahn 1987, p. 83). Along similar lines, Cooper suggests that the principle of unity underlying spirit's various manifestations is a combination of competitiveness and desire for self-esteem and esteem by others. On this account, anger is spirit's reaction to the frustration of its desire for victory and esteem (Cooper 1984, pp. 14–15). Ardor and combativeness are also attributed to spirit by Frère, although his treatment tends to emphasize the variety of spirit's manifestations rather than the underlying unity (Frère 2004, in particular his conclusion at p. 187). In all of these interpretations, spirit has an eminently social character in that the kinds of actions, values, and behavior patterns through which it expresses its self-assertiveness and desire for esteem are determined by social norms, to which spirit is particularly sensitive (Burnyeat 2006, pp. 8–13). A second alternative consists in identifying the fundamental desire of the spirited part in the desire for the fine (καλόν), to which the feeling of shame is connected. In particular, Jessica Moss and Rachel Singpurwalla have suggested that it is because of this desire that spirit is a natural ally of reason, in that it can keep in check appetitive desires through the feeling of shame. Moss agrees with the general consensus that the content of the καλόν to which spirit aspires is determined by social norms. Singpurwalla, on the contrary, challenges the idea that spirit is constitutively responsive to social norms and suggests instead that the object of its desire is the fine in the sense of acting and living in accordance with reason (Moss 2005; Singpurwalla 2013). A slightly different solution that identifies the unity underlying spirit by addressing the function it plays within the tripartite soul is that suggested by Tad Brennan. In his view, the spirited part of the soul is best understood as a necessary response to the existence of appetitive souls in the world, and spirit's essential role consists in constraining the appetitive souls of other people, as well as one's own appetitive part, through spirit's attachment

suggested that spirit is fundamentally a desire for self-assertion,[16] and in these readings the desire for self-assertion is often constitutively intertwined with the desire for recognition. This interpretation, however, faces some textual difficulties, for in Book IV Socrates attributes spirit to animals.[17] After stating that the spirited part always takes reason's side in the conflict with the appetitive part, Socrates asks whether the spirited part is not just a form of the rational part (λογιστικοῦ τι εἶδος; *Rep.* 440e8). This option is immediately discarded on the basis of two probative arguments. We should take these two arguments seriously, for the alternative is rather unappealing: if the two arguments do not work or are to be taken as simple metaphors, then the conclusion is that Socrates in fact does not articulate any argument in support of the distinction between reason and spirit within a section of the dialogue in which—on the

to an honor system that must be understood, in somewhat projectivist terms, as a system for the distribution of appetitive goods (Brennan 2012). Finally, in his extensive treatment of spirit, Renaut argues that the nature of spirit appears "vague" precisely because spirit is an intermediary between reason and appetites, and as such it cannot be properly defined if not in relation to the cognitive function of reason and to the conative function of the appetitive part. In his interpretation, spirit plays the function of valorization, of mediation between affects and values, and of enabling the soul to have moral emotions (Renaut 2014, pp. 169–185).

16. My outline of an explanation of spirit's nature is indebted in particular to Tait's article, while that of spirit's function is indebted in particular to Moss' and Brennan's contributions. Although my reading has some differences with theirs concerning the nature of spirit, their detailed explanation of the mechanisms through which spirit becomes an ally of reason and controls the appetitive part, as well as their clarification of spirit's relation to social norms, is enlightening.

17. Angela Hobbs argues that the essence of human spirit is the need to believe that one counts for something and a tendency to form an ideal image of oneself according to one's conception of the fine and noble, while self-assertion is only required to obtain this recognition from others. Coherently, she suggests that the similarity between human spirit and the assertive drive of some animals should not be emphasized and we should not look for an exact parallel. Her reading, however, does not account for Socrates' argument for the distinction of spirit from reason based on the presence of spirit in wild animals. Moreover, it is textually problematic; for example, it downplays the frequent use of comparisons with animals and the fact that τὸ κρατεῖν and νικᾶν are the two first objects of spirit's desire in a series of three, at 581a9–10. See Hobbs 2000, p. 31.

contrary—he does provide a set of robust arguments in support of the distinction between reason and the appetites.

The first of the two arguments is that spirit is also present in living beings that do not have reason, like little children (441a7–b1) and beasts.[18] This argument rests on the assumption that the spirit observable in wild beasts must be the same as human spirit. This does not entail that spirit will be in the same condition in human beings as in wild beasts, for spirit is malleable and can be guided and reoriented by reason and apprehended social norms. However, this argument implies that spirit in wild animals must count as spirit in the full sense and must be essentially defined in the same terms. If this is the case, then, it is hard to see how spirit could be defined as a desire for recognition.[19]

A possible reading of this passage may suggest that Socrates is only referring to animals who live in packs or herds, and who are teachable and interact within social structures; in this view, there would not be spirited sharks, for example.[20] However, this alternative reading runs against serious textual difficulties, for in the passage there is no textual indication of this qualification (ἔτι δὲ ἐν τοῖς

---

18. The second argument is modeled on that already employed for the distinction between appetitive and rational part, that is the observation of conflict between spirit and reason, as illustrated by the quotation of a verse from Homer's *Odyssey* (*Rep.* 441b4–c2).

19. Singpurwalla mentions this passage at the beginning of her article (Singpurwalla 2013, p. 44), but she does not address it when she articulates her thesis, nor does she try to solve the problem this passage raises for her main claim. Indeed, it is difficult to see how wild beasts could have an innate desire to be fine in the sense of acting in accordance with reason. Contrary to Singpurwalla, Hobbs correctly sees the problem that this passage raises and suggests that an untrained spirit and a trained one appear as two very different entities. But, as already mentioned, she also suggests that we should not look for an exact parallel between the spirit of animals and human spirit, a suggestion I do not share for the reasons explained above: Hobbs 2000, pp. 20–21. Along similar lines, Renaut also downplays the relevance of this passage, as it would seem to run against his definition of spirit as essentially an intermediary between appetites and reason: Renaut 2014, p. 175.

20. This reading was suggested to me by an anonymous reader, whom I thank for carefully reading my text and raising several perspicuous objections.

θηρίοις ἄν τις ἴδοι ὃ λέγεις, ὅτι οὕτως ἔχει; 441b2–3) and, moreover, when Socrates introduces spirit in Book II, at 375a10–b2, he argues that horses, dogs, and *whatever other* animals (ἄλλο ὁτιοῦν ζῷον) must be spirited if they are courageous. The latter passage entails that all animals displaying "courageous" behavior—that is, the disposition to enter into combat with other individuals *at the risk of their own death*—owe this disposition to spirit. This includes animals that do not live in packs or herds. Finally, the comparison of spirit to a snake in Book IX (590b1) contributes to challenging the exclusive association of spirit with pack animals.

One way to solve the difficulty is to narrow down what is included in the definition of spirit as a desire for self-assertion and to take it to be the mere *tendency to forcefully act in such a way as to establish one's superiority over others.* As such, self-assertion is conative and does not require a rational grasp of oneself or concerns for honor and esteem but only some basic form of awareness of oneself, of the kind many nonhuman animals have. The drive to self-assertion, moreover, should be carefully distinguished from that of mere self-preservation. The latter indeed can entail behavior that is not self-assertive or that contradicts a self-assertive attitude—for example, hiding, running away from a danger, or passivity. In contrast, self-assertion can motivate to the extent of risking death, hence it is the psychic basis for courage. As we will see later, accounting for the tension and conflict between the desires of spirit and appetitive desires necessitates this distinction.

In Book IX, spirit is defined as the desire to dominate, win, and be held in high repute (τὸ κρατεῖν . . . νικᾶν καὶ εὐδοκιμεῖν; 581a9–10).[21] Self-assertion is the best candidate for the factor unifying desire for power over others, victory, and high esteem, for, according to the circumstances, it can be realized by following any or all of these

---

21. The spirited part is also defined as φιλόνικον in Plat. *Tim.* 70a2–3.

three patterns. In the first two objects of desire, the spirit's drive toward self-assertion focuses on the pursuit of control over others, on force, and on competition. The verb κρατεῖν, indeed, has an array of meanings turning around the idea of a power, with possible despotic traits, based on greater force, conquest, and superiority.[22] The third object of desire and source of pleasure, εὐδοκιμεῖν, on the contrary, expresses its search for self-assertion through the recognition of others. As self-assertion can be achieved through recognition by others, and not only through their violent oppression, the spirit of people living in a society is particularly sensitive to social norms. Indeed, recognition has to take place within the context of a set of shared evaluative standards—that is, within a specific normative framework. Since self-assertion takes place in relation to something or somebody that is external to (and possibly in competition with) oneself, for people living in a society, the patterns of behavior through which one asserts oneself fundamentally depend on the framework of social norms that regulate one's exchanges with others. As noted by Moss, one of spirit's central features is its malleability.[23] In the case of wild animals, spirit's drive to self-assertion will be ultimately based on force, although for animals living in packs or herds this superiority will tend to be articulated within a social structure. Within human societies that value honor, political courage, agonism, and nobility, spirit will tend to follow this pattern of behavior in order to achieve the desired self-assertion and will tend to desire honor and what is socially defined as fine. The orientation and content of this sensitivity to the fine is the outcome of education, as is clear from Socrates' claim that through music and poetry children will learn to discriminate between the fine and the shameful and develop an affective disposition

---

22. Kratos, for example, is the executor of the orders of the tyrant Zeus in Aesch. (?) *PB*.
23. Moss 2005, pp. 162–165.

toward these two objects before being able to grasp the reason for this distinction (401e1–402a2).

In conclusion, the desire for esteem is one of the possible patterns spirit takes to satisfy its drive to self-assertion. This does not mean that all these possible patterns of realizing spirit's desire are normatively equivalent. Indeed, as we will see in the next section, in human beings spirit can pursue its fundamental desire in ways that unleash its most dangerous and least noble aspects, destroying its natural capacity for a normatively optimal alliance with reason. Keeping this definition of spirit as a drive to self-assertion in mind, it is now time to address its relation to the other parts of the soul in human beings, by focusing in particular on the notions of its malleability, alliance with reason, and enslavement to appetites.

5.2 ALLY OF REASON, SLAVE OF APPETITES, OR SAVAGE BEAST?

Spirit's health within human beings depends to a large extent on its dynamic relation to the other parts of the soul. For example, spirit's rule over the soul is incapable of establishing that harmony among the various parts that only reason's normative rule can assure. The timocratic man's secret adoration for gold and silver testifies to his spirit's inability to effectively persuade and control his appetitive part (548a–b). Moreover, his fixation on power, competition, and honor based only on physical and warlike exploits, as well as his deficient training in music to the detriment of reason, will incline him to waging perpetual war (547e–548a, 548e–549a). In other words, without reason's normative guidance, the aspects of spirit that will be unleashed in a man with a particularly stirred spirited part are the savage, harsh, and violent ones. In contrast, spirit's attunement to reason is its normatively optimal condition, achieved through a proper and harmonious education that nurtures and stimulates the rational part while soothing and making the spirited part gentle (441e8–442b3).

As an ally of reason, spirit that has been educated to love the fine acts as an inner police force by restraining appetites, and reacts with anger against a perceived injustice, while at the same time accepting a punishment when justified (440a–d).[24] The section of the dialogue on spirit's alliance with reason raises a number of interpretive problems that are relevant to understanding the relation between spirit and the other two parts of the soul in the tyrannical man. In this section, Socrates first says that Glaucon has probably never seen spirit, either in himself or in others, acting as an ally of appetites against what reason has decided. Following this, Socrates goes to the extent of claiming that spirit, unless it is corrupted by a bad upbringing, is a natural ally of reason (441a3). However, despite Socrates' earlier claims, in Books VIII and IX we discover that the spirited part can actually work for the appetites, in the case of the oligarchic man and—as we will see—in that of the tyrannical man. Moreover, it is unclear why spirit, which is represented in other parts of the dialogue as so dangerous that it has to be tamed through a complex educational process, is said here to be a natural ally of reason.

The term employed by Socrates to indicate this alliance, ἐπίκουρος, has a military connotation in addition to echoing the role of the auxiliaries in the beautiful city. Spirit is an ally of reason in its struggle against appetites; it is a companion in a fight that takes place in a person who still has to acquire all the virtues (440e4–6). Thus, spirit's "alliance" with reason indicates a relationship between these two parts of the soul beyond mere friendship or harmonious

---

24. This aspect is present in Plat. *Tim.* 70a4–7 as well: here spirit listens to reason and cooperates with it in order to hold in check, through force, the appetitive desires when they do not want to be persuaded by reason.

interaction. In a virtuous person, the appetitive part comes to accept the rule of reason and has a relationship of friendship with reason as harmonious as spirit's. But the passage at 441a2–3 refers to the specific role that spirit can play in the case of an inner conflict in a not-yet-virtuous person rather than to the harmonious relationship established among all three parts of the soul in a virtuous person. Appetites, contrary to spirit, are never characterized in the dialogue as the military aid of reason in the case of such a conflict.

Once this point is clarified, we may be tempted to interpret the passage as indicating that spirit has an innate disposition to side with reason in its struggle against the appetites, independent of whether it has been educated to honor the fine or not. According to this interpretation, only a bad upbringing could carry it away from this natural alliance. But in this case, it is not clear why the spirited part would need education and taming at all, given that avoiding a bad upbringing should already be sufficient to bring it into accord with reason.[25] On a more plausible interpretation, suggested by Moss, spirit is a natural ally of reason, not because it is always already its ally and tends to align with it even in the absence of good education, but because unlike the appetites, it can be morally educated and is malleable, as spirit's preferences do not depend on facts about its brute constitution.[26] A possible objection to this interpretation could be that spirit's malleability is still too vague of a concept: it may be sufficient to explain why, if educated, spirit will align with reason, but it is not sufficient to explain why spirit is not instead the natural ally of appetites in their struggle against reason. Indeed, spirit could, precisely *because* it is malleable, come to identify the satisfaction of appetites with a privileged pattern to self-assertion or even honor, as

---

25. This is how Singpurwalla reads this passage: spirit has an inherent tendency to align with reason, which a good education does not necessarily create (Singpurwalla 2013, p. 48).
26. Moss 2005, pp. 162–164.

in the case of the oligarchic man and his desire for wealth (553d). In other words, the reference to the natural alliance of spirit with reason can be explained through its malleability only if we show that spirit's malleability is not bidirectional.

This objection can be resolved by analyzing the extent to which spirit is malleable and the reasons for the limitations of its malleability; indeed, spirit is not so malleable as to become the *willing ally* of appetites against reason.[27] Socrates' observation that spirit never allies itself with appetites (440b–c) is not in contradiction with either the subsequent passage at 441a3, where spirit can fail to be the helper of nature because of a bad upbringing, or the description of the oligarchic man in Book VIII. At 441a3, Socrates only says that the spirited part of the soul can fail to be the natural ally of reason owing to bad education, but he does not say that through a bad upbringing it can become the *ally* of appetites. Moreover, when he discusses the oligarchic man, at 553d1–7, he does not say that in the oligarchic soul the spirited part will be the *ally* of the appetitive part but, rather, that it will be *enslaved* to it:

> I suppose that, after making the rational and spirited parts sit on the ground on both sides next to him and enslaving them (καταδουλωσάμενος), he allows the first to reason and investigate only about the ways to make more money and the second to admire and honor (θαυμάζειν καὶ τιμᾶν) only wealth and the wealthy and to find pride (φιλοτιμεῖσθαι) only in the possession of wealth and in anything that happens to contribute to it.

---

27. In his interpretation of spirit as an intermediary between reason and appetites, Renaut argues that spirit can indeed become an ally of the appetitive part: Renaut 2014, p. 177. This reading, however, is not textually supported, as I show in this section.

The spirit so enslaved will play a useful role for the oligarchic man, as it will hold in check, through compulsion and fear, the evil appetites that might jeopardize the realization of the oligarchical man's fundamental desire—namely, the accumulation of wealth (554c1–2). In this way, spirit's inner role as a police force of appetitive desires is maintained but instrumentalized for the sake of a specific appetite.

The language employed here by Plato is significant. At several points throughout the dialogue, Socrates contrasts harmonization of the three parts of the city and of the soul and civil war in both the city and the soul. The rule of the guardians in the ideal city is characterized by harmony and persuasion: the guardians are allies and friends of the citizens instead of their masters (see, for example, 417a–b; 462e–463b). But rule can be despotic and stir conflicts, and such is the rule of the appetitive part of the soul in the oligarchical man. For this reason, he will never be free from inner civil war (554d9–e1 and 554e3–5). Enslaving spirit, therefore, will not ensure harmony within his soul. It would seem, then, that spirit is not so malleable that it can willingly accept the rule of the appetitive part and be attuned to it. This observation is confirmed by the image of the lion and of the multiform beast in Book IX:

> We should therefore say to the one who claims that it is profitable for this human being to commit injustice, while it is not profitable to do just things, that what he is actually claiming is that it is profitable for him to strengthen the manifold beast, the lion, and what is connected to the lion by feeding them well, while starving and weakening the human being so that he can be pulled wherever either of those leads. And he doesn't make them accustomed to each other or friends, but allows them to bite and devour each other in their fight. (588e3–589a4)

Here it appears that the normative rule of reason is the precondition for the friendship between the two beasts within the soul. Without such rule, they will naturally be inclined to fight each other. The metaphor of enslavement is not in contradiction with this image of perpetual struggle, as enslavement is the outcome of one part violently overcoming and oppressing another. We may therefore say that in the oligarchic soul, the appetitive part has managed to win the struggle, which does not grant any real harmony, given that oppression is a sign of ongoing conflict.

To return to our problem of the equivocal nature of malleability, this trait of spirit is a persuasive candidate for the basis of Socrates' claim that spirit is a natural ally of reason only if we understand this malleability to be limited. Spirit can be educated and influenced in such a way as to willingly obey reason's orders and help it control the appetites, but it cannot be corrupted into becoming a *willing* ally of the appetites against reason. In this worst-case scenario, it will be enslaved.[28]

The asymmetry between spirit's willing alliance with reason and its possible subjugation to the appetites stems from reason's and appetite's different capacities to optimize spirit's fundamental desire for self-assertion. On the one hand, the alliance with reason allows a tamed spirit to satisfy its fundamental desire for self-assertion in a normatively optimal way, by channeling it into love for the fine and honor, sensitivity to justice, or into the desire to preserve the correct rational doctrine that it has apprehended. On the other hand, spirit's desire entails a conflict with appetitive desires.[29] And indeed, the guardians' way of life can satisfy their spirited desire for self-assertion

---

28. The opposition of θυμός and ἐπιθυμία is stated by Socrates in *Cra.* 419d as well, as the word ἐπιθυμία is interpreted as deriving from ἐπὶ τὸν θυμὸν, that is from the fact that appetite runs against spirit.

29. On the fact that only if guided by reason the spirited and the appetitive parts can enjoy their own pleasures in the best and truest possible way, see *Rep.* 586e4–587a1.

in all of its three forms: the guardians have power over the producers, they have an agonistic relationship to external enemies and a healthy competition among each other, and they have recognitions based on their honor (as, for example, in the distribution of sexual partners).

With the rule of appetites, such a satisfaction of spirit's desire would not be possible. Desire for power, competitiveness, and desire for others' recognition—the three possible developments of the underlying desire for self-assertion—can turn out to be incompatible with some appetites at any time. As the desire for self-assertion expresses and requires activity, for example, it is in conflict with some specific appetitive pleasures that, on the contrary, demand passivity. This is clearly shown by the exchange between Socrates and Callicles about catamites in the *Gorgias*. Here, as already addressed in chapter 4, Socrates resorts to the example of the passive partners in a homosexual sexual act in order to shame Callicles, who abides by traditional beliefs concerning the identification of manliness and activity, and to push him to question his hedonistic belief that pleasure is identical with the good (*Gorg.* 494e).[30] Moreover, because of its active character, spirit can be in conflict with the appetitive desire to avoid pain or death in circumstances in which facing these risks is necessary to self-assertion. Enslavement to appetites, then, is frustrating to spirit not only because it does not grant spirit the possibility of always satisfying its natural desire but also because it forces spirit to act contrary to its natural predisposition.

To summarize, spirit is the natural ally of reason, not because it always actively tends to align with reason, nor because it has an innate desire for what is truly fine, but, rather, because its nature entails the capacity of being educated and shaped in such a way as to both

---

30. Callicles, indeed, is outraged by Socrates' suggestion that a coherent hedonist should also praise the life of a catamite, as he is deeply ashamed by it. On Socrates' strategy in shaming Callicles see Moss 2005 and Tarnopolsky 2010, pp. 79–88. For a different interpretation of the refutation of Callicles, which assumes that Callicles has no shame, see Klosko 1984.

harmoniously align with reason's normative orders and help it in the struggle against the appetites, while not entailing an equal capacity to willingly align with the appetitive part's rule. The reference to nature, moreover, contains a normative perspective as well. By aligning with reason and holding the appetites in check, spirit can fully satisfy its fundamental desire in such a way as to contribute to the well-being and harmony of the entire soul, while enslavement to appetites is against nature and hence stirs intra-psychic conflicts. As I will illustrate, in spite of the scant references to spirit in the treatment of the tyrannical man, the consequences of this enslavement are crucial to understanding what is so wrong with him, psychologically and morally.

5.3 THE WEREWOLF AND OTHER ANIMAL METAPHORS

After arguing for the natural derivation of tyranny from the extreme, anarchic freedom characterizing the democratic regime, Socrates employs a metaphor, describing the transformation of the democratic leader into a tyrant through a myth concerning werewolves and the temple of Zeus Lykaios in Arcadia (*Rep.* 565d4–566a4). The festival of Lykaia, celebrated in Arcadia on the slopes of Mount Lykaion, was linked to the founding myth of the bloodthirsty king Lycaon, who according to Ovid, in order to test Zeus' divinity, served human flesh mixed with the meat of other animals in a banquet prepared for him. Lycaon was therefore turned into a wolf by the enraged god (Ov. *Met.* 1.163–252). The Arcadian people reportedly practiced human sacrifices to Zeus during the festival of Lykaia, and in Plato's account, human flesh was mixed in the offerings to the god: whoever happened to taste it, says Socrates, would be immediately turned into a wolf.[31]

---

31. Plato's account of this myth is the oldest extant in Greek literature. Other accounts of the Lycaon myth are given in Paus. 8, 2.3–4, where Lycaon is turned into a wolf for having

The same, argues Socrates, goes for the tyrant who, metaphorically speaking, tastes the blood of the docile mob he dominates. As I will show, the metaphor of the tyrant's transformation into a werewolf refers to the corruption of his spirit. If read against the background of the other animal metaphors representing spirit, the image of the werewolf can help us understand the nature of the tyrannical spirit's corruption and its consequences for the tyrant's subjects. Moreover, an analysis of this metaphor allows us to appraise both the dangers entailed by spirit's nature and the extent of its malleability through education and social conventions.

Plato's use of animal metaphors in the *Republic* should not be downplayed or neglected, as throughout the dialogue spirit is the part of the soul most closely associated with both domestic animals and wild beasts.[32] It is compared to dogs, wolves, lions, and serpents: all these animals are also mentioned by Homer as images of his heroes, where they serve the purpose of emphasizing the violence of the struggle, force, courage, blood-thirst, and rapidity in the attack against the enemy.[33] In the *Iliad*, just a few moments before confronting Achilles, Hector is compared to a mountain snake (δράκων) gorged with poisons and filled with anger, holding its ground and waiting to confront a man (*Il.* 22.93).[34] The most important heroes are

practiced human sacrifice and poured the blood of an infant on Zeus' altar, and in Apollod. *Bibl.* 3.8.1, where the responsibility for the human sacrifice is rather attributed to Lycaon's fifty children, all of whom Zeus punishes by striking them dead with lightning. The practice of human sacrifice in Lycia is attested in *Minos* 315b and later sources. For a discussion of this myth, see Mainoldi 1984, pp. 11–17.

32. On Plato's use of animal metaphors, see Frère 1998. On political animals in Plato, see Vegetti 2009a.

33. Another animal metaphor one can find in the dialogue is that of the ape (*Rep.* 590b6–9); even in this case, Plato suggests a Homeric reference, for Thersites chooses the life of a monkey in the myth of Er (620c2–3).

34. The term δράκων in Homer is interchangeable with ὄφις. In *Il.* 12.200–209, a serpent caught by an eagle is described as a monstrous beast still fighting to the point that it forces the eagle to drop it; the beast is called δράκων at v. 202 and ὄφις at v. 208. The term used by Plato in reference to spirit is ὀφεῶδες, which is a *hapax* (590b1). The use of the term ὀφεῶδες has raised some perplexities among commentators of the *Republic*. Nettleship suggests that

frequently compared to lions within the context of individual fights, where the lion is an image for force, ferocity, and proud egoism, but also of individual nobility and heroic exploits.[35] Comparisons with wolves are employed to describe the ardor in the fight between the Trojans and Achaeans in *Il.* 4.471–2 and the Danaans' ferocity and force in the fight against the Trojans, who are depicted as the wolf's prey, lambs, and goats with a weak θυμός, in *Il.* 16.352–7.[36] Finally, the hunting dog is employed as a model of tenacity, speediness, steadfastness, and courage for the most important heroes.[37] Given Plato's indebtedness to the Homeric portrayal of heroic θυμός, his use of animal metaphors that we find so often in the Homeric poems deserves careful attention.[38]

ὀφεῶδες is the outcome of a transcription mistake and that we should, rather, read ὀχλῶδες, unruly, a term applied to the appetitive part at 590b7 (Nettleship [1897] 1964, p. 335), while Jaeger suggests that we should read it as ὀργῶδες, which would be another Platonic *hapax*, but referring to ὀργή (Jaeger 1945, p. 126). For a useful discussion of this point, see Gastaldi 2005b, pp. 617–620. Gastaldi does not discuss the Homeric comparison between Hector and a δρακών and the interchangeability of δρακών and ὄφις in the *Iliad*.

35. Among others, see, on Achilles: Hom. *Il.* 18.318–321, 20.164–175, 24.41–44, 24.572. On Agamemnon: *Il.* 11.129, 11.172–178, 11.239. On Ajax: *Il.* 11.548–557, 17.133–137, 17.281–285. On Hector: *Il.* 7.256–257, 12.41–50, 15.271–280, 15.630–637, 15.751–754 and 823–828, 18.161–164. The Homeric Hymn to Heracles calls him the λεοντόθυμος, the lion-hearted: Hom. *Hymn* 15. On the nobility and courage of the lion, see Aristot. *Hist. an.* 488b. See also Gastaldi 2005b, pp. 601–603, and Hobbs 2000, p. 25.

36. For the analysis of the image of the wolf in the *Iliad*, see Mainoldi 1984, pp. 98–102.

37. See *Il.* 8.338–340, 10.360–362, 11.414–420, 22.189–192. See also Mainoldi 1984, pp. 109–111. These are only some of the aspects of the image of the dog in the *Iliad*, for, as shown by Mainoldi, the dog is also the animal most connected to the underworld (the dog as eater of corpses, for example), and it is sometimes portrayed as being filled with fear in front of savage beasts. According to Mainoldi, in his depiction of the guardians as dogs, Plato re-elaborates some elements coming from Homeric poems by combining some essential features characterizing hunting dogs in Homer with others characterizing watchdogs (for example, loyalty to the master): Mainoldi 1984, pp. 187–188.

38. In Homer, θυμός has a wider meaning than in Plato, as it is the substrate of an array of passions, but it also indicates life and vitality. Plato privileges only some select aspects of Homeric θυμός—in particular, its connection to courage, temperament, and anger, and its heroic aspects. On Homeric θυμός and its influence on Plato, see, for example, Cooper 1984; Calabi 1998; Frère 2004, pp. 15–25; Renaut 2014, ch. 1. On the medical origin of the term θυμοειδές, see Jaeger 1945.

spirit compared to lion & serpent

In Book IX, Socrates resorts twice to the comparison of spirit to a lion and once to a serpent (*Rep.* 588d3 and 590b1). We have no persuasive reasons to think that the spirit described here as a wild beast is a corrupt one.[39] Given that this passage poetically portrays the soul to refute the claim that injustice profits it, we can take the image of the lion and the serpent as figuring a spirit in its "raw state"—that is, a spirit that has not been trained yet and hence one that has not been corrupted by a bad upbringing, either. And indeed, at 589b3–4, Socrates insists that reason must make an ally of the lion by taming it. Spirit, as fundamentally a drive to self-assertion, is both a potential ally of reason (insofar as it can be guided through beliefs and social norms) and a potential threat (insofar as it could be inclined to pursue a pattern of behavior leading to the violent oppression of others). This ambivalence of spirit is emphasized by these two animal metaphors. The serpent is a dangerous and aggressive animal, but it can be charmed, as is Thrasymachus, who—as Glaucon jokingly notices—is enthralled by Socrates' arguments (358b2–3). The lion embodies a combination of savagery and kingliness, violence and courage. Moreover, the figure of the lion unifies the three different patterns of self-assertion indicated at 581a9–10: pursuit of domination over others, competitiveness, and pursuit of honor. Indeed, in Greek literature, the lion was also associated with, while expressing an ambivalence toward, legitimate monarchic power: it showed the danger—implicit in the monarch's use of force and violence—that monarchic power may turn into a tyranny.[40]

---

39. This is what Hobbs suggests, but her interpretation exacerbates a textual problem instead of solving it, as she takes the lion to be uneducable, in spite of the fact that Socrates clearly says that reason needs to make an ally of the lion (589b): Hobbs 2000, p. 26.

40. In Aesop's fables, for example, the lion is usually portrayed as the king ruling over the other animals, but his rule is based on his greater force, which the lion tends to use to oppress others in a tyrannical fashion: see, for example, *Fable* 142, 187, 339, 341, 372 (Perry); and Dumont 2001, p. 108. Agamemnon is called a noble lion in Aeschylus' tragedy, which both insists on his legitimate monarchic power and emphasizes his violence and ruthlessness: see

The two other animals associated with spirit—the dog and the wolf—express two possible and opposed developments of its drive to self-assertion. The wolf, as we will see, is associated with the possible degeneration of spirit into political savagery, of which the tyrant is the worst and most dangerous extreme. The dog models two aspects of the ideal combination of reason and spirit: the potentiality of a harmonious relation between spirit and reason inherent to a specific kind of nature, and the realization of this potentiality through domestication. This specific kind of nature is characterized by the combined presence of a strong spirit and of a strong love for learning (φιλομαθές). In this sense, the dog as an animal metaphor is distinct from the lion, which corresponds to spirit in its raw state without any further specification about the kind of soul or nature of which it is part.

The image of the dog is introduced in the dialogue for the first time in response to the problem raised by the necessity of introducing spirited citizens to the inflamed city. While the dog, as a lover of learning, is both a philosophical animal and an anticipation of the introduction of philosopher-kings later on in the dialogue, it is also a spirited one. In Book II, 375b9–11, both Socrates and Glaucon recognize that while a spirited nature is necessary to the defense of the city and must therefore characterize the guardians, it is extremely difficult for someone who has a spirited nature not to be savage (ἄγριος). Indeed, spirit has a potentially destructive character (375c2–3). The

---

Aesch. *Ag.* 824–825 on the beast of Argo, which attacked Troy like a lion devouring raw flesh, and Aesch. *Ag.* 1259 on Agamemnon as a noble lion. On this ambiguity of the regality associated to the lion, see Catenacci 2012, pp. 177–178. There is at least one notable comparison of a leader of democratic Athens to a lion expressing a similar meaning—that is, the ambivalence of the combination of nobility and possible ferocity: in Aristophanes' *Frogs*, Alcibiades is the lion cub that Athens reared at its own risk: Aristoph. *Frogs*, 1431–1432. Pericles was also famously associated with a lion: see Hdt. 6.131.2, where his mother, Agariste, dreams to give birth to a lion. In Aristophanes' *Knights*, Paphlagon/Cleon presents himself as a lion, comparing himself, by the same token, to Pericles: Aristoph. *Kn.* 1036–1043. Demos, being hard of hearing, misunderstands him and thinks that Cleon has become Antileon, the tyrant of Chalcis: *Kn.* 1044.

example of watchdogs serves the purpose of showing that a combination of gentleness and spiritedness, albeit rare to find, is not contrary to nature (375e6–7).[41] The watchdog's gentleness depends on its tendency to develop attachments to those it recognizes as its own (376a–b). This observation is developed in two directions in the dialogue. On the one hand, it serves the purpose of emphasizing the "philosophical" nature of dogs as animals that love learning. On the other, it refers to the possibility of taming spirit, which will be one of the main tasks of the educational program of Books II and III and of the collectivist arrangements introduced at the end of Book III and developed further in Book V. These collectivist arrangements should be taken as an example of how spirit can be tamed, educated, and molded through specific social conditions and through specific notions of what is honorable and fine.

In Book III, while discussing the process for selecting the rulers among the guardians, Socrates includes the coincidence between one's own private interests and the interests of the city as a condition for being taken into consideration. Only those who will love and care for the city—because they both have a deeply engrained belief that what is advantageous to the city is advantageous to themselves and will preserve this belief against all temptations to the contrary—will be fit for the task of ruling (412d–e). Later on, in Book V, Socrates insists that, in order to achieve unity in the city, it is necessary that its citizens say the words "mine" and "not mine" in unison and with regard to the same things, which is to say that the privatization of pleasures and pains needs to be entirely overcome (462b–c). This commonality of pleasures and pains is expressed a few lines later through the famous metaphor of the city as an ensouled body that feels the pain

---

41. Tait correctly noticed that the sense of this analogy is not to infer the nature of the guardians from that of watchdogs but, rather, to show that there is a basis in nature for the requisite combination of apparently opposed qualities, gentleness and spiritedness, which at first appeared contrary to nature: Tait 1949, p. 204.

affecting one of its members as its own pain (462c–d). These passages are particularly relevant for the interpretation of spirit's fundamental drive as a drive to self-assertion that can be transformed and educated through social conventions and arrangements. Indeed, in both passages, the notion of what is one's own in the sense of belonging to a community can be so enlarged as to comprehend the whole city. Shifting the main site of affective identification from the family to the city is the fundamental goal of the abolition of private families and of the establishment of the collective education of children articulated in Book V. But affective identification is connected to self-assertion, in the sense that it enlarges the notion of what is to be considered as one's own in terms of self-identification and belonging to a community. If what identifies someone in a fundamental way is not just oneself but also her kinship network or homeland, to assert the interest of her family or of her country will be the same as to assert her own interest, and the frustration or pain felt by her family or her country will be her own frustration or pain as well. The dog is a good animal example of the way spirit can come to consider somebody else as a part of one's own identity, as a watchdog is ready to fight and even to die for those it knows and considers as its own.

The tyrannical wolf is in this respect the polar opposite of the dog, as the wolf considers every external object as possible prey—that is, as a possible object of private appropriation and possession. As it does not have an enlarged sense of belonging, its only attitude to the flock is predatory. The wolf was an animal frequently associated with the tyrant in Greek literature, and references to wolves in relation to excessive violence and misuse of power are dispersed throughout the *Republic* and in other dialogues.[42] While in Homer the image

---

42. See, for example, Aesch. *Ag.* 1258–1260; and Diod. 10.29. For a good collection of occurrences, see Catenacci 2012, pp. 174–178. Catenacci also remarks that λύκος (wolf) is an onomastic component recurring in the names of various tyrants and, perhaps, also in the name of Peisistratus' bodyguards, λυκόποδες: Catenacci 2012, p. 176.

of the wolf is associated with combativeness, aggression, and force, in the classical period, more decisively negative features were progressively attributed to it. In addition to being wild and violent, the wolf was depicted as a clever deceiver (Aesch. *Ag.* 1258–1260), as savage, bloodthirsty, and unreliable (Aristoph. *Lys.* 628–629), and as a robber (Aristoph. *Clouds* 351–352). As noted by Mainoldi, in the classical period the wolf became the animal metaphor for a kind of savagery that was not only incompatible with social and political norms but also considered a threat to the city as such.[43] It was thus a symbol for a particular kind of savagery—the political one.

In line with this common depiction of wolves, Plato's own interpretation of the myth of the werewolf aims at emphasizing two main features related to the condition and operation of the tyrant's spirit: ferocity and unrestrained thirst for power.[44] The possible transformation of a political leader or soldier into a wolf attacking the flock he was meant to protect had already been evoked in Book III, in the discussion of the education and taming of the spirit of the guardians, famously compared to watchdogs. These dogs, having transformed into wolves, would act as savage despots (δεσπόταις ἀγρίοις) toward the citizens by taking advantage of their greater force (416b3). This is why

[T]he most terrible and shameful thing of all for a shepherd is to rear such dogs to assist him with the flocks in such a way that they will attempt to harm the cattle out of licentiousness, hunger, or some other bad habit and will become similar to wolves instead of dogs. (416a2–7)[45]

43. Mainoldi 1984, p. 139.
44. The tyrant is associated with a wolf in *Phaedo* 82a as well, while in *Laws* 906d, wolves are a metaphor for criminal and unjust men.
45. On the uncanny similarity of dogs and wolves (and of sophists and philosophers), see *Soph.* 231a.

Since one of the main concerns of the educational program articulated in Books II and III is taming the guardians' spirit so that it does not endanger the city they are supposed to protect, a plausible case can be made that the wolf is to be taken as one of the animal metaphors indicating spirit in the dialogue. It may be significant in this sense that Thrasymachus, the supporter of a tyrannical conception of power, is compared to three animals, two of which are explicitly associated with spirit. He is first implicitly and jokingly compared to a wolf, as Socrates says that if he hadn't seen him before Thrasymachus stared at him, he would have been dumbstruck—a reference to a legend involving wolves (336d5–7). Then he is explicitly referred to as a lion, when Socrates ironically says that it would be crazy to shave a lion—that is, to bear false witness against Thrasymachus (341c1–2). Finally—as already mentioned—he is described by Glaucon as a snake charmed by Socrates' arguments (358b2–3).

Throughout the discussion of the educational program of Books II and III, the dog serves as a normative metaphor for a potentially well-tempered spirited nature and for the realization of this potentiality through domestication. In other words, the image of the dog does not express spirit in its "raw" form but, rather, spirit in specific conditions depending both on a particular kind of nature, characterized by a strong φιλομαθές part, and on an adequate educational process. By contrast, the wolf is the dog's polar opposite, but also the dog's possible degeneration: it does not express the negative and dangerous aspects of spirit in its uneducated state but, rather, those related to spirit as corrupted by a bad upbringing or influences in the city. Moreover, it is important to note that among the causes for the transformation of dogs into wolves, licentiousness and hunger are the only ones directly mentioned, which may be taken as an indication that the lupine spirit is corrupted by the appetites.

In sum, the four main animal metaphors adopted in the dialogue in reference to spirit, while drawing from some Homeric themes and other common depictions of these animals in Greek literature, describe three different states of the spirited part: the lion and the snake correspond to spirit in its "raw" state—that is, to an untrained but also uncorrupted spirit, images that express the ambivalence between aggressiveness and predisposition to be charmed, nobility, and savagery; the dog expresses the potentiality for a normatively optimal condition of spirit within a nature in which a strong spirit and a strong rational part coexist, as well as the realization of this potentiality through taming and education; the wolf corresponds to a spirit utterly corrupted through bad upbringing, social conditions, and appetites. This predatory spirit deprived of all nobility is the spirit of the tyrant.

5.4 SAVAGERY IN THE CITY

The suggestion that the wolf is an animal symbol indicating a corrupt spirit is further corroborated by the fact that the metaphor returns in Book VIII, to introduce the theme of the tyrant's brutality and violence in his attachment to political power. The combination of attachment to political power and excessive violence cannot but recall the most dangerous potential aspects of the spirited part, which Socrates proposes to tame through his educational program in Books II and III. This theme is developed in two distinct explanatory patterns. First, in Book VIII, the savagery of the tyrant's behavior is presented as a necessity dictated by the *external* circumstances created by the tyrant's rule. However, when Socrates describes the tyrannical man, his savagery is presented as a consequence of the bad *internal* state of his soul in a manner that is consistent with the theory of the soul's tripartition. This apparent tension can be resolved by taking into account the dynamic of externalization and internalization characterizing the exchange between the soul and the city.

In his rejection of Bernard Williams' critique of Plato's analogy between city and soul, Jonathan Lear insists that the *Republic* offers an account of the structure of the human psyche based on the notion that human beings enter the world with a capacity, on the one hand, to absorb cultural influences and, on the other, to shape their own social and political environment. The relationship between city and individual soul, then, is a dynamic one, based on what Lear, adopting psychoanalytic terminology, calls "externalization" and "internalization." This means that, rather than suggesting an analogical relationship, Plato's parallel treatment of the city and the individual soul charts the dynamic transaction between a person's inner life and his cultural environment—that is, the outside and the inside of a person's psyche.[46] Lear's idea of externalization and internalization as a main feature of Plato's treatment of the relation between soul and city is enlightening for understanding the dialogue as a whole and Plato's treatment of the corrupt regimes and their corresponding men in particular. Here the soul is constantly exposed to the corrupting effects of societal and political conditions, and at the same time it externalizes its corrupt nature in deeds and behaviors that further shape those very conditions. Moreover, to reconcile these different explanatory patterns, we need to consider that Plato's argumentative strategy consists in combining a political account of the tyrant's origin, a sociopsychological account of the origin and nature of tyrannical souls, and a psycho-political account of the effects of political power on the tyrant's soul.

The description of the bloodthirsty character of the tyrannical regime addresses the constraints imposed on a ruler's behavior by the mechanisms proper to absolute power: the emphasis is put on the "happy necessity" (ἐν μακαρίᾳ ... ἀνάγκῃ; 567d1) presiding over the

---

46. Lear 1992. See also Williams [1973] 2006; and Ferrari's criticism of both Williams and Lear in Ferrari 2005.

process of transformation of the tyrant into a wolf. However, this description is not in tension with but, rather, complements, and is in turn complemented by, the subsequent treatment of the tyrannical man in Book IX. While in Book IX the savagery of the tyrannical man is explained on the basis of the exceptionally unhealthy state of his soul, this extreme sickness is in turn the effect that mechanisms of internalization vis-à-vis his familial and social context have had on an already disordered soul. Moreover, when Glaucon suggests that the tyrannical man just described is the most miserable of all, Socrates corrects him: rather than the private tyrannical man, the most unhappy is the tyrannical man who, instead of living a private life, has the misfortune to have the opportunity to become an actual tyrant (578c1–3). Socrates then continues by describing the very same constraints already addressed in Book VIII, but this time with specific attention to their effects on the tyrant's soul. In this case, the tyrannical man becomes like a body without self-control fighting with other bodies for all its life (579c8–d2). The bloodthirsty character of the tyrannical man is only increased and nourished by the constraints of absolute power, which include his complete isolation and the necessity of a perpetual war with everybody else.

The first explanatory pattern runs from 565d to 569c. As already mentioned, the myth of the werewolf at 565d is introduced as a metaphor for the transformation of the προστάτης—that is, the democratic leader—into a complete tyrant. In a situation of civil strife caused by the exploitation of the city's rich by its demagogic drones and the consequent transformation of the former into oligarchs plotting against democracy, the προστάτης begins taking bloodthirsty measures in order to preserve his power. These include false accusations, trials, exiles, and assassinations (565e3–566a). It is at this point that Plato mobilizes the Arcadian themes remarked on in the previous section. The leader, after tasting the blood of his fellow citizens (that is, of the rich), turns into a wolf, becoming a full-fledged tyrant (τύραννος ἀπειργασμένος) and beginning an endless spiral of violence.

After an initial period in which he alternates between measures of internal pacification and violent repression, both aimed at stopping internal conflicts that may jeopardize his rule (566d–568e), the tyrant rapidly reveals his true new nature: he wages perpetual wars against external enemies in order to both make himself indispensable in the eyes of the demos (566e7–9) and to push common people to stay away from active politics by impoverishing them through war taxes (566a1–3). Then, as soon as he starts fearing that these measures may cause opposition or discontent among the demos, he leaves those whom he suspects of aspiring to freedom at the mercy of the enemies, to which end he stirs up more wars (567a5–8). After that, he turns against his former allies as soon as they begin criticizing the current state of affairs, once again compelled by the necessity to preserve his power (εἰ μέλλει ἄρξειν; 567b8–9), and therefore becomes, willingly or unwillingly, everyone's enemy (567c1–3). When the demos gets angry and finally rebels, trying to chase the tyrant away, then and only then will the citizens fully realize what kind of creature (θρέμμα) they have generated, welcomed, and let grow (569a8–b2). This creature, which was supposed to be a domestic animal,[47] turns out to be, rather, a θηρίον, a wild beast, a wolf. This transformation of what was supposed to be a tame animal into a wild beast echoes literary depictions comparing the tyrant's rise to power to a wild beast revolting against the city that has nourished it.[48] But the passage also

---

47. The word θρέμμα, literally "nursling," was most often used in reference to tame animals.
48. See, for example, Hdt. 5.92.β15–21 in reference to Cypselus. The image of the lion growing in the city into a wild beast that will devour it is employed by the Chorus in reference to Troy's destiny of destruction in Aesch. *Ag.* 717–736. Cassandra uses a similar metaphor later in reference to the destiny of the House of Atrides, caused by the contamination of Atreus' atrocious and impious vengeance against his brother Thyestes, who had slept with Atreus' wife: Atreus killed Thyestes' children and fed them to their father: Aesch. *Ag.* 1223–1226.

recalls the discussion of the transformation of dogs into wolves already addressed in Book III, 416a2–7.

While spirit is not explicitly mentioned in this section, the use of the image of the wolf, as well as the insistence on the two aspects of attachment to power and excessive violence, is a plausible basis for arguing that spirit is involved in the tyrant's behavior. This theme is developed from two main perspectives: in terms of the effects that the constraints posed by social conditions and the possession of arbitrary power have on an already deranged soul; and of the consequences of the tyrant's disordered spirit for his subjects.

5.5 THE TYRANT'S ENSLAVED SPIRIT: SHAMELESSNESS AND BRUTALITY

The relation between the tyrant's spirit and his propensity to violence, brutality, and unaccountable power, which is only implicit in Book VIII, emerges more clearly in a passage in Book IX, where we encounter the sole mention of spirit in the treatment of the tyrannical man. At 572a3–5, Socrates discusses the appropriate cure for the lawless dreams that all people happen to have. This cure entails two main measures: quieting the two irrational parts of the soul, and arousing reason with fine arguments and speculations before going to sleep. Thanks to these preparations, dreams will be at their least lawless. Here we find the only explicit reference to τὸ θυμοειδές and θυμός:

> [H]e soothes the spirited part as well in the same way and does not fall asleep with his spirit still aroused because he had an outburst of anger against someone. (572a3–5)

This passage is extremely significant because it raises some problems for the common reading of the nature of lawless desires among Plato's interpreters—namely, that they are only appetitive in nature.[49] This common reading is justified by claiming that the division between lawless and lawful desires in 571b6–7 is a subdivision of the distinction between necessary and unnecessary appetitive desires in Book VIII (558d–559a). However, while the logic of this division does seem to imply that only appetitive desires can be independently lawless, it nonetheless does not exclude the possibility that spirit's desires can acquire a lawless character because of spirit's enslavement to the appetites, and that these desires can combine with lawless appetitive desires. In fact, the mention of spirit at 572a3–5 does suggest that anger or an excessive arousal of spirit contributes to having lawless dreams. With this insight in mind, we can now turn to examining the much-discussed passage about lawless dreams and lawless desires.[50]

At the very beginning of Book IX, Socrates notices that the distinction between necessary and unnecessary desires has not been correctly dealt with previously in the conversation. In particular, the discussants have forgotten to add a crucial distinction—that between lawful and lawless (παράνομοι) desires. These appetites are present in everybody, but "they are repressed (κολαζόμεναι) by the laws and by the better desires in alliance with reason (τῶν βελτιόνων ἐπιθυμιῶν μετὰ λόγου)" (571b6–7). In this passage, Socrates claims that, if held in check, these criminal desires may even disappear or be significantly weakened in some people, while in others they will remain strong and many. The verb κολάζω indeed indicates punishment and retribution, hence forced repression of criminal desires through the laws and better desires. Forced repression of these desires, which should be carefully distinguished from their disappearance or weakening, may occur in people who are not fully virtuous and in whose soul there is

---

49. For an excellent articulation of this position, see Reeve 2006, pp. 43–50.
50. The use of the term ἐπιθυμία in the discussion about lawless desires is not an acceptable basis for an objection to my claim, for, as already argued, this term is employed throughout the dialogue to indicate an array of desires that are not appetitive in nature.

still a conflict. Disappearance and weakening, on the contrary, occur only in some people (likely, those who are always normatively guided by reason and are entirely virtuous).

One may be tempted to take these better desires to be only appetites. This reading, however, is problematic because it would suggest that appetites can directly restrain other appetites, which would undermine the rationale for the soul's partition articulated in Book IV: inner conflict of the kind "do this" versus "do not do this" is the main basis for the argument for the existence of distinct parts within the soul.[51] Appetites cannot directly restrain other appetites; they can, at most, play an indirect role in holding other appetites in check. In the case of the oligarchic man, for example, better appetitive desires play a role in checking other appetites only insofar as they influence reason and spirit. It is reason that has the ability to recognize the possible incompatibility between different kinds of appetites in his soul, and it is spirit that has the ability to repress them. Given both the difficulties that follow from holding the view that appetites restrain each other and the fact that the role of repressing the appetites is attributed to spirit in the *Republic*, there are good reasons to think that "better desires" include the desires of spirit. This reading is corroborated by the passage's reference to laws, given spirit's ability to internalize and adhere to laws and social norms.

The interpretive problem of determining what part of the soul is responsible for lawless desires and what part for the activity of control is raised again by the following passage, where Adeimantus asks Socrates to specify what counts as a criminal appetite. Socrates gives the following answer:

Those that are awakened in sleep . . . when the rest of the soul—
the rational, gentle, and ruling part—is asleep, the beastly and

51. For an array of good reasons against such an option, see Lorenz's discussion of the logic of tripartition in Lorenz 2006, pp. 41–52.

savage part (τὸ δὲ θηριῶδές τε καὶ ἄγριον), full of food and strong drinks, is unruly and, repelling sleep, seeks to go and satisfy its habits. You know that in this state it dares to do anything, as released and liberated from any *shame and reason* (αἰσχύνης καὶ φρονήσεως). In its fantasies it doesn't shrink from trying to have sex with its mother or with anyone else, whether a human being, a god, or a beast. It commits any murder and does not abstain from any food. In a word it doesn't lack any folly and shamelessness. (571c3–d4)

The reference to shame may be taken to corroborate that the better desires responsible for the activity of control include those of spirit. On this basis, we can argue that in a non-virtuous person, whose spirit is not entirely corrupt, the activity of control belongs to reason and spirit *together*. Moreover, the reference to shame may indicate that if spirit does not play its role of inner control, lawless dreams will likely occur.

So far, I have argued for spirit's role in the repression and control of lawless appetites and dreams. We have seen, however, that at 572a3–5, Socrates refers to the necessity of soothing the spirited part of the soul before going to sleep. This passage can plausibly been taken as indicating that the activity of control is not the only role spirit can play in dreams. In this passage on dreams, reason is the only part explicitly asleep, which leaves us with the possibility that spirit, if both left alone without the normative guidance of reason and enslaved to appetites and inflamed by them, behaves like a beast and contributes to the generation of savage desires. This reading is not refuted by the content of these lawless dreams. Murder does not seem to be specifically appetitive and may instead refer to bloodthirstiness, a potential feature of spirit. Sexual dreams are clearly appetitive, but some of the peculiar sexual dreams at stake in our passage may entail participation of spirit: incest is explicitly associated with either desire for or a prediction of possession of the motherland in a passage by Herodotus concerning the tyrant Hippias,[52] and sex with the gods is hubristic, as is the illusion of being able to rule over the gods, mentioned later.

To summarize, lawless desires, while primarily appetitive, may entail a distinctive contribution and participation by a spirit entirely enslaved to the appetites. If the normative rule of reason or laws is missing and the appetites rule it, θυμός can, like the ἐπιθυμητικόν, be unleashed and seek ways of gratification through unlawful objects. In the case of dreams, this is possible because reason is not awake and because θυμός has been excessively stirred before going to sleep. In these conditions, spirit is incapable of shame because it is both too aroused and not properly guided, either by internalized laws or by reason's orders. Consequently, spirit is not fighting the appetites of the desiderative part, and what remains of it is its savagery and thirst for power. This passage is particularly important for our analysis because, as we will discover some lines later, the tyrannical man permanently lives while awake as if he were dreaming such dreams (574e2–4). We can, therefore, take the passage on lawless dreams to exemplify the condition of the tyrannical man's soul while he is awake.

An analysis of the genesis of the tyrannical man's soul will help understand how his spirit has become so corrupted. Both the democratic father and his son (i.e., the would-be tyrant) share the characteristic of being driven by their appetitive part. In contrast to the case of the oligarchic man, the tyranny of the appetitive part characteristic of the democratic men is not focused on a dominant and exclusive object of desire. As already seen in chapter 4, the decisive shift from the democratic to the tyrannical ethos occurs when, driven

---

52. See Hdt. 6. 107.1–2, and the interpretation of this passage in Holt 1998, pp. 222–224. Among later sources, see Artem. 1.79, who interprets in this way incest dreams had by politicians, Suet. *Iul.* 7.2., and Dio Cass. 37.52.2, 41.24.2.

by a new and powerful eros, the would-be tyrannical man abandons the respect for the laws that still characterize his father and instead endorses complete παρανομία—that is, lawlessness (572c9–e1). The acquisition of a lawless attitude and behavior does not go without a struggle, as the potential tyrant is conflicted and pulled in opposite directions; this conflict derives from the power that the social conventions and norms that he has learned in his childhood still have on his soul. This is why the introduction of μανία plays a crucial role:

> And when the other appetites—filled with incense, myrrh, crowns, wine, and the other unbridled pleasures found in such companies—buzz around the drone, making it grow as much as possible and nurturing it, they cause the sting of longing in it. Then this popular leader of the soul (οὗτος ὁ προστάτης τῆς ψυχῆς) takes madness as its bodyguard (δορυφορεῖταί τε ὑπὸ μανίας) and is driven into a frenzy. If it detects in the man any beliefs or desires (δόξας ἢ ἐπιθυμίας) that are considered to be good or that still show a sense of shame (ποιουμένας χρηστὰς καὶ ἔτι ἐπαισχυνομένας), it kills them and banishes them from him until he is purged of moderation (καθήρῃ σωφροσύνης) and filled with _imported madness_. (573a4–b4)

Although spirit is not explicitly mentioned, this passage contains some indications about the way the tyrant's spirit becomes completely corrupted and loses its capacity for shame. It is indeed shame that prevents the would-be tyrannical man from endorsing absolute lawlessness. This shame derives from the fact that, during his education, he has acquired a set of beliefs and corresponding desires that, while not truly noble, are still thought to be good or useful (χρηστὰς), albeit in the sense of being socially deemed as such. These opinions are useful because they stir nobler desires than those of the appetitive part of the soul (for example, the desire for honor and esteem), enabling the man raised with such beliefs to keep his baser appetites under control. These useful desires that still show some sense of shame should include those of spirit. Once they disappear, together with the beliefs that nourished them, the tyrannical man's soul is left with no possible aid against appetites, and all moderation is lost. These useful old δόξαι and ἐπιθυμίαι are destroyed through "imported" madness.

We discover something else about this madness a few lines later. At 574d5–e1, Socrates says:

> And in all these circumstances, the opinions recently released from slavery—the ones that once when he still had a democratic constitution within himself under the influence of the laws and of his father, were released only in sleep—are now the body-guard of Eros (δορυφοροῦσαι τὸν Ἔρωτα) and with its help over-come the traditional opinions that he had held from childhood about what is fine or shameful (πάλαι εἶχεν δόξας ἐκ παιδὸς περὶ καλῶν τε καὶ αἰσχρῶν), opinions deemed to be just (τὰς δικαίας ποιουμένας).

If we combine this passage with the previous one, it appears clear that μανία includes a new set of opinions and desires that the ty-rannical man only dared to have when he was asleep. These new opinions are, so to speak, his reason's nightmares.[53] Previously, the old traditional opinions determined what is fine and shameful for the future tyrant. As we have already discussed, the fine and the shameful are, respectively, the spirit's object of desire and disgust in its pursuit of self-assertion through recognition. Indeed, in its search for self-assertion, spirit adapts itself to follow the existing

---

53. I will further address the nature of this madness and the content of these beliefs when I will analyze the tyrannical man's reason, in chapter 6, this volume.

beliefs (i.e., those that are held to be just) that determine the framework of social norms within which it can gain recognition. The introduction of new beliefs is necessary to free spirit from the restraints that these beliefs impose on its savagery. Madness plays the role of introducing these new beliefs.

Accounting for this transition requires recognizing the role that spirit's drive for self-assertion plays in the constitution of the tyrannical soul. Based on this analysis, one could conclude that with the acquisition of these new beliefs and the loss of the capacity for shame, spirit loses its control of the appetites and thus ceases to have any function within the soul. However, while its job as an ally of reason in the control of the ἐπιθυμητικόν is over, spirit still does have an important, albeit negative, psychic function. At 573c3–5, Socrates says that a madman (μαινόμενος) tries to rule not only over human beings but also over gods, and supposes that he is able to do so. His madness consists of his desire for absolute domination exacerbated by his illusion of being able to rule over the divine, which is to say that this madman is fundamentally hubristic. But desire for absolute power and illusions of omnipotence are characteristic of spirit rather than of the appetitive part of the soul. In our tyrannical man, because of the replacement of old traditional beliefs about the fine and the shameful by the new maddening beliefs, the ambivalence inherent to spirit (which is both a natural ally and a potential enemy of reason) is resolved to the advantage of the thirst for power and desire for victory based on mere force. When sensitivity to honor fades away together with the feeling of shame, what remains in the tyrannical soul is the most savage aspect of spirit—that is, its propensity to oppress everybody else and resort to violence. Moreover, this propensity to violence and domination of others is put primarily in the service of appetitive desires, and especially erotic love.

By examining the features of spirit's enslavement to the appetitive part, we can throw some light both on the nature of the role played by this mutilated spirit and on the kind of new beliefs that may have corrupted it. Tad Brennan has insisted on the unity of (what he defines as) the external and the internal role of spirit: in both cases, the role proper to spirit is to confront appetitive souls, both one's own and others'. These two roles are unified in that the only way for spirit to act as an internal police force is through the internalization of the representation of the rival appetites and claims of others.[54] In my view, the unity of these two roles and the consequent virtuous regulation of appetites express a normatively good working of spirit—that is, spirit in its pursuit of its fundamental desire in a normatively good way. But spirit can go seriously astray. In the case of the tyrant, because of the enslavement of spirit to lawless appetites, these internal and external roles are completely decoupled, and there is no internal representation of the appetites of others. From the tyrant's perspective, everything is the legitimate object of his appetite, and there is no space left for the claims of others. What remains is the external violent control over the appetites of others for the sake of the gratification of the tyrannical man's insatiable appetitive part. And indeed, the tyrannical man becomes madly enraged and does not hesitate to resort to violence whenever his endless striving toward the gratification of his appetites is frustrated by external circumstances. At 573e7–574a1, the frustration of his appetitive striving enrages him (οἰστρᾶν) to the point that he will not hesitate to steal from others what may satisfy his appetite, by resorting either to deception (ἀπατ ήσαντα) or even to violence (βιασάμενον). Later, he will use the same violence against his own parents, after having unsuccessfully tried to deceive them with the goal of taking possession of their wealth for the sake of the gratification of his uncontrollable eros (574a6–b5). Finally, he will treat his motherland in the same way he treated his parents, enslaving the city that tries to resist him (575d3–9).

54. Brennan 2012, pp. 105–106, and 127.

In all these circumstances, the tyrannical man resorts to violence and oppression of others as a response to the frustration of his appetites caused by external constraints. The enslavement of the city—that is, the possession of arbitrary, unaccountable, and unrestrained political power—is the natural outcome of this dynamic for the tyrannical man who finds the external circumstances propitious to becoming an actual, political tyrant. Indeed, by enslaving the city, the political tyrant can appropriate what belongs both to the individual citizens and to the city as a whole.

5.6 AGGRESSIVE COWARDICE

A possible difficulty with this interpretation of the tyrannical man's spirit is raised by another aspect of his psychopathology—namely, his fear.[55] The paranoid terrors that characterize tyrants may seem to corroborate the interpretive option that holds that the tyrannical man has a weak spirit rather than a violently stirred one.

In the description of the violent measures taken by the tyrant in Book VIII, the tyrant is compelled to act in a brutal and ruthless way by the very logic of his absolute power. In each instance, his acts are dictated by the fear of losing his power to a growing internal opposition. Moreover, the tyrant appears to be suspicious even of his own former supporters; he constantly monitors those who may represent a threat to him—that is, those who have intellect, courage, conspicuous wealth, or greatness of soul—and ends up becoming the enemy of them all (576b12–c3). This topic is developed in the description of the tyrant of Book IX by emphasizing the paranoid terror characterizing his life. Rather than the private tyrannical man, it is the man with both a tyrannical disposition and the misfortune to

55. On the tyrant's paranoia, see Vegetti 2007.

become an actual tyrant that is the most wretched of all men, because possession of actual political power exacerbates the negative traits and sickness that the tyrannical soul has already acquired. The tyrant lives in a constant state of fear and generalized suspicion, stirred by his isolation, absolute lack of friends, and the hatred he inspires in his subjects. This is why he has less freedom than his subjects, for he does not even have the possibility to travel abroad, freely circulate in the city, or enjoy the simple pleasures that common people do: he lives the life of a woman, confined to his own house (579b–e).[56] Seizing and trying to maintain a tyrannical power, then, exacerbates the fear that already characterizes the private tyrannical man (578a4–5).

In Book IV, Socrates gives a definition of political courage as the disposition to preserve the doctrine that one has learned during the educational process from the legislator concerning what is to be feared and what is not (429b8–d2). Someone with a proper nature and education absorbs the laws into his soul like a dye, acquiring in this way beliefs to which he holds fast in spite of all adverse circumstances and all temptations coming from appetitive pleasures. Spirit is the part of the soul responsible for this endurance in preserving the learned doctrine. This definition does not require a complete absence of fear and should be carefully distinguished from mere boldness, as it includes holding fast to correct beliefs about what is to be feared. The same observation applies to the definition of courage given later on in Book IV, 442b5–9, where courage is described as the endurance of the spirited part in obeying reason's orders and in fighting in order to accomplish what the rational part has decided. This specific endurance that is courage requires a process of harmonization of the spirited and the rational part, achieved through an educational process entailing

---

56. This is the same point made in Xen. *Hiero* 3.1–4.2. The consequences the unsuccessful tyrant risks suffering are graphically illustrated by Polus in the *Gorgias*, and include torture, castration, watching his relatives being tortured, and having his eyes burned out: Plat. *Gorg.* 473c–d. On the idea that a tyrant cannot abdicate, see also Pericles' speech in Thuc. 2.63.

the correct dose of music, poetry, and physical training. While the spirited part is the one primarily responsible for a courageous disposition, the latter nevertheless requires the spirit's harmonization either with the laws or with reason's orders. On this definition, having a spirited nature may be a precondition for courage, but it is not alone sufficient to make someone courageous. The fact that the tyrant has both a stirred spirit and paranoid terrors is clearly not in tension with this definition of courage, for as we have seen, the enslavement of his deranged spirit to his appetites makes him incapable of preserving acquired useful beliefs or of obeying reason. The tyrannical man may be savage, audacious, and daring, but he is certainly not courageous in this sense.

But if the tyrannical man has a stirred and savage spirit, how can we combine the description of the tyrant's paranoid terrors with the observation in Book II (375a11) that spirit is the psychic precondition for the lack of fear? Here indeed Socrates says that a spirited soul will tend to be ἄφοβος and ἀήττητος with regard to external affections and circumstances, and this is why the guardians of the beautiful city need to be spirited (375b7). In particular, the guardians will need to be unafraid of death (386a6–b2), as it is proper for free men to fear slavery more than dying (387b4–6): someone courageous will be able to face death on the battlefield and stay firm in all possible circumstances (399a–b). The tyrant, on the contrary, is not only afraid of dying but also is filled with fears of all kinds. The comparison to a woman at 579b8 indicates that he falls short not only of courage as defined by Socrates but also of more traditional understandings of ἀνδρεῖα as manliness.

The tyrant's pervasive cowardice, lack of manliness, and womanly life could be taken as indicators of an excessively weakened spirit. There are several passages in the dialogue indicating that the excessive softening of spirit is a cause of cowardice. In the discussion on music and gymnastic in Book III (410c8–d5; 411b1–4), where the weakening of spirit is due to excess of musical education and to the lack of an adequate corresponding physical training, spirit does not harmonize with the φιλομαθές part, leading to softness of the soul (μαλακία); in this way, one becomes excessively cultivated and soft. This process goes smoothly in the case of souls that already have a weak spirit by nature, while it is more painful for people who have thumoeidic nature. In this case, spirit does not quickly disappear, but having been softened, it becomes unstable, easily irritated, prone to anger, and filled with discontent (411b7–c2). It is interesting to notice that discontent (δυσκολία) coupled with stubbornness (αὐθάδεια) characterizes an excessively strained spirit as well (590a9–b1). This indicates that the same traits of characters can be caused by different psychic dynamics, depending on the various modes of relations between the three parts of the soul and on the different conditions and states of these parts. While in Book III excess of softness and weakness of spirit are both due to musical overstimulation and the focus is on the relation between the part of the soul that is a lover of learning and spirit, in Book IX they are linked to the domination of the appetitive part. Here softness is coupled with luxuriousness (τρυφή) and is indicated as the cause of vileness or cowardice (δειλία) within the soul (590b3–4).

These references to cowardice link it to the softness of the soul. However, as we have seen, softness is not a character trait of the tyrannical man, who is described as savage as a lycanthrope. Consequently, the tyrant's cowardice cannot be caused by a simple weakening of his spirit caused by excessive musical education or excess of luxuriousness. In fact, it should be noted that spirit can be corrupted in various ways according to specific processes: it can become either too savage or too soft, music can make it weakened, unstable, prone to anger, and irritable at the same time while flattery, slavishness, and subjugation to appetitive desires can even transform it into an ape (590b6–9). This apelike spirit is probably the one belonging to base figures of the likes of Thersites, whom Er sees choosing the life of a monkey in Book X (620c2–3), and hence corresponds to a specific form of degradation.

While the tyrannical man's life is filled with terrors, cowardice and fear are only one aspect of his deranged spirit, for, as I have argued, the tyrannical man is also characterized by impious audacity. Thus, the tyrant is sick with two diseases at the same time, as he has both aspects of a disharmonic soul indicated in Book III: savagery and cowardice (411a3). As Socrates argues, the possibility of the simultaneous presence of two contradictory illnesses of the soul is attested to by the case of Achilles, who is accused both of slavishness (caused by his love for money) and of arrogance toward gods and humans (391c4–6). Since the tyrannical man is the most deranged and disharmonic of all types of man—the unhappiest and most intemperate—it is not surprising that two different illnesses caused by a badly functioning spirit are present in his soul. He is, therefore, not simply a coward but also an aggressive one: someone who deals with presumed or real menaces through violence and aggression, who does not disdain to resort to manipulation, evil plots, false trials, and illegal killings in order to prevent his own fall and death, and who isolates himself in order to try to alleviate his fear of others. He is similar in this respect to another aggressive coward of Greek literature: the tyrannical Aegysthus, whom Cassandra calls a "wolf" in Aeschylus' *Agamemnon* (1258–1260).

Chapter 6

Clever Villains

The Tyrant's Reason

But it was I, the know-nothing Oedipus, who went and stopped her, hitting the mark by intelligence alone, and not by being taught by birds.

Sophocles, Oedipus Tyrannus

Cunning, cleverness, quick-wittedness, and resourcefulness appear prominently in several classical depictions of tyrants. From the mythological Oedipus to historical despots such as Peisistratus, being quick to grasp situations, accurately appraising people, contriving plans, and finding appropriate solutions to crises seems to be a necessary requirement for the job. As the tyrant is never a legitimate ruler, a certain capacity for plotting; a predisposition to foresight; the ability to calculate possible outcomes, decipher signs and quickly grasp allusions and hints, guess people's motivations and ambitions; and cunningly maneuver between internal and external enemies are necessary for both taking and maintaining power. As we learn from the story of Periander and Lycophron, limited intellectual capabilities are incompatible with holding absolute power: Periander preferred to recall his estranged younger son Lycophron to Corinth rather than allow his foolish elder son to succeed him as a tyrant (Hdt. 3.50–53).

As we have seen, Plato's depiction of the tyrant mobilizes an array of traditional literary tropes on the subject. In particular, the *Republic* adopts two of the main features of the tyrannical man common in literary depictions—namely, erotic excess and a predisposition for violence—while systematizing them within Plato's overall moral psychology. Whether a strong rational part should also be considered one of the features of Plato's tyrant, however, is a controversial issue. On certain accounts of the soul's tripartition, this would be incompatible with the role attributed to reason in the dialogue, and the tyrant's instrumental reasoning should, rather, be attributed to the lower parts of his soul (more specifically, to his appetitive part). Moreover, as is the case of the spirited part of the soul, the lack of explicit mention of reason's role in the tyrant's psychology and his management of political power may be taken to suggest that the tyrant has a weak rational part of the soul, that his reason is asleep, and therefore that it does not play any significant role in his corruption. Julia Annas, who persuasively distinguishes between the role played by reason in planning and reason's normative guidance, argues that while in both the democratic and the oligarchic men, reason, in spite of not being in charge in a moral sense, is still able to contrive life plans, this is not the case for the tyrannical man.[1] In fact, any rational pattern is disrupted by the tyrant's obsessive lust for the particular objects of his desire, to the point that he "would not last a week."[2]

As I will show, however, there are good reasons to think that the tyrant is naturally endowed with great rational capabilities and that he belongs among the "wicked, but clever people" mentioned by Socrates in Book VII. More specifically, Plato's tyrant is the *alter ego* of the philosopher or, in other words, a man with a philosophical nature gone astray.

1. Annas 1981, p. 135.
2. Annas 1981, p. 304.

6.1 THE DANGER OF BEING SMART

Before searching for traces of the tyrant's intellectual prowess in the discussion of tyranny in Books VIII and IX, it is worth pausing a moment on two earlier passages that can provide us with evidence that the tyrant not only cannot be unintelligent but must even have some special intellectual capabilities. The first passage, from Book VII, concerns wicked villains:

> On the contrary, the virtue of thought (ἡ δὲ τοῦ φρονῆσαι), it seems, happens to belong above all to something more divine, which never loses its power but—according to the direction in which it is turned— becomes *either useful and advantageous or useless and harmful*. Or have you never considered, about the people who are said to be wicked but clever (πονηρῶν μέν, σοφῶν δέ), how sharp the vision of their little soul is and how keenly it sees through the things toward which it is turned? This is evidence of the fact that it doesn't have poor vision, but rather is forced to be at the service of vice, so that the keener it sees, the more evil it does. (*Rep.* 518d11–519a5)

This passage dispels any doubts we may have about the fact that intellectually endowed people—that is, people with a strong rational part of the soul—can become evil and harmful *without* losing their intellectual capabilities. On the contrary, it is precisely because of the fact that they do have sharpness of mind that they can accomplish great evils. This notion had already been established in the second passage under examination, from Book VI:

> Such are the dimension and character of the ruin and corruption of the best nature with respect to the noblest pursuit, a nature that—as we argue—is at any rate rare. And it is particularly

from these men that come those who do the greatest evil to cities and private men, as well as those who do the greatest good, if by chance the flow draws them in that direction. But a little nature doesn't ever do anything great either to private men or to cities. (495a10–b6)

As mentioned in chapter 3, this passage is part of a lengthy discussion about philosophical natures and their corruption. It indicates that it is not easy to qualify as a philosophical nature, for this character requires an array of specific natural predispositions such as mental sharpness, good memory, quick wits, ease at learning, and high-mindedness. In the passage quoted here, in addition to claiming that this kind of great nature can be the source of the worst evils to the city, Socrates excludes the possibility that people with a petty nature and mediocre capabilities could cause great harm to their community: in order to cause great harm, one needs to have some exceptional qualities such as those mentioned here. As tyranny *is* the greatest danger and the greatest harm for a city, we may take this passage to indicate that these qualities, albeit in a corrupt form, are present in the tyrant's soul.

Keeping these two passages in mind may help us make sense of a potentially misleading aspect of the discussion of tyranny in Books VIII and IX—that is, the fact that the rational part of the soul is never mentioned, with the exception of the passage concerning dreams, where reason appears to be asleep (571c3–5). However, it would seem that Plato's tyrant needs specific cognitive skills in order to do what he does. Taking power requires plotting and deception: the tyrant has to present himself as the champion of the people while hiding his real intentions, to keep the people at bay through careful political maneuvering, to deliberate about which concessions can be made and which should just be hinted at, and to use cunning ruses such as making up false accusations with which to get rid of his enemies

(565c–566a). The same requirement applies to his rule. While the tyrant may not actually be able to govern in Plato's sense—for he has no knowledge of the good, is entirely mistaken about what his advantage is, and is, moreover, incapable of governing himself—his rule does have a clear logic: he does anything necessary to preserve his power in order to be able to satisfy his πλεονεξία and insatiable eros and appetites. This would seem to require some skills and rational calculation, for systematic political maneuvering, using deception, waging opportunistic wars, eliminating internal enemies, and repressing the populace (566d–567b) in order to maintain power are different from mindless and arbitrary acting out or mere rudimentary means–end reasoning. These acts are not simple outbursts of passion, and they are not the outcome of basic thought processes. Rather, they are the result of careful deliberation and entail means–end calculations of a highly complex nature. Moreover, if the tyrant is to successfully maintain his power, he ought to utilize some particularly developed cognitive skills for grasping complex situations and people's hidden motivations, and for foreseeing outcomes of actions and political orders.

If the tyrant is endowed with a strong rational part, and if this part is put at the service of his appetitive desires and contributes to his psychic disorder, then it is necessary to investigate the nature of its corruption, as well as its relation to the other parts of the soul. However, meeting this task requires a preliminary digression into the nature of reason in the *Republic*.

6.2 THE MOTIVATIONAL AND COGNITIVE ASPECT OF REASON

The relevant asymmetries between reason and the other two parts of the soul give it a peculiar status in the *Republic*. The nonrational parts of the soul are best understood as sources of motivation endowed with some nonrational cognitive abilities. Their status as specific cognitive faculties, however, is less clear. They are both bearers of specific kinds of desire and conducive to specific kinds of pleasures. While they do not participate in reason, they can be guided by the rule of reason and can have nonrational cognitive access to perceptions mediated by reason, and therefore can both be habituated and have their desires shaped accordingly. They are also particularly sensitive to sensory appearances and yield their assent to them unreflectively, as they are unable to weigh evidence and calculate.[3] We learn from the discussion of education in Books II and III that spirit can be triggered or tamed by kinds of harmony and rhythm, as well as images, while Book X insists on the reactions of the nonrational part of the soul[4] to perceptual phenomena such as visual illusions (*Rep.* 602e–603b and 604–605c). Furthermore, there are good grounds to think that, while the nonrational parts of the soul cannot form the rational beliefs and engage in the means–end reasoning that belongs only to reason, they do have the cognitive ability to form nonrational beliefs.[5] But there is no textual evidence that they play a specific and unique constitutive function in the organization of sense-perception and in the formation of perceptual data. In other words, there is no evidence that the two nonrational parts of the souls should be understood as specific cognitive faculties.

On the contrary, the cognitive function and abilities of reason are better delineated. The rational part of the soul is indicated through

---

3. Lorenz 2006, p. 68; Moss 2008; and Ganson 2009.

4. I take this to be an umbrella term including both appetite and spirit. For interpretations along the lines of this reading that support the consistency between the tripartition of Book IV and the partition of the soul in Book X, see Adam 1963, vol. 2, p. 40; Penner 1971, pp. 96–118; Lorenz 2006, p. 65; Moss 2008; Ganson 2009. For an argument against the notion of a division of the rational part, see Siewert 2001. For the opposite view, that the division of the soul in Book X is inconsistent with that of Book IV, arguing for a partition of reason, see Nehamas 1982; Burnyeat 1997, p. 223. For a reading of the passage as presenting a bipartition between reason and appetite, see Annas 1981, p. 131.

5. Lorenz 2006, part 2.

an array of terms, some appearing more frequently in the context of discussions concerning motivation, others emphasizing reason's distinctive cognitive role. The pair of interchangeable terms τὸ φιλομαθές and τὸ φιλόσοφον (indicating, respectively, desire for learning and desire for wisdom) stresses reason's motivational role and its moral significance.[6] As love of learning, wisdom, and truth are all labels for reason, it can be argued that in a certain respect reason *is* a kind of desire. Reason also has the ability to generate rational desires, or evaluative desires, which depend on the judgment and rational belief that the object of the desire under discussion is a good of some sort.[7] On a restrictive reading of this point, the desires of reason, which are generated by its activity of seeking goodness and truth, are rational only if reason is not mistaken in pursuing these goals and choosing the appropriate means.[8] However, whether reason *as* desire can also be interpreted in this limited manner is another matter. Rather than depending on a rational belief, it seems that the desire to inquire and discover the truth is of a *conative* nature, which means that whoever has a rational part within her soul will, by the same token, have this inborn desire, albeit in varying degrees.[9] As we will see, this inborn conative desire can be corrupted and misfire entirely.

The term τὸ λογιστικόν, together with the terms διάνοια and νοῦς (used both in their generic sense to indicate mind or thought and in their specific meaning to indicate two specific and distinct kinds of thought—i.e., discursive reason and understanding), stress the role of reason as the faculty of reasoning. Therefore, we calculate, learn, understand intelligible realities, make rational deliberations, and give orders through the rational part of the soul. These, however, are not

---

6. See, for example, *Rep.* 411e4–6, 435e6, 581b10, 581c5.
7. Siewert 2001.
8. Ganson 2009, p. 188.
9. Cooper 1984, p. 5, defines the desires of reason as impulses that one has merely in virtue of having a mind.

its only cognitive activities, for Socrates attributes a further role to reason, a role that combines its motivational and cognitive aspect, as well as its practical and theoretical activity. In contrast to the nonrational parts, reason has both the ability and the task to acquire knowledge of what is good for each part of the soul and for the soul as a whole, to deliberate accordingly, and to give orders to the other parts of the soul (442c4–7). This entails that reason be able to take into account the desires and pleasures proper to the other parts of the soul, discriminate between the ones that should be pursued and the ones that shouldn't, and lead the other two parts in such a way as to make the soul harmonious:

> Then let's not fear to say that even those desires of the money-loving and of the honor-loving part that receive the pleasures prescribed by the rational part by following knowledge and reason and by pursuing them with their help, will receive the truest pleasures—to the extent that it is possible for them to receive true pleasures—because they follow truth. And they will receive the pleasures that are proper to them, if indeed what is best for each thing is what it's proper to it. (586d4–e2)[10]

To actually grasp what is good for the whole soul, reason needs a philosophical education. Going through the laborious educational process culminating in dialectics and knowledge of the Good requires a specific kind of motivation, provided by the inborn love of learning belonging to reason. In fact, this desire also determines how far an individual will go in his studies and whether he will actually be able to grasp intelligible realities or contrarily whether he will incorrectly identify the Good.[11] The unity of practical and theoretical activity is

10. See also *Rep.* 431c5–7.
11. Reeve 2006, pp. 96–99.

apparent in the educational curriculum articulated in Book VII, as this course of study is not meant just to transmit content but also to operate both as a progressive conversion of the soul away from the prioritization of sensible experience and as a progressive redirection of the inner sight already present in each soul (518b–d).[12] Finally, theoretical knowledge of the Good and the other forms, on the one hand, and practical self-transformation and self-rule, on the other, are virtually inseparable, as once reason begets truth and understanding (490b2–b6) and possesses them, it also by the same token imitates it, ordering and unifying the soul to create a likeness of the Good within it (500c–d).[13] The long section of the dialogue running across Books VI and VIII dedicated to the discussion of the Form of the Good, the divided line, the allegory of the cave, and the educational curriculum of the would-be philosophers is the *locus* where the imbrication of metaphysics, moral psychology, epistemology, and politics is most explicitly articulated. While in these pages we learn what reason can achieve when oriented toward the proper object and properly educated in appropriate philosophical natures, we must now analyze what happens to reason in the tyrant.

6.3 THE CORRUPTION OF REASON

As outlined here, it is possible to identify three main characteristics of the rational part of the soul: (i) reason is the faculty of reasoning or calculating; (ii) it has the capacity and tasks of evaluating what is good for itself and for the entire soul and of giving orders to the other two parts of the soul; and finally (iii) it is itself a form of desire, the

---

12. Miller 2007.

13. For a discussion of the union of practical and theoretical activity in Plato's conception of reason and knowledge, see Peters 1989.

desire for learning, wisdom, and truth. When addressing the corruption of reason in the tyrant's soul it is therefore necessary to investigate whether all three sides are involved in and perverted by this process.

Socrates' discussion of the case of the oligarchic man suggests that the calculative part can be corrupted if enslaved to the appetites (*Rep.* 553d1–4). The oligarchic man utilizes the calculative faculties of reason to realize the life goal (i.e., the accumulation of wealth) set by the appetitive part. In this case, once the appetitive part of the soul establishes the goals and values to be pursued, it is the work of reason to contrive a plan conducive to the satisfaction of these goals. In this case, reason has entirely abdicated its normative rule, although, as argued by Klosko, in a sense it still leads the soul, for it elaborates and presides over the plan while also defending it from drives and desires that may challenge it.[14] In the case of the oligarchic man, reason has to oppose appetitive desires that would entail unnecessary expenditures or excessive greed that would cause loss of social prestige, for both of these desires would jeopardize the life-goal of accumulating wealth (554c11–d3).

We may imagine a similar role for reason in the tyrannical soul. For example, it is reason that—enslaved to the appetites—contrives the plan to take power and calculates the means to maintain it in order to enable the tyrannical man to unleash and satisfy his inexhaustible appetitive desires. While the text does not explicitly extend this consideration to the case of the tyrant, there is no reason to believe that this extension is unjustified. Rather, the fact that managing a tyranny requires skills in rational calculation equally (if not more) complex than those required for a successful businessman would

---

14. Klosko expresses this point by distinguishing between the direct and the normative rule of reason. Reason directly rules in every soul, but in nonphilosophical souls it only plays an instrumental role akin to Humean reason: Klosko 1988.

seem to warrant attributing an active role to the calculative aspect of reason, even in its subordination to the tyrant's appetites.

Despite playing this active role, reason does not rule normatively in either the oligarchic man or in the tyrant, for it does not autonomously set values and goals for itself and for the whole soul. This, however, does not mean that the motivational aspect of reason is not involved in the process of moral corruption, or that it is merely forced into silence and ineffectuality. As I will show in what follows, both reason as the bearer of moral beliefs concerning the good of the whole soul and its conative aspect as desire of learning and truth are corrupted, too. Moreover, they do contribute to the moral disorder of the tyrannical soul.

There are several passages scattered throughout the dialogue that mention dangerous beliefs and their nefarious impact on young, intelligent people. In Book II, for example, Adeimantus mentions the belief (supported by both private individuals and poets) that unjust deeds are more profitable than just ones, and he proceeds to discuss the effect that such beliefs have on young people endowed with intellectual skills:

> All such things that are said concerning virtue and vice as well as concerning the consideration that gods and humans have of them, what effect shall we think they have on the souls of young people, dear Socrates? I mean *those who are smart by nature and who, jumping on all of these sayings*—so to speak—*are able to draw conclusions from them* about what sort of man one should be and what road one should travel to lead his life as best as possible. (*Rep.* 365a4–b1)

As Adeimantus argues, these smart young people will reach the conclusion that it is profitable to act on these beliefs and will therefore form secret societies and political clubs in order to manipulate assemblies and courts through persuasion and force (365c–d). In chapter 2, I discussed the political significance of these references to secret clubs and their underlying reference to the crisis of Athenian democracy in the last third of the fifth century. If read in the light of the present discussion about the rational part of the soul and the overarching political context of the *Republic*, this passage further conveys interesting insights about the political dangers deriving from the moral corruption of young elites endowed with intellectual capabilities and hence from the moral corruption of reason itself.

A further passage from Book VII expands on the effects of moral relativism on young minds. In this exchange, Socrates is discussing the educational curriculum for the philosopher-kings and articulates the reasons why the study of dialectics may turn out to be a dangerous business and is, therefore, best postponed to a mature age. This passage is particularly relevant because, contrary to the discussion of poetry and music in Books II, III, and X, it addresses a different form of corruption based not on images, rhythms, and harmonies appealing to the nonrational parts of the soul but, rather, on rational arguments and the misuse of refutation. A person who approaches dialectics too young not only runs the risk of indulging in the game of refutation for its own sake or to satisfy his competitiveness but is also potentially drawn to lawlessness, owing to the refutation and consequent abandonment of the traditional beliefs given by the lawgiver which he had previously held:

> After this, what do you think he will do with regard to honoring and obeying these beliefs? —It's inevitable that he will not honor and obey them in the same way anymore. —Then, when he no longer considers these beliefs either honorable or suitable to him and can't find out the true ones, to what other kind of life will he likely give himself up if not to the one that flatters him? . . . *Then, I suppose, from being law-abiding he will appear to have become lawless.* (538e3–539a3)

This passage parallels the discussion of madness and beliefs in the case of the tyrannical man (573a–b and 574d–e). In this case, too, new beliefs conveyed by the flatterers supplant old ones that the tyrannical man had learned from his father, leading to lawlessness. The relevant difference is that in this case, the tyrannical man is ready to adopt these new beliefs because he is already stung by eros and an array of uncontrollable appetites. But like in the passage from Book VII, the tyrannical man adopts the beliefs that flatter him—that is, those that allow him to justify the satisfaction of every appetite, and in particular of those that are against the law. We are now in a better position to interpret the reference to the sleep of reason in lawless dreams. Far from indicating a mere absence of reason or a lack of activity on its part, the sleep of reason should be understood as reason abdicating its task of autonomously setting the moral goals to be pursued in the life of an individual. In a sense, one may say that the sleep of reason is madness, understood as the new lawless beliefs adopted by reason because of its enslavement to appetites and eros.

While Socrates does not offer a full-fledged discussion of the content of these maddening beliefs, it is likely that these are (mistaken) beliefs about the good. These mistakes of judgment make the tyrant delusional, as he lives his whole life as if it were a megalomaniacal dream of incest, paraphilia, murders, and cannibalism (576b). It is reason that, enslaved to the appetitive part, endorses these mad beliefs, as it misidentifies what is good and what makes one happy. Socrates' characterization of the birth of tyranny as the natural outcome of the principle of freedom that dominates in the democratic regime helps identify the specific content of these beliefs. Democratic freedom is interpreted as the freedom to do whatever one wishes. Plato attributes to Thrasymachus and Callicles the belief that the tyrant is supremely happy because he alone enjoys a freedom that can be compared to Zeus' freedom in *Prometheus Bound*: unaccountable and unrestrained. In Book II, Glaucon eloquently voices this belief through the story of Gyges, and Adeimantus refers to the belief that unjust deeds are more profitable than just ones. The viewpoint that complete impunity and having the power to do whatever one wishes make the tyrant a blessedly happy man is a good candidate for the μανία, or new set of beliefs that replace the old, traditional ones in the tyrannical man's soul. And people like Thrasymachus, the supporters of this conception of freedom and of its appropriation by those who hold tyrannical power (whether the demos as a whole or a single man), are good candidates for the role of tyrant-makers (τυραννοποιοί; 572e4–5). These tyrant-makers persuade the would-be tyrannical man that complete lawlessness equates to complete freedom (572d9–e1). It is this belief—the belief in one's entitlement to a form of happiness that can only be achieved by raising oneself above both human and divine law—that mutilates spirit's capacity for internal control of the appetites and to feel shame.

In fact, these mistaken beliefs about the good are not just a consequence of the corrupting effect of the combination of eros, unrestrained appetites, bad education, city life under democracy, and sophistic arguments. They also act as an ancillary cause in the moral and psychic disorder of the tyrannical man, as they offer a pseudorational justification of his behavior, provide a life-plan in terms of (im)moral goals, and free the spirit from its attachment to received laws and customs and therefore from shame. This interpretation necessitates explaining how spirit accesses reason's mad beliefs.[15] To at least begin a solution, one must notice that nothing in the psychic dynamic just described requires spirit to have an autonomous capacity to interpret and evaluate ethical notions or to make rational or proto-rational judgments of a moral sort. It is sufficient for it to

---

15. For a discussion of the cognitive faculties of the nonrational parts of the soul, see Irwin 1977; Moline 1978; Kahn 1987, particularly p. 85; Klosko 1988; Boeri 2010; Lorenz 2006; Blackson 2010.

have the capacity for passively gaining *some* access to reason's beliefs and judgments and to affectively respond to them while occasionally influencing reason in turn. In other words, spirit must have some passive cognitive capacity that does not constitute a capacity for reasoning. Reason's madness—that is, the acquisition of new tyrannical beliefs—is sufficient to unleash a spirit that is already influenced by the appetitive part's violent domination.

The active corruptive role played by these beliefs of reason is hinted at by Socrates' adoption of the metaphor of the bodyguard in his depiction of the soul of the tyrant, as the new beliefs released from slavery become the bodyguard of erotic love and *rule* (κρατήσουσι) along with it (574d7–8). This passage indicates that reason still plays the role that naturally belongs to it (that of giving orders to the other parts of the soul), but that it is doing this as a sort of *proxy*—that is, acting on behalf of the appetites and eros to which it is truly enslaved. While reason does rationally articulate the (im)moral goals to be pursued, it does so by yielding to the appetitive part's and appetitive eros' inclinations, rather than by grasping these goals on its own by virtue of philosophical education.

So far we have seen that the corruption of reason concerns both the instrumentalization of rational capabilities and the perversion of reason's role of ruling the soul by identifying what the good for the whole soul is. But what about the conative side of reason—that is, its nature as a specific form of desire for learning, knowledge, and the good? The passage from Book VII quoted earlier, concerning the corruption of reason through a precocious education in dialectic, may provide some further useful indication to answer this question. The impact of the misuse of refutation on a young mind appeals to the youth's desire for learning and finding the truth. The discussion about the dangers of the early study of dialectics—which provides the context from the passage from Book VII—revolves around a specific kind of youth, one endowed not only with good rational cognitive skills but also with a strong φιλομαθὲς. These are the kind of people who, when learning dialectic too early, will tend to misuse it, enjoying the art of refutation for its own sake rather than for the sake of truth (539c). However, it takes some rational talent, some willingness to learn how to play with arguments, some pleasure in discovering contradictions, in order to indulge in the sport of refutation, rather than spending time in other more intuitively pleasurable activities.[16] Even if we admit that spirited competition is the main source of pleasure in such an endeavor, given that the desire for victory can be satisfied through an array of alternative agonistic activities that do not entail the hassle of going through a laborious intellectual education, the conative aspect of reason must play an active role in this specific form of corruption. Thus, the discussion about the dangers of dialectic and the lawlessness it can generate is a discussion concerning—among other things—cases in which the very desire of learning that is reason can be corrupted and oriented toward the wrong objects. In the case of the youth approaching dialectic too early, refutation becomes a competitive game, and the desire to learn—which is still necessary to the study of dialectic—is subordinated to the desire for victory and honor.

The case of the tyrannical man is clearly different insofar as he is enslaved not to spirit but to appetites and eros. However, this insight concerning the possible corruption of reason's desire for learning and truth may also be applied to his case. While there is no hint of his predisposition for the game of refutation or intellectual interests in the discussion of the tyrannical man, there is a specific kind of will to knowledge

---

16. According to Reeve, the desire for the pleasure of knowing also determines the level of technical and intellectual skills that one is able to muster, and this is why a honor-lover will never experience the pleasure of knowing the truth: Reeve 2006, pp. 96–97. However, precisely because desire determines the kind of intellectual skills one can develop, some love of learning must be involved whenever some dialectical skills are acquired, albeit they end up being misused in futile competitive games and do not yield knowledge as a result.

displayed in the description of the tyrant's paranoia and obsession with his real and alleged enemies. The tyrant lives his life suspecting others of being opposed to him and plotting against him: "He must, therefore, observe with a sharp eye (ὀξέως ἄρα δεῖ ὁρᾶν) anyone who is brave, high-minded, smart, or rich" (567b10–c1). The tyrant will therefore be—in a sense—keen-sighted. Keen sight, a quality that Socrates attributes to the guardians in Book VI (ὀξὺ ὁρῶντα; 484c1–2), recurs here, but with an altogether different meaning. In the case of the guardians, being keen-sighted means being oriented to the knowledge of the forms necessary to establish and guard just laws and customs in the beautiful city, while in the case of the tyrant, it means being constantly alert to the motivations and actions of his subjects for the sake of guarding his own power. This paranoid will to knowledge is a parody of the orientation to knowledge of the guardians, but it is nevertheless the result of the corruption of the same conative aspect of reason as desire of learning and truth.

Based on this analysis, it would appear that all aspects of reason are deeply corrupt, to the point that even reason's desire for knowledge is reshaped into its caricature. However, adopting this interpretation may seem to leave the tyrant's psychic conflict unexplained. The fact that eros leads his whole soul has even been taken as indicating that—paradoxically enough—the tyrant's soul is more unified than other corrupt souls and the tyrannical life is characterized by greater coherence than the other vicious lives.[17] This view, however, is problematic, insofar as harmony and unity are virtues, and the tyrant has no shred of virtue left in his soul. In order to find an alternative solution, we need to refer to the nature of the appetitive part of the soul and to examine why, in spite of enslaving reason, appetites will still be in conflict with it.

---

17. See, for example, Nucci 2001 and Pappas 2013, pp. 191–192.

Not by chance, the depiction of appetites in Book IX is much more colorful and somber than what we had found in Book IV: the appetitive part is akin to an enormous hydra with a multitude of heads, some of gentle animals and others of savage ones, that can grow and change at will (588c–d). While the human being who is in control of itself and has received the proper education will feed and domesticate the gentle beasts, the tyrant consistently feeds the savage ones. As argued in chapter 4, his appetites are multiplied and intensified (or eroticized) by eros. The multiplicity of appetites and their savagery are the source of his psychic conflict, for the limitations of spatio-temporal existence make it impossible to satisfy all these savage appetites at once. Moreover, prudential considerations— primarily, concerns for self-preservation and for the preservation of his power—make it impossible for the tyrant to satisfy at least some of them in his given circumstances. In both cases, reason—at times with the help of spirit, at times against spirit—will need to express aversion to some appetites and their objects, and a conflict will ensue. Reason will need to express aversion to some appetites for the sake of satisfying others that cannot be satisfied at the same time or to maintain the possibility of limitless appetitive enjoyment open by preserving the tyrant's life and his political power. As argued by Siewert, reason gives mental commands based on the evaluation that to do a given course of action is best on the whole considering the available information about circumstances and conditions. These mental commands are active desires of reason formed on the basis of beliefs concerning the good or what is best in given circumstances.[18] Therefore, while the tyrant's savage appetites are self-referential and do not take into account enabling conditions, his reason will (mis)calculate for the good of the whole soul and express aversions to appetites that, in given circumstances, would endanger the possibility

18. Siewert 2001.

of continuing appetitive enjoyment (for example, by causing death). Socrates' insight about the conflict between reason and appetites, therefore, applies to the tyrant's soul, in spite of reason's enslavement to the appetitive part. The more savage and numerous the tyrant's appetites, the more violent the conflict and the greater the amount of psychic suffering.

While the mechanisms of the interaction between the parts of the soul are not mentioned, this conflict appears quite clear from the passages referring to the unhappiness of the tyrant:

> And isn't the tyrant tied in this kind of prison, being naturally such as we described him, filled with many fears and erotic loves of all kinds? *Even though he is really curious in his soul,* he is the only one in the whole city who cannot go anywhere abroad or see the sights that the other free people desire to see. Instead, he lives like a woman, buried at home most of the time, and envious of the other citizen whenever they travel abroad and see something good. (579b1–c2)

This inner conflict is evidenced by the fact that the tyrant is greedy for traveling abroad and enjoying various sights, but *instead* is confined to his house. In order to be confined to his house, an order must have been given against his desire to travel, and reason is the most likely candidate for expressing this aversion and giving this order. Moreover, as the reference to the tyrant's many erotic loves suggests, abiding by the order of reason to preserve his own life does not tame or appease his appetitive desires, which therefore keep tormenting him with their sting.

In conclusion, all aspects of the tyrant's reason are corrupt because of its enslavement to a lawless appetitive part, but corruption and enslavement do not translate into a greater unity of the tyrant's soul, for reason will constantly need to fight against one appetite or another because of prudential considerations and because of the limitations inherent to spatiotemporal existence, which set objective limits to the possibility of satisfying his endless and savage appetites.

6.4 THE TYRANT AND THE PHILOSOPHER

In the *Gorgias*, while speaking of the superior man, Callicles makes the prescriptive point that a man who wants to live correctly must allow his appetites to grow and multiply, and also have sufficient intelligence to find the ways to satisfy them (*Gorg.* 491e5–492a3). Callicles' idealized tyrant is a man superior to others on account of his political skills, intelligence, and courage, entitled on the basis of such natural endowments to be slave to no one and to devote his life to the satisfaction of increasingly numerous and large appetites by *employing his skills* for such a purpose. A similar point is made by Thrasymachus in Book I of the *Republic*, for his tyrannical ruler makes no mistakes in the management of power to his own advantage and his own injustice qualifies as good judgment (εὐβουλία; 348d2). Accordingly, Socrates refutes Thrasymachus and Callicles by portraying a tyrannical figure who would, indeed, be endowed with the natural goods they ascribed to him and would be capable of good judgment, but instead squanders his natural qualities to end up the most wretched of all men. Consistent with traditional depictions, Plato's tyrant is characterized by exceptionality. Not only are his appetites exceptionally lawless but he also possesses a strong spirit and rational part, which, once corrupted by the appetites, further contribute to his moral corruption and its dangerous nature, for himself and for others. The tyrant is, therefore, an appetitive figure of a very different kind from the appetitive money-makers of Kallipolis, who do not have the natural rational endowment necessary to pursue the superior form of life destined to the guardians and philosophers. On the contrary, if he had not been corrupted by the ethos of the demos and by the beliefs propagated by the tyrant-makers who flourish in democratic cities, the tyrant could have become a philosopher. This man with extraordinary intellectual resources is far more dangerous than one dominated by his appetites out of intellectual weakness. The latter will never be capable of great misdeeds. The former, on the contrary, will utilize his rare intellectual capabilities and put them at the service of his basest desires and the terrible crimes needed to satisfy them.

That the tyrant is a denatured philosopher or a man with a philosophical nature gone astray is suggested by the claim that only great natures can cause great harm, in the discussion in Book VI concerning the corruption of philosophical natures within the democratic city (*Rep.* 495a10–b6).[19] These great natures are characterized by both a predisposition to courage (hence a strong spirited part of the soul) and a set of intellectual skills and strong desire for learning. The distinction that Socrates makes between nature (φύσις) and character (ἦθος) (for example, when he speaks of becoming what one ought to be; 493a1) explains how men of great character can fall to such a level of corruption. At 496a11–5, Socrates argues that a well-reared ἦθος is the one who remains consistent with φύσις, because the philosopher is in exile and hence cannot participate in political affairs, because there are no corruptors, or because the city is too small to corrupt such a great soul. Resorting for a moment to an Aristotelian terminology, we might understand nature in terms of a set of inborn capacities and predispositions that require actualization and development in order to become a character or stable disposition, and may therefore not be realized if the environment, the education, or the

---

19. The identification of the tyrant with a corrupt philosophical nature has been suggested by Nucci 2001; Giorgini 2005; Larivée 2005. See especially the excellent discussion of this point in Larivée 2012.

way of life of a person is not suitable to its realization. This reading is confirmed by the metaphor of the seed at 491d1–5, where it appears clear that the philosophical nature ought to be planted and nourished in appropriate ways and in suitable seasons and conditions in order to develop well. Furthermore, a few lines later (497a3–5), Socrates says that someone with a philosophical nature will grow (αὐξήσεται) more fully within a community that has a suitable constitution and will save the community as well as himself. The verb αὐξήσεται indicates natural growth, along the lines of the earlier metaphor of the seed, hence it can be taken as a reference to the idea of the actualization of a natural potentiality.[20] It must also be noted that this passage conveys the idea that participation in ruling a city with a suitable constitution provides the favorable conditions for a fuller flourishing of a philosophical nature.

In general, the thrust of Socrates' discussion about the degradation of philosophical natures is that under the existing constitutions only a small number of philosophical men escape corruption. Those who escape this fate cannot do it alone, but are saved only by a divine dispensation (θεοῦ μοῖρα): divine intervention is needed in order to realize a philosophical nature. It is precisely the array of natural goods belonging to them (*Rep.* 491b7–c4) that puts philosophical natures in such a danger. A young man with talent and goods of such a rare kind will be the privileged object of flattery for politicians and fellow citizens, who will want to use his talent for their own purposes and will not hesitate to resort to persuasion and, when necessary, to compulsion (494b8–e7). The main source of corruption identified by Socrates in this discussion is the political life of the city and, only in the second instance, the private education imparted by the sophists. Indeed, even if one received a proper private education, one would

---

20. I'm grateful to Melissa Lane for pointing out the relevance of the verb αὐξήσεται in this passage.

hardly escape corruption because of the morbid character of the city and its political life as such. Moreover, a young man with such a rare nature, good family connections, and wealth, but flattered by corruptors, will tend to become utterly ambitious and systematically overestimate his own capabilities (494c7–d1).

This corruption also explains why the eros of the philosopher and that of the tyrant—both of whom are passionate lovers *by nature*—take opposite paths. While the eros of the first is tamed through education and is channeled toward the proper object, the eros of the second is untamed and channeled toward improper objects because the tyrant has not received the appropriate education and is exposed to the corruption of city life. In the first case, eros becomes a powerful ally of reason; in the second, it is degraded into a large winged drone ruling over appetites, which together with madness blinds the tyrant. In this light we can better see how a mistaken understanding of freedom as the license to do whatever one wishes breeds tyranny. The lack of proper boundaries between the permitted and the forbidden, and the absence of the limiting effects that a strong collective ethos has on an individual, contributes to the unrestrained character acquired by the eros of the tyrant, who appropriates for himself all the liberties of his fellow citizens.

6.5 SUMMARY REMARKS

The analysis of the tyrant's psyche articulated in these pages has presented a figure characterized by exceptionality that can rightly play the role of the philosopher's *alter ego*. The tyrant is a figure of extreme moral corruption in whom exceptional natural talents are perverted and put at the service of unrestrained appetitive passions, and in whose soul psychic conflict rages as reason has entirely abdicated its normative rule over the soul while still enabling the tyrannical man to do great harm to himself and others. If we take the tyrant to be a denatured philosopher, it appears clear that Plato's intention in describing such a type of man was not to provide a generalization of the features belonging to tyrants based on empirical observation of actual tyrannies. Certainly, we cannot take Plato to argue that all—or even most—historical tyrants were denatured philosophers. As discussed in Part I, Plato's depiction of tyranny mobilizes anti-tyrannical democratic tropes in order to subvert democratic discourse and undermine the purported polar opposition between the values of democracy and those of tyranny. Alcibiades, while not explicitly mentioned, lurks behind the pages devoted to the corruption of philosophical natures and represents the figure of an exceptionally talented man who, instead of following Socrates' advice to take care of his soul and practice philosophy, developed into a greedy, licentious, appetitive, and overly ambitious demagogue and scoundrel, causing great harm to Athens. While in Book VI, Socrates speaks of existing corrupt constitutions in general, it is clear that Athenian democracy is what he actually has in mind, as emerges from the reference to the corrupting effects of public gatherings, such as assemblies, courts, and theaters (492b), and from the famous passage comparing the demos gathered in assembly or in courts to a huge, moody beast (493a6–b5).

The analysis of the tyrant's psyche in these pages therefore confirms the interpretation of Plato's treatment of tyranny as a critique of democracy, for the political and moral problem addressed throughout the dialogue is precisely that of the emergence of tyrannical figures out of the ethos and institutions of democracy, of the formation of a tyrannical kind of political leader of the demos, and of the corruption by democracy of elite young citizens, endowed with the skills and abilities to pursue a philosophical life.

Conclusion

In Book IX, Socrates triumphantly announces that he has success-fully demonstrated that a tyrant lives a life 729 times more wretched than that of a kingly man (*Rep.* 587d11–e4). This is the final mo-ment of the refutation of Thrasymachus, Glaucon, and Adeimantus' thesis that the tyrant is the happiest man in virtue of his license to do whatever he wants and satisfy his greed with impunity. With this final move, Socrates also completes the subversion of the democratic tenet concerning the polar relationship of democracy and tyranny as opposition between freedom and slavery. Rule by the philosopher-king replaces democracy in this antagonism. While democracy is the natural parent of tyranny, the beautiful city ruled philosophically is the genuinely free city opposed to tyrannical slavery. While the freedom cherished by the democratic city is nothing but license of appetitive enjoyment and serves as fertile soil for the private appro-priation of this license by a tyrant, the freedom of the kingly person and of the city ruled philosophically is the only kind of freedom gen-uinely opposed to tyranny.

Plato's critique of Athenian democracy is, therefore, neither a benevolent critique aimed at highlighting its limitations and at stim-ulating reforms and correctives within this particular form of govern-ment, nor a secondary concern of a text otherwise mostly preoccupied with moral psychology. As my analysis has shown, Plato's opposition to democracy is straightforward and internally connected to his moral arguments and preoccupations. As discussed in chapter 3, interpreters who have defended Plato from accusations of being a proto-totalitarian thinker have emphasized the openness and dialogical character of Plato's philosophy, the pluralism characterizing the figure of Socrates in his ability to speak in multiple voices and represent others' positions, the gentleness of the democracy depicted in Book VIII, or the incorporation in Plato's dialogues of democratic practices such as *parrhesia*. However, the emphasis on these features of Plato's philosophy—and of the *Republic*—misses the target. The case can be made that some liberal principles characterize Plato's practice of philosophy as it is articulated in the dialogues. And certainly philosophical practice as understood by Plato would be impossible without open confrontation between differing positions, rational justification of claims, and persuasion based on the notion that philosophical ideas cannot be inculcated but can only be grasped by an individual through maieutic help. However, extending the preceding points in order to characterize Plato as a democratic thinker, or at least as not hostile to democracy, neglects the distinction between liberalism and democracy.

Liberalism—in its minimal definition—is a doctrine of individual rights, which identifies in individual liberty the primary political value and allows restrictions on liberty only if justified. Democracy, however, is a form of government, a method of decision-making based on the presupposition of the equality of the participants at one stage or another of the collective process of deliberation. While democracy does have a relation to liberalism, this relation is contingent and not constitutive; in fact, not all democratic theory (and reality) is liberal and, vice versa, liberalism without democracy is both a conceptual possibility and a historical reality.

Athenian democracy did have features that may qualify as *liberal*. In Pericles' *Funeral Oration*, for example, we find notions akin to tolerance and a defense of privacy. Athenian democracy, however, was fundamentally a specific form of government, the core of which was popular rule and the sovereignty of the Athenian demos, both in the Assemblies and in the Courts. The freedom that was central to its ideology can hardly be decoupled from the key tenet of popular rule as the absence of a master. But it is precisely the principle of popular rule that Plato attacks over and over again in the *Republic*. His treatment of tyranny is meant to show that popular rule "naturally" breeds tyranny and creates tyrannical figures in the form of democratic leaders, both because of the corrupt ethos of the demos and because of the institutional mechanisms of democracy. Insofar as Plato's critique addresses precisely the relation between the demos and its leaders, even a more restricted version of democracy than the direct democracy of fifth- and fourth-century Athens—one, for example, recognizing the citizens' equal right to select competent representatives—would be incompatible with the political argument of the *Republic*, or at least with its analysis of the ethos of the masses and its disdain for their political incompetence.

However, while Plato does articulate a straightforwardly antidemocratic argument in the *Republic*, he is certainly not the proto-totalitarian thinker that Popper saw. Moreover, his critique of democracy raises relevant questions even for readers such as myself, who defend the validity of democratic principles in their most radical version. In particular, Plato's analysis of the demagogic leaders' manipulation of the masses and use of military force resembles the modern phenomenon of Bonapartism—that is, of authoritarian centralized governments revolving around a charismatic leader appealing to the anti-elitist sentiments of the masses and supported by the army. His psychopathology of the tyrannical leader could serve as the faithful psychological portrait of a number of contemporary tyrants. And his harmonization of political government with the principle of justice appeals to the necessity for political theory to articulate the connection between political organization and ethical concerns. Finally, to use Mario Vegetti's expression, in the *Republic*, Plato elaborates a "big politics" in which moral philosophy intersects with political utopianism, envisaging the necessity and possibility of radical transformation.[1]

This analysis of Plato's anti-tyrannical (and anti-democratic) argument in the dialogue shows that, in fact, the *Republic*'s appeals to radical change and to philosophers' participation in it should be taken seriously. The conclusion of my analysis of the tyrannical man's psyche argues that Plato's tyrant is a potential philosopher gone bad. This interpretation bears relevant consequences for the question of the relationship between philosophy and politics in the *Republic*. Several passages appear to provide some textual ground for a depoliticized reading of the dialogue as putting forward the idea that philosophers should stay away from engagement in political activity *tout court*. In the final conversation of Book IX, after having conclusively stated the immense superiority of the pleasure and way of the life of the kingly man (the philosopher) in comparison with the tyrannical man, Socrates argues that those who shape their souls on the model of the ideal constitution will not care for the honors and recognition they may obtain from a corrupt city by assimilating the ideas about the good and happiness held by the many. They will, instead, refuse to participate in its political affairs and consider themselves inhabitants of the ideal city, *unless some divine chance intervenes* (591d–592b). Similarly, in Book VI, when addressing those rare cases of philosophical natures that, in spite of the adverse political circumstances in which they find themselves, develop into good characters out of luck or divine intervention, Socrates claims that these worthy philosophers will live a quiet life, cultivating their souls away from politics, as if taking refuge behind a little wall (496a–e).

---

1. Vegetti 2009b, p. 174. On what Plato can still teach us, see also Lane 2011.

In Book VII, Socrates argues that those who have dwelled among intelligible realities are unwilling to take care of human affairs, and are instead eager to spend all their time above, among the Forms (517c–d). Moreover, if the philosopher happened to turn from the study of the true beings to human evils, the prisoners of the cave would gladly kill him, not recognizing him as someone who had a grasp of the truth but, rather, taking him as a fool (517d). As this remark does not fit well with the idea that the class of the money-makers will willingly accept the rule of the philosopher-kings, it would seem that at this stage Socrates is addressing the ascent from and descent into a corrupt city.

In a famous passage from Book V (*Rep.* 473c11–e1), Socrates claims that the beautiful city can be realized only if philosophers come to power. Since Kallipolis is not in place yet, this passage refers to those very rare men who became philosophers by divine chance in spite of the surrounding corruption. These men do not have any obligation whatsoever to the city they are going to rule and, for some interpreters, it is unclear why they should aspire to power.[2]

This question is taken up again in the discussion of the allegory of the cave in Book VII. Philosophers who have become such in spite of the city in which they live, have no obligation to take care of the political affairs of a corrupt city and are allowed to remain in the "Isles of the Blessed": they are like plants that have grown spontaneously, without being sown and tended by the constitution of their city, and hence have no moral obligation to their city (520b1–5). On the contrary, the founders of the beautiful city will compel the philosophers who have been reared by the city itself to pay back their debt by taking charge of its political affairs (520b6–c1). The

---

2. Leo Strauss even suggests that this passage is the decisive proof that Kallipolis was not meant as a serious project, since neither would the philosophers be willing to rule nor would their fellow citizens be willing to compel them to rule: Strauss 1978, pp. 121–127.

interpretation of this passage is one of the most controversial issues in recent scholarship. A literal interpretation of the compulsion at stake as an external compulsion exercised by the founders or the current rulers of Kallipolis, an external law, or some other unspecified agents is unattractive, for what characterizes the philosopher-kings is precisely their ability to rationally determine their own courses of action and ways of life, and therefore to be genuinely free, in contrast with the slavish tyrant.[3]

Two more credible alternatives have been suggested. The first argues that although they have no desire to,[4] the philosopher-kings rule for instrumental reasons—that is, in order to avoid either rule by someone less worthy than themselves or the fall of the ideal city. Despite its plausibility, this solution does not sufficiently account for the references within the text to duty and justice.[5] The second alternative holds that the philosophers rule because it is just to do so, and the philosopher-kings are just people. This can entail either that the philosophers *desire* to rule in order to imitate the Forms, insofar as ruling is an expression of one's knowledge of the Forms in actions,[6] or that the philosophers *do not* desire to rule, but are compelled to do so by internal moral reasons.[7] The former variation of this interpretation, insofar as it holds that the philosopher-kings desire to rule (for whatever reason), is refuted by the indications to the contrary provided by the text itself (519d4–7; 520d1–4). Moreover, what this interpretation cannot really account for is one of the central tenets of the dialogue's discussion of political rule— namely, that for a city to be ruled in a just way, holding political power cannot be the object of the desire (or erotic love) of the rulers. One of the reasons why

---

3. See also Caluori's refutation of this kind of interpretations: Caluori 2011, pp. 17–18.
4. See *Rep.* 517c7–d2, 519c4–6; see Brown 2000.
5. See, for example, Reeve 2006, pp. 95ff. and 202ff.
6. See, for example, Irwin 1977, pp. 236–237; and Kraut 1991.
7. See, for example, Caluori 2011.

the philosopher-kings are just rulers is precisely that their eros has a different object, the Forms, an object that is adequate to the intensity and insatiability of their eros. While the tyrant's eros is turned downward, and political arbitrary power becomes an object of desire *qua* the means through which he tries to satisfy his insatiable appetites, the philosopher-king's eros is turned upward. However, his explicit aversion to ruling does not entail that he will not be available to rule, provided that ruling the city is a demand of justice and that neglecting to rule would run counter to the philosopher's nature as an eminently just person.[8]

Seeing political rule as a demand of justice gives a rationale not only for the return to the cave of the philosopher-kings educated within the just polis but also for the political intervention of those rare philosophers living in an unjust city and seizing the *kairos* for a radical political transformation of their city, insofar as realizing the possibility of reforming a city according to the ideal constitution is a demand of justice. The interpretation of Plato's critique of tyranny put forward in this volume strengthens this reading of the descent. The philosophers not only ought to rule but also they *must* rule whenever the appropriate circumstances allow it, both for the sake of the city and for the sake of philosophy itself. While it is possible that some philosophical natures will develop well even when planted in bad soil, these amount only to rare exceptions, to the intervention of a divine chance. In a democracy, the large part of the philosophically talented youth will be corrupt. As we have seen, the main source of corruption is not private education but, rather, life in the democratic city per se, and in particular the influence of the demos on ambitious and talented youth. A good private education can hardly counter the effects of an entire political, social, and cultural environment on the souls of the citizens, as the case of Alcibiades shows.

---

8. And indeed, this is precisely what Glaucon answers to Socrates at 520d7–e2.

The identification of the tyrant as a philosopher *manqué* shows the extent to which philosophy and politics are entangled, even if this relationship entails a tension that Plato has not solved in the *Republic*. This entanglement is not simply instrumental and extrinsic. The problem is not only that if the philosophers do not rule the city will suffer civil war and hence make their blessed life of contemplation very difficult, if not impossible, out of extrinsic reasons. The problem is, also, that in an unjust city (such as the democratic one), the fruitful transaction between the individual soul and the city so fundamental to the educational process of a philosophical nature is impossible. A corrupt city is unjust insofar as it dooms philosophy and education to failure, and without education and philosophy, there is no justice. Educational failures are not of little importance, insofar as for Plato, philosophically educating people who have a natural talent for it is a constitutive and essential part of what it is to be a philosopher. This means that the relationship between the city and philosophy is much less extrinsic than it may appear. Seizing the *kairos* for a political change, taking advantage of a divine fate that is improbable but not impossible, and that will allow the realization of a regime similar to the ideal city depicted in the dialogue, is a demand of justice. Moreover, as we have seen, a corrupt philosophical nature is a danger for the city: Socrates seems to be warning Athens that it has a vested interest in offering the proper environment for the flourishing of philosophy, as historically some of these corrupt philosophical natures turned out to be a great liability to its own interests.

In this light, withdrawing from political commitment is morally impossible in the ideal city. In the case of a corrupt city, it can be a secondary and necessary solution, to which those who have had the good luck to become philosophers in spite of the difficulties must adapt because of the absence of the proper circumstances for taking action. However, whenever the appropriate circumstances are there, philosophers must seize this *kairos* in order to save their city.

REFERENCES

Abbate, Michele, ed. 2004. *Proclo. Commento alla* Repubblica *di Platone (Dissertazioni I, III–V, VII–XII, XIV–XV, XVII)*. Milan: Bompiani.

Adam, James, ed. 1963. *The Republic of Plato*. 2 vols., 2nd ed. Cambridge: Cambridge University Press.

Adkins, Arthur. 1960. *Merit and Responsibility: A Study in Greek Values*. Oxford: Clarendon Press.

Ahrensdorf, Peter J. 2009. *Greek Tragedy and Political Philosophy: Rationalism and Religion in Sophocles' Theban Plays*. Cambridge and New York: Cambridge University Press.

Andrewes, Antony. 1963. *The Greek Tyrants*. New York: Harper and Row.

Annas, Julia. 1981. *An Introduction to Plato's* Republic. Oxford and New York: Oxford University Press.

Annas, Julia. 1997. "Politics and Ethics in Plato's *Republic*." In *Platons Politeia*, edited by Otfried Höffe, pp. 141–160. Berlin: Akademie Verlag.

Annas, Julia. 2000. "Politics in Plato's *Republic*: His and Ours." *Apeiron* 33, no. 4, pp. 303–325.

Arends, Jacob F. M. 1988. *Die Einheit der Polis: Eine Studie über Platons "Staat"*. Leiden: Brill.

Arruzza, Cinzia. 2011. "The Private and the Common in Plato's *Republic*." *History of Political Thought* 33, no. 2, pp. 215–233.

Arruzza, Cinzia. 2012. "'Cleaning the City': Plato and Popper on Political Change." *Polis: The Journal of the Society for Greek Political Thought* 29, no. 2, pp. 259–285.

Balot, Ryan K. 2001. *Greed and Injustice in Classical Athens*. Princeton, NJ: Princeton University Press.

Bambrough, Renford. 1967. *Plato, Popper, and Politics: Some Contributions to a Modern Controversy*. New York: Barnes and Noble.

Bearzot, Cinzia. 1981. *Platone e i moderati ateniesi*. Milan: Istituto lombardo di scienze e lettere.

Bearzot, Cinzia. 2009. "La sovversione dell'ordine costituito nei discorsi degli oligarchici ateniesi." In *Ordine e sovversione nel mondo greco e romano. Atti del convegno internazionale Cividale del Friuli 25-27 settembre 2008*, edited by Gianpaolo Urso, pp. 69–86. Pisa: Edizioni ETS.

Bearzot, Cinzia. 2013. *Come si abbatte una democrazia. Tecniche di colpo di Stato nell'Atene antica*. Bari-Rome: Laterza.

Blackson, Thomas. 2010. "Early Work on Rationality: The Lorenz-Frede Interpretation." *History of Philosophy Quarterly* 27, no. 2, pp. 101–124.

Bloom, Allan, ed. 1991. *The Republic of Plato*. New York: Basic Books.

Bobonich, Christopher. 2002. *Plato's Utopia Recast: His Later Ethics and Politics*. Oxford and New York: Oxford University Press.

Boeri, Marcelo D. 2010. "¿Por qué el Θυμός es un "aliado" de la razón en la batalla contra los apetitos irracionales?" *Rivista di Cultura Classica e Medioevale* 52, pp. 289–306.

Brennan, Tad. 2012. "The Nature of the Spirited Part of the Soul and its Object." In *Plato and the Divided Self*, edited by Rachel Barney, Tad Brennan, and Charles Brittain, pp. 102–127. Cambridge and New York: Cambridge University Press.

Brill, Sara. 2013. *Plato on the Limits of Human Life*. Bloomington: Indiana University Press.

Brinckman, August. 1911. "Ein Brief Platons." *Rheinisches Museum für Philologie* 66, 226–230.

Brisson, Luc, ed. 1987. *Platon: Lettres*. Paris: Garnier-Flammarion.

Brown, Eric. 2000. "Justice and Compulsion for Plato's Philosopher-Rulers." *Ancient Philosophy* 20, pp. 1–17.

Bultrighini, Umberto. 1999. *"Maledetta democrazia". Studi su Crizia*. Alessandria: Edizioni dell'Orso.

Burnet, John, ed. 1900–07. *Platonis Opera*. 5 vols. Oxford: Clarendon Press.

Burnet, John. 1950. *Greek Philosophy. Vol. I: From Thales to Plato*. London: Macmillan.

Burnyeat, Myles. 1979. "The Virtues of Plato." *New York Review of Books* 26, no. 4. http://www.nybooks.com/articles/1979/09/27/the-virtues-of-plato/.

Burnyeat, Myles. 1997. "Culture and Society in Plato's *Republic*." In *The Tanner Lectures on Human Values*, edited by G. P. Peterson, pp. 215–324. Salt Lake City: University of Utah Press.

Burnyeat, Myles. 2006. "The Truth of Tripartition." *Proceedings of the Aristotelian Society*, NS, 106, pp. 1–23.

Burnyeat, Myles, and Michael Frede. 2015. *The Pseudo-Platonic Seventh Letter: A Seminar*. Oxford and New York: Oxford University Press.

Calabi, Francesca. 1998. "Andreia/thymoeides." In *Platone, La Repubblica, Vol. III (Libro IV)*, edited by Mario Vegetti, pp. 187–203. Naples: Bibliopolis.

Caluori, Damian. 2011. "Reason and Necessity: The Descent of the Philosopher-Kings." *Oxford Studies in Ancient Philosophy* 40, pp. 7–27.

Campese, Silvia, and Silvia Gastaldi. 1998. "Bendidie e Panatenee." In *Platone, La Repubblica, Vol. I (Libro I)*, edited by Mario Vegetti, pp. 105–132. Naples: Bibliopolis.

Canfora, Luciano. 2013. *La guerra civile ateniese*. Milan: Rizzoli.

Catenacci, Carmine. 2012. *Il tiranno e l'eroe. Storia e mito nella Grecia antica*. Rome: Carocci editore.

Chappell, T. D. J. 1993. "The Virtues of Thrasymachus." *Phronesis* 38, no. 1, pp. 1–17.

Connor, Robert W. 1971. *The New Politicians of Fifth-Century Athens*. Indianapolis/Cambridge: Hackett Publishing.

Connor, Robert. W. 1977. "Tyrannos Polis." In *Ancient and Modern: Essays in Honor of Gerald F. Else*, edited by John H. D'Arms and John E. Eardie, pp. 95–109. Ann Arbor: University of Michigan Press.

Cooper, John. 1984. "Plato's Theory of Human Motivation." *History of Philosophy Quarterly* 1, no. 1, pp. 3–21.

Cornford, F. M. 1971. "The Doctrine of *Eros* in Plato's *Symposium*." In *Plato: A Collection of Critical Essays. Vol. 2: Ethics, Politics, and Philosophy of Art and Religion*, edited by Gregory Vlastos, pp. 119–131. New York: Anchor Books.

Cummins, W. Joseph. 1981. "'Eros', 'Epithumia,' and 'Philia' in Plato." *Apeiron* 15, no. 1, pp. 10–18.

Danzig, Gabriel. 2008. "Rhetoric and the Ring: Herodotus and Plato on the Story of Gyges as a Politically Expendient Tale." *Greece & Rome* (Second Series) 55, no. 2, pp. 169–192.

Danzig, Gabriel. 2013. "Plato's *Charmides* as a Political Act: Apologetics and the Promotion of Ideology." *Greek, Roman, and Byzantine Studies* 53, pp. 486–519.

Danzig, Gabriel. 2014. "The Use and Abuse of Critias: Conflicting Portraits in Plato and Xenophon." *Classical Quarterly* 64, no. 2, pp. 507–524.

Davidson, James N. 1997. *Courtesans and Fishcakes: The Consuming Passion of Classical Athens*. New York: St. Martin's Press.

De Romilly, Jacqueline. 1995. *Alcibiade. Ou les dangers de l'ambition*. Paris: Éditions de Fallois.

Diès, Auguste, ed. 1932. *Platon, La République*, vol. 1. Paris: Les Belles Lettres.

Dover, Kenneth K. 1989. *Homosexuality in Ancient Greece*. Cambridge, MA: Harvard University Press.

Dumont, Jacques. 2001. *Les Animaux dans l'Antiquité grecque*. Paris: L'Harmattan.

Dušanič, Slobodan. 2000. "Critias in the *Charmides*." *Aevum* 70, no.1, pp. 53–63.

Eagleton, Terry. 2007. *Ideology: An Introduction*. London and New York: Verso.

Edmunds, Lowell. 2006. *Oedipus*. New York: Routledge.

Euben, Peter J. 1996. "Reading Democracy: 'Socratic' Dialogues and the Political Education of Democratic Citizens." In *Demokratia. A Conversation on Democracies, Ancient and Modern*, edited by Josiah Ober and Charles Hedrick, pp. 327–359. Princeton, NJ: Princeton University Press.

Farrar, Cynthia. 1988. *The Origins of Democratic Thinking: The Invention of Politics in Classical Athens*. Cambridge and New York: Cambridge University Press.

Ferrari, Giovanni R. F. 1992. "Platonic Love." In *The Cambridge Companion to Plato*, edited by Richard Kraut, pp. 248–274. Cambridge: Cambridge University Press.

Ferrari, Giovanni R. F. 2005. *City and Soul in Plato's* Republic. Chicago: University of Chicago Press.

Field, G. L. 1946. "The Open Society and its Enemies." *Philosophy* 21, pp. 271–276.

Finley, Moses I. 1973. *Democracy Ancient and Modern*. New Brunswick, NJ: Rutgers University Press.

Finley, Moses I. 1974. "Athenian Demagogues." In *Studies in Ancient Society*, edited by Moses I. Finley, pp. 1–25. London: Routledge.

Foucault, Michel. 1990. *The History of Sexuality. Vol 2: The Use of Pleasure*. New York: Vintage Books.

Frede, Dorothea. 1996. "Plato, Popper, and Historicism." *Proceedings of the Boston Area Colloquium* 12, pp. 247–276.

Frère, Jean. 1998. *Le Bestiaire de Platon*. Paris: Éditions Kimé.

Frère, Jean. 2004. *Ardeur et colère. Le θυμός platonicien*. Paris: Éditions Kimé.

Fronterotta, Francesco. 2010. "Plato's *Republic* in the Recent Debate." *Journal of the History of Philosophy* 48, no. 2, pp. 125–151.

Ganson, Todd Stuart. 2009. "The Rational/Non-Rational Distinction in Plato's *Republic*." *Oxford Studies in Ancient Philosophy* 34, pp. 179–197.

Gastaldi, Silvia. 2005a. "L'infelicità dell'ingiusto: il caso del tiranno." In *Platone, La Repubblica, Vol. VI (Libri VIII e IX)*, edited by Mario Vegetti, pp. 499–538. Naples: Bibliopolis.

Gastaldi, Silvia. 2005b. "L'immagine dell'anima e la felicità del giusto." In *Platone, La Repubblica, Vol. VI (Libri VIII e IX)*, edited by Mario Vegetti, pp. 593–633. Naples: Bibliopolis.

Gavrielides, Era. 2010. "What Is Wrong with Degenerate Souls in the *Republic*." *Phronesis* 55, pp. 203–227.

Giorgini, Giovanni. 1993. *La città e il tiranno. Il concetto di tirannide nella Grecia del VII-IV secolo a.c.* Milan: Giuffré editore.

Giorgini, Giovanni. 2005. "Il tiranno." In *Platone, La Repubblica, Vol. VI (Libri VIII e IX)*, edited by Mario Vegetti, pp. 423–470. Naples: Bibliopolis.

Giorgini, Giovanni. 2009. "Plato and the Ailing Soul of the Tyrant." In *Le philosophe, le roi, le tyran*, edited by Silvia Gastaldi and Jean-François Pradeau, pp. 113–127. Sankt Augustin: Academia Verlag.

Gomme, Arnold Wycombe. 1962. "The Working of the Athenian Democracy." In *More Essays in Greek History and Literature*, edited by David A. Campbell, pp. 177–193. Oxford: Blackwell.

Gray, Vivienne J. 1996. "Herodotus and Images of Tyranny." *American Journal of Philology*, 117, no. 3, pp. 361–389.

Griswold, Charles L. 1995. "Le libéralisme platonicien: de la perfection individuelle comme fondement d'une théorie politique." In *Contre Platon. Vol. 2: Renverser le platonisme*, edited by Monique Dixsaut, pp. 155–95. Paris: Vrin.

Hackfort, Reginald. 1947. "Plato's Political Philosophy." *Classical Review* 61, pp. 55–57.

Halperin, David M. 1985. "Platonic Eros and What Men Call Love." *Ancient Philosophy* 5, pp. 161–204.

Halperin, David M. 1986. "Plato and Erotic Reciprocity." *Classical Antiquity* 5, no. 1, pp. 60–80.

Hamal, Debra. 2015. *The Battle of the Arginusae: Victory at Sea and Its Tragic Aftermath in the Final Years of the Peloponnesian War*. Baltimore, MD: John Hopkins University Press.

Hardie W. F. R. 1936. *A Study on Plato*. Oxford: Oxford Clarendon Press.

Hatzfeld, Jean. 1951. *Alcibiade. Études sur l'histoire d'Athènes à la fin du Ve siècle*. Paris: Presses Universitaires de France.

Havelock, Eric A. 1963. *Preface to Plato*. Cambridge, MA: Belknap Press of Harvard University Press.

Heintzeler, Gerhard. 1927. *Das Bild des Tyrannen bei Platon. Ein Beitrag zur Geschichte der Griechischen Staatsethik*. Stuttgart: Verlag Von W. Kohlhammer.

Henderson, Jeffrey. 2003. "Demos, Demagogue, Tyrant in Attic Old Comedy." In *Popular Tyranny: Sovereignty and its Discontents in Ancient Greece*, edited by Kathryn A. Morgan, pp. 155–179. Austin: University of Texas Press.

Hobbs, Angela. 2000. *Plato and the Hero: Courage, Manliness, and the Impersonal Good*. Cambridge and New York: Cambridge University Press.

Holt, Philip. 1998. "Sex, Tyranny, and Hippias' Incest Dream (Herodotus 6.107)." *Greek, Roman, and Byzantine Studies* 39, pp. 221–241.

Huffman, Carl A. 2005. *Archytas of Tarentum: Pythagorean, Philosopher and Mathematician King*. Cambridge and New York: Cambridge University Press.

Hyland Drew A. 1968. "*Eros, Epithumia*, and *Philia* in Plato." *Phronesis* 13, no. 1, pp. 32–46.

Iannucci, Alessandro, ed. 2002. *La parola e l'azione. I frammenti simposiali di Crizia*. Bologna: Ed. Nautilus.

Irwin, Terence. 1977. *Plato's Moral Theory: The Early and Middle Dialogues*. Oxford: Clarendon Press.

Irwin, Terence, ed. 1979. *Plato: Gorgias*. Oxford and New York: Clarendon Press.

Irwin, Terence. 1995. *Plato's Ethics*. Oxford and New York: Oxford University Press.

Isnardi, Margherita. 1955. "L'Accademia e le lettere platoniche." *La Parola del Passato* 10, pp. 241–273.

Isnardi Parente, Margherita. 1970. *Filosofia e politica nelle lettere di Platone*. Naples: Guida.

Isnardi Parente, Margherita, and Maria Grazia Ciani, eds. 2002. *Platone. Lettere.* Milan: Fondazione Lorenzo Valla.

Jaeger, Werner. 1945. "A New Greek Word in Plato's *Republic.* The Medical Origin of the Thymoeides." *Eranos* 45, pp. 123–130.

Jaeger, Werner. 1955. *Aristoteles: Grundlegung einer Geschichte seiner Entwicklung.* Berlin: Weidmann.

Johnstone, Mark. 2013. "Anarchic Souls: Plato's Depiction of the 'Democratic Man.'" *Phronesis* 58, pp. 139–159.

Johnstone, Mark. 2015. "Tyrannized Souls: Plato's Depiction of the 'Tyrannical Man.'" *British Journal for the History of Philosophy* 23, no. 3, pp. 423–437.

Jones A. H. M. 1953. "The Athenian Democracy and its Critics." *Cambridge Historical Journal* 11, no. 1, pp. 1–26.

Kahn, Charles. 1983. "Drama and Dialectic in Plato's *Gorgias.*" *Oxford Studies in Ancient Philosophy* 1, pp. 75–121.

Kahn, Charles. 1987. "Plato's Theory of Desire." *Review of Metaphysics* 41, no. 1, pp. 77–103.

Kahn Charles. 1998. *Plato and the Socratic Dialogue: The Philosophical Use of a Literary Form.* Cambridge and New York: Cambridge University Press.

Kallet, Lisa. 2001. *Money and the Corrosion of Power in Thucydides: The Sicilian Expedition and its Aftermath.* Berkeley: University of California Press.

Kallet, Lisa. 2003. "Dēmos Tyrannos: Wealth, Power, and Economic Patronage." In *Popular Tyranny. Sovereignty and its Discontents in Ancient Greece,* edited by Kathryn A. Morgan, pp. 117–153. Austin: University of Texas Press.

Kamtekar, Rachana. 2005. "The Profession of Friendship: Callicles, Democratic Politics, and Rhetorical Education in Plato's *Gorgias.*" *Ancient Philosophy* 25, pp. 319–339.

Keyt, David. 2006. "Plato and the Ship of State." In *The Blackwell Guide to Plato's Republic,* edited by Geronimos Santas, pp. 189–213. Oxford: Blackwell.

Klosko, George. 1984. "The Refutation of Callicles in Plato's *Gorgias.*" *Greece & Rome* 31, no. 2, pp. 126–139.

Klosko, George. 1988. "The 'Rule' of Reason in Plato's Psychology." *History of Philosophy Quarterly* 5, no. 4, pp. 341–356.

Kosman, Arieh. 2007. "Justice and Virtue: The Republic's Inquiry into Proper Difference." In *The Cambridge Companion to Plato's Republic,* edited by G. R. F. Ferrari, pp. 116–137. Cambridge and New York: Cambridge University Press.

Krentz, Peter. 1982. *The Thirty at Athens.* Ithaca, NY: Cornell University Press.

Kraut, Richard. 1991. "Return to the Cave: *Republic 519–521.*" In *Proceedings of the Boston Area Colloquium in Ancient Philosophy* 7, edited by J. J. Cleary, pp. 43–62. Leiden: Brill.

Labarbe, Jules. 1990. "Quel Critias dans le *Timée* et le *Critias* de Platon?" *Sacris Erudiri* 31, pp. 239–255.

Laird, Andrew. 2001. "Ringing the Changes on Gyges: Philosophy and the Formation of Fiction in Plato's *Republic*." *Journal of Hellenic Studies* 121, pp. 12–29.

Lane, Melissa. 2011. *Eco-Republic: What the Ancients Can Teach Us about Ethics, Virtues, and Sustainable Living*. Princeton, NJ: Princeton University Press.

Lanza, Diego. 1977. *Il tiranno e il suo pubblico*. Turin: Einaudi.

Larivée, Annie. 2005. "Malaise dans la cité. Eros et tyrannie au livre IX de la *République*." In *Etudes sur la République de Platon. I. La justice*, edited by Monique Dixsaut and Annie Larivée, pp. 169–197. Paris: Vrin.

Larivée, Annie. 2012. "*Eros Tyrannos*: Alcibiades and the Model of the Tyrant in Book IX of the *Republic*." *International Journal of the Platonic Tradition* 6, pp. 1–26.

Lear, Jonathan. 1992. "Inside and Outside the *Republic*." *Phronesis* 37, no. 2, pp. 184–215.

Lentini, Giuseppe. 2002. "I simposi del tiranno: sui frammenti 70-72 V. di Alceo." *Zeitschrift für Papyrologie und Epigraphik* 139, pp. 3–17.

Lesses, Glenn. 1987. "Weakness, Reason, and the Divided Soul in Plato's *Republic*." *History of Philosophy Quarterly* 4, no. 2, pp. 147–161.

Levinson, Roland B. 1953. *In Defense of Plato*. Cambridge, MA: Harvard University Press.

Lewis, Sian. 2009. *Greek Tyranny*. Exeter: Bristol Phoenix.

Loraux, Nicole. 2001. *The Divided City. On Memory and Forgetting in Ancient Athens*. New York: Zone Books.

Loraux, Nicole. 2006. *The Invention of Athens: The Funeral Oration in the Classical City*. New York: Zone Books.

Lorenz, Hendrik. 2006. *The Brute Within. Appetitive Desire in Plato and Aristotle*. Oxford and New York: Oxford University Press.

Ludwig, Paul W. 2002. *Eros and Polis: Desire and Community in Greek Political Theory*. Cambridge and New York: Cambridge University Press.

Ludwig, Paul W. 2007. "Eros in the *Republic*." In *The Cambridge Companion to Plato's Republic*, edited by G. R. F. Ferrari, pp. 202–231. Cambridge and New York: Cambridge University Press.

Mainoldi, Carla. 1984. *L'Image du loup et du chien dans la Grèce ancienne d'Homère à Platon*. Paris: Éditions Ophrys.

Marshall, Mason, and Shane A. Bilsborough. 2010. "The *Republic*'s Ambiguous Democracy." *History of Philosophy Quarterly* 27, no. 1, pp. 301–316.

McGlew, James F. 1993. *Tyranny and Political Culture in Ancient Greece*. Ithaca, NY: Cornell University Press.

McGlew, James F. 1999. "The Athenian 'Hetaireiai' in 415 BC." *Historia: Zeitschrift für Alte Geschichte* 48, no. 1, pp. 1–22.

McNeill, David N. 2001. "Eros and Madness in Plato's *Republic*." *Review of Metaphysics* 55, pp. 235–268.

Meulder, Marcel. 1989. "Est-il possible d'identifier le tyran décrit par Platon dans la *République?*" *Revue Belge de Philologie et d'Histoire* 67, no. 1, pp. 30–52.

Miller, Mitchell. 2007. "Beginning the 'Longer Way.'" In *The Cambridge Companion to Plato's Republic*, edited by G. R. F. Ferrari, pp. 310–344. Cambridge and New York: Cambridge University Press.

Moline, Jon. 1978. "Plato on the Complexity of the Psyche." *Archiv für Geschichte der Philosophie* 60, no. 1, pp. 1–26.

Monoson, Sara S. 2000. *Plato's Democratic Entanglements: Athenian Politics and the Practice of Philosophy*. Princeton, NJ: Princeton University Press.

Morgan, Kathryn A. 1998. "Designer History: Plato's Atlantis and Fourth-Century Ideology." *Journal of Hellenic Studies* 118, pp. 101–118.

Moss, Jessica. 2005. "Shame, Pleasure, and the Divided Soul." *Oxford Studies in Ancient Philosophy* 29, pp. 137–170.

Moss, Jessica. 2008. "Appearances and Calculations: Plato's Division of the Soul." *Oxford Studies in Ancient Philosophy* 34, pp. 35–68.

Nails, Debra. 1998. "The Dramatic Date of Plato's *Republic*." *Classical Journal* 93, no. 4, pp. 383–396.

Nehamas, Alexander. 1982. "Plato on Imitation and Poetry." In *Plato on Beauty, Wisdom and the Arts*, edited by J.M.E. Moravcsik and Philip Temko, pp. 47–78. Totowa (NJ): Rowman & Littlefield.

Németh, György. 2006. *Kritias und die Dreißig Tyrannen*. Stuttgart: Franz Steiner.

Nettleship, Richard Lewis. [1897] 1964. *Lectures on the 'Republic' of Plato*. London: Macmillan.

Nichols, Mary P. 1987. *Socrates and the Political Community: An Ancient Debate*. Albany: State University of New York Press.

Nucci, Matteo. 2001. "La posizione di eros nell'anima. Un caso esemplare: l'eros tiranno." *Elenchos* 22, pp. 39–73.

Nussbaum, Martha C. 1986. *The Fragility of Goodness: Luck and Ethics in Greek Tragedy and Philosophy*. Cambridge and New York: Cambridge University Press.

Ober, Josiah. 1989. *Mass and Elite in Democratic Athens: Rhetoric, Ideology, and the Power of the People*. Princeton, NJ: Princeton University Press.

Ober, Josiah 1993. "Thucydides' Criticism of Democratic Knowledge." In *Nomodeiktes: Greek Studies in Honor of Martin Ostwald*, edited by Ralph Mark Rosen and Joseph Farrell, pp. 81–89. Ann Arbor: University of Michigan Press.

Ober, Josiah. 1998. *Political Dissent in Democratic Athens: Intellectual Critics of Popular Rule*. Princeton, NJ: Princeton University Press.

Ober, Josiah. 2003. "Tyrant Killing as Therapeutic *Stasis*: A Political Debate in Images and Texts." In *Popular Tyranny: Sovereignty and its Discontents in Ancient Greece*, edited by Kathryn A. Morgan, pp. 215–250. Austin: University of Texas Press.

Ober, Josiah. 2017. *Demopolis: Democracy before Liberalism in Theory and in Practice*. Cambridge and New York: Cambridge University Press.

Osborne, Robin. 1985. "The Erection and Mutilation of the Hermai." *Proceedings of the Cambridge Philological Society* 31, pp. 47–73.

Osborne, Robin. 2003. "Changing the Discourse." In *Popular Tyranny: Sovereignty and its Discontents in Ancient Greece*, edited by Kathryn A. Morgan, pp. 251–272. Austin: University of Texas Press.

Pappas, Nickolas. 2013. *The Routledge Guidebook to Plato's* Republic. London and New York: Routledge.

Parry, Richard D. 2007. "The Unhappy Tyrant and the Craft of Inner Rule." In *The Cambridge Companion to Plato's* Republic, edited by G. R. F. Ferrari, pp. 386–414. Cambridge and New York: Cambridge University Press.

Pasquali, Giorgio, ed. 1938. *Le lettere di Platone*. Florence: Le Monnier.

Penner, Terry. 1971. "Thought and Desire in Plato." In *Plato: A Collection of Critical Essays. Vol. II: Ethics, Politics, and Philosophy of Art and Religion*, edited by Gregory Vlastos, pp. 96–118. New York: Anchor Books.

Peters, James Robert. 1989. "Reason and Passion in Plato's *Republic*." *Ancient Philosophy* 9, no. 2, pp. 173–187.

Popper, Karl R. 1945. *The Open Society and its Enemies. Volume I: The Spell of Plato*. London: George Routledge & Sons.

Price, A. W. 1995. *Mental Conflict*. New York: Routledge.

Raaflaub, Kurt. 1979. "Polis tyrannos: Zur Entstehung einer politischen Metapher." In *Arktouros: Studies Presented to B.M.W. Knox*, edited by G. W. Bowersock, pp. 237–252. Berlin and New York: Walter de Gruyter.

Raaflaub, Kurt A. 1990. "Contemporary Perceptions of Democracy in Fifth-Century Athens." In *Aspects of Athenian Democracy*, edited by W. R. Connor, M. H. Hansen, K. A. Raaflaub, and B. S. Strauss, pp. 33–70. Copenhagen: Museum Tusculanum Press.

Raaflaub, Kurt A. 2003. "Stick and Glue: The Function of Tyranny in Fifth Century Athenian Democracy." In *Popular Tyranny: Sovereignty and its Discontents in Ancient Greece*, edited by Kathryn A. Morgan, pp. 59–93. Austin: University of Texas Press.

Recco, Greg. 2009. *Athens Victorious. Democracy in Plato's* Republic. Lanham, MD: Lexington Books.

Reeve, C. D. C. 2006. *Philosopher-Kings: The Argument of Plato's* Republic. Indianapolis, IN: Hackett Publishing.

Renaut, Olivier. 2014. *Platon. La médiation des émotions. L'éducation du θυμός dans les dialogues*. Paris: Vrin.

Robinson, Eric W. 2011. *Democracy Beyond Athens: Popular Government in the Greek Classical Age*. Cambridge and New York: Cambridge University Press.

Roochnik, David. 2003. *Beautiful City: The Dialectical Character of Plato's* Republic. Ithaca, NY: Cornell University Press.

Rosen, Stanley. 1965. "The Role of Eros in Plato's *Republic*." *Review of Metaphysics* 18, 452–475.

Rosenmeyer, Thomas G. 1949. "The Numbers in Plato's *Critias*: A Reply." *Classical Philology* 44, no. 2, pp. 117–120.

Rosenstock, Bruce. 1994. "Athena's Cloak. Plato's Critique of the Democratic City in the *Republic*." *Political Theory* 22, no. 3, pp. 363–390.

Roux, Sylvain. 2001. "Entre mythe et tragédie: l'origine de la tyrannie selon Platon." *Revue des Études Grecques* 114, pp. 140–159.

Rowe, Christopher. 1998. "Democracy and Socratic-Platonic Philosophy." In *Democracy, Empire, and the Arts in Fifth-Century Athens*, edited by Deborah Boedeker and Kurt A. Raaflaub, pp. 241–253. Cambridge, MA: Harvard University Press.

Santas, Gerasimos Xenophon. 1988. *Plato and Freud: Two Theories of Love*. Oxford and New York: Basil Blackwell.

Santas, Gerasimos Xenophon. 2007. "Plato's Criticism of Democracy in the *Republic*." In *Freedom, Reason, and the Polis: Essays in Ancient Greek Political Philosophy*, edited by David Keyt and Fred Miller Jr., pp. 70–89. Cambridge and New York: Cambridge University Press.

Sartori, Franco. 1957. *Le eterie nella vita politica ateniese del VI e V secolo A.C.* Rome: L' "Erma" di Bretschneider.

Sartori, Franco. 1958. "Platone e le eterie." *Historia: Zeitschrift für Alte Geschichte* 7, no. 2, pp. 157–171.

Saxonhouse, Arlene W. 1996. *Athenian Democracy: Modern Mythmakers and Ancient Theorists*. Notre Dame, IN: University of Notre Dame Press.

Saxonhouse, Arlene W. 1998. "Democracy, Equality, and Eidê: A Radical View from Book 8 of Plato's *Republic*." *American Political Science Review* 92, no. 2, pp. 273–283.

Saxonhouse, Arlene W. 2009. "The Socratic Narrative: A Democratic Reading of Plato's Dialogues." *Political Theory* 37, no. 6, pp. 728–753.

Scanlon, Thomas F. 1987. "Thucydides and Tyranny." *Classical Antiquity* 6, no. 2, pp. 286–301.

Schmid, Walter T. 1998. *Plato's Charmides and the Socratic Ideal of Rationality*. Albany: State University of New York Press.

Schofield, Malcolm. 2006. *Plato: Political Philosophy*. Oxford and New York: Oxford University Press.

Schriefl, Anna. 2013. *Platons Kritik an Geld und Reichtum*. Berlin: de Gruyter.

Schuhl, Pierre-Maxime. 1946. "Platon et l'activité politique de l'Académie." *Revue des Études Grecques* 59/60, nos. 279–283, pp. 46–53.

Schuller, W. 1978. *Die Stadt als Tyrann: Athens Herrschaft über seine Bundesgenossen*. Konstanz: Universitätsverlag Konstanz.

Scott, Dominic. 2000. "Plato's Critique of the Democratic Character." *Phronesis* 45, no. 1, pp. 19–37.

Scott, Dominic. 2007. "Erōs, Philosophy, and Tyranny." In *Maieusis. Essays on Ancient Philosophy in Honour of Myles Burnyeat*, edited by D. Scott, pp. 136–153. Oxford and New York: Oxford University Press.

Seaford, Richard. 2003. "Tragic Tyranny." In *Popular Tyranny: Sovereignty and its Discontents in Ancient Greece*, edited by Kathryn A. Morgan, pp. 95–115. Austin: University of Texas Press.

Shear, Julia. 2011. *Polis and Revolution: Responding to Oligarchy in Classical Athens.* Cambridge and New York: Cambridge University Press.

Sheffield, Frisbee. 2012. "Erôs Before and After Tripartition." In *Plato and the Divided Self,* edited by Rachel Barney, Tad Brennan, and Charles Brittain, pp. 211–237. Cambridge and New York: Cambridge University Press.

Shorey, Paul. 1979. *What Plato Said.* Chicago: University of Chicago Press.

Siewert, Charles. 2001. "Plato's Division of Reason and Appetite." *History of Philosophy Quarterly* 18, no. 4, pp. 329–352.

Singpurwalla, Rachel. 2013. "Why Spirit Is the Natural Ally of Reason: Spirit, Reason, and the Fine in Plato's *Republic.*" *Oxford Studies in Ancient Philosophy* 44, pp. 41–65.

Sissa, Giulia. 2008. *Sex and Sensuality in the Ancient World.* New Haven, CT: Yale University Press.

Slings, S. R., ed. 2003. *Platonis Rempublicam.* Oxford: Oxford University Press.

Smith, David G. 2009. "Alcibiades, Athens, and the Tyranny of Sicily (Thuc. 6.16)." *Greek, Roman, and Byzantine Studies* 49, pp. 363–389.

Solinas, Marco. 2005. "Desideri: fenomenologia degenerative e strategie di controllo." In *Platone, La repubblica, Vol. VI,* edited by Mario Vegetti, pp. 471–498. Naples: Bibliopolis.

Solinas, Marco. 2008. *Psiche: Platone e Freud. Desiderio, sogno, mania, eros.* Florence: Firenze University Press.

Strauss, Leo. 1978. *The City and Man.* Chicago: University of Chicago Press.

Tait, M. D. C. 1949. "Spirit, Gentleness and the Philosophic Nature in the Republic." In *Transactions and Proceedings of the American Philological Association* 80, pp. 203–211. Baltimore, MD: John Hopkins University Press.

Tarnopolsky, Christina H. 2010, *Prudes, Perverts, and Tyrants. Plato's Gorgias and the Politics of Shame.* Princeton, NJ: Princeton University Press.

Tate, J. 1958. "Plato's Political Philosophy." *Classical Review,* n. s., 8, pp. 241–242.

Taylor, Alfred E. 1928. *A Commentary on Plato's* Timaeus. Oxford: Clarendon Press.

Thesleff, Holger 1982. *Studies in Platonic Chronology.* Helsinki: Societas Scientiarum Fennica.

Thornton, Bruce S. 1997. *Eros: The Myth of Ancient Greek Sexuality.* Boulder, CO: Westview of HarperCollins.

Tuozzo, Thomas. 2011. *Plato's* Charmides: *Positive Elenchus in a "Socratic Dialogue."* Cambridge and New York: Cambridge University Press.

Tuplin, Christopher. 1985. "Imperial Tyranny: Some Reflections on a Classical Greek Political Metaphor." In *Crux: Essays in Greek History Presented to G.E.M. de St. Croix on his 75th Birthday,* edited by P. A. Cartledge and F. D. Harvey, pp. 348–375. London: Duckworh/Imprint Academic.

Vegetti, M. 1998a. "Introduzione al libro I." In *Platone, La Repubblica, Vol. 1 (Libro I),* edited by Mario Vegetti, pp. 15–38. Naples: Bibliopolis.

Vegetti, M. 1998b. "Trasimaco." In *Platone, La Repubblica, Vol. 1 (Libro I),* edited by Mario Vegetti, pp. 233–256. Naples: Bibliopolis.

Vegetti, M. 1998c. "Ricchezza/povertà e l'unità della polis." In *Platone, La Repubblica, Vol. 3 (Libro IV)*, edited by Mario Vegetti, pp. 151–158. Naples: Bibliopolis.

Vegetti, Mario, ed. 2006. *Platone, La Repubblica*. Milan: BUR.

Vegetti, Mario. 2007. "Paranoia nella tirannide antica." In *Paranoia e politica*, edited by Simona Forti and Marco Revelli, pp. 43–57. Turin: Bollati Boringhieri.

Vegetti, Mario. 2009a. "Animali politici e altri animali in Platone." In *Gli antichi e noi: scritti in onore di Antonio Mario Battegazzore*, edited by Walter Lapini, Luciano Malusa, and Letterio Mauro, pp. 75–92. Genoa: G. Brigati.

Vegetti, Mario. 2009b. *Un paradigma in cielo. Platone politico da Aristotele al Novecento*. Rome: Carocci editore.

Vernant, Jean-Pierre. 1982. "From Oedipus to Periander: Lameness, Tyranny, Incest in Legend and History." *Arethusa* 15, pp. 19–38.

Von Fritz, Kurt. 1968. *Platon in Sizilien und das Problem der Philosophenherrschaft*. Berlin: de Gruyter.

Wallach, John R. 2001. *The Platonic Political Art. A Study of Critical Reason and Democracy*. University Park: Pennsylvania State University Press.

Weiss, Roslyn. 2007. "Wise Guys and Smart Alecks in *Republic* I and 2." In *The Cambridge Companion to Plato's Republic*, edited by G. R. F. Ferrari, pp. 90–115. Cambridge and New York: Cambridge University Press.

Welliver, Warmann. 1977. *Character, Plot and Thought in Plato's* Timaeus-Critias. Leinde: Brill.

White, Nicholas. 1979. *A Companion to Plato's Republic*. Indianapolis, IN: Hackett Publishing.

Williams, Bernard. [1973] 2006. "The Analogy of City and Soul in Plato's *Republic*." In *The Sense of the Past: Essays in the History of Philosophy*, edited by Myles Burnyeat, pp. 108–117. Princeton, NJ: Princeton University Press.

Wilson, J. R. S. 1995. "Thrasymachus and the *Thumos*: A Further Case of Prolepsis in *Republic* I." *Classical Quarterly* 45, no. 1, pp. 58–67.

Wohl, Victoria. 1999. "The Eros of Alcibiades." *Classical Antiquity* 18, no. 2, pp. 349–385.

Zeitlin, Froma I. 1990. "Thebes: Theater of the Self and Society in Athenian Drama." In *Nothing to Do with Dionysos? Athenian Drama in Its Social Context*, edited by John J. Winkler and Froma I. Zeitlin, pp. 130–167. Princeton, NJ: Princeton University Press.

INDEX LOCORUM

GENERAL INDEX

Academy of Plato (385), 54, 59, 63n24, 158n39
acquisitiveness. *See* greed
Adeimantus, 72–73, 77–79, 87, 106, 215, 237, 240, 251
Adkins, Arthur, 144, 144n8, 147n20
Aelianus, 59
Aeschylus, 15, 40, 203n40, 226
Against Alcibiades (Lysias), 93
Against Eratosthenes (Lysias), 25, 71, 76, 79
Against Timarchus (Aeschines), 155
Agamemnon (Aeschylus), 40, 226
Alcibiades
    corruption of, 90n71, 93, 250, 257
    demos, relation to, 89–90, 147, 158, 160n43, 161
    denouncement of, 89n68
    eros of, 92–93, 158–60, 158n39, 180–81
    greed of, 90n71, 147
    as inspiration for Plato's tyrant, 63
    lawlessness of, 90, 93, 160
    lineage of, 90n71
    political involvement of, 23, 30, 74, 82, 91–93, 145n12
    scholarship on, 90
    sexual license of, 46, 93, 160, 180
    Socrates, relation to, 77, 77n49, 93, 160
    as symbol of Athenian democracy, 89–90
    traits of, 46, 90n71, 160

    tyrannical aspirations of, 23, 45, 93, 160, 160nn42–43
Alcibiades (Plato ?), 158n39
Andrewes, Antony, 19n11
animals
    apes, 201n33, 225
    appetitive part and, 164, 244
    dogs, 109, 191, 201–2, 202n37, 204–6, 205n41, 207–9, 213
    drones, 169, 175, 211
    education and, 208
    horses, 165n47, 191
    lions, 39–40, 40n48, 164, 197, 201–4, 203–4nn39–40, 208–9, 212n48
    literature and, 154, 203, 206, 209, 212
    philosophers and, 204–5
    rational part and, 203n39
    serpents, 191, 201–3, 201n34, 208–9
    spirited part and, 11, 189–92, 189n17, 190n19, 201–3, 208–9, 213, 225–26
    tyrants and, 39–40, 171, 211–12, 244
    wolves (*see* wolf metaphor)
Annas, Julia, 2n2, 228
Antenor, 20
Antiphon, 89
Anytus, 67–68
Aphrodisia, 158
Apology (Plato), 77, 120–21
aporia, 84

GREEK TERMS